S0-CFU-744

Sea Stories

of

Cape Cod
and the Islands

To Paul —
Welcome to Cape Cod —
Enjoy your retirement

Admont G. Clark

Admont Gulick Clark
Captain, USCGR (Retired)

Lower Cape Publishing

To my wife Ruth, who bore this next imposition with grace.

Orleans, Massachusetts
First Edition

ISBN 0-936972-17-3

Library of Congress Control Number 00-090746

Acknowledgments

The experience of writing this book has been enriched by the courtesy and generosity of many of my sources— in a number of instances by permission to draw upon whole histories or biographies, or permission to draw upon many different articles from a historical society journal, as well as individual articles.

I wish therefore to express due gratitude to those many people and organizations who have made this book possible. Their names are listed below:

Dr. W. Randolph Bartlett, my colleague at Cape Cod Community College, for his research on Lorenzo Dow Baker of Wellfleet, who invented and developed the Caribbean banana trade.

Dr. Delores Bird, another colleague of mine, for her work as editor of *Early Encounters,* the papers of W. Sears Nickerson.

The Bishop Museum of Honolulu, for valuable photographs on early whaling.

Janet Bosworth, of the Cuttyhunk Historical Society, for her many contributions of historical material from the island, including some of her own research.

The Falmouth Historical Society (and especially Florence Fitts) for generosity with their materials and permissions to use photographs and publications.

The Greenwood Press of Westbury, CT, for permission to use the excerpt from *Mad Jack Percival,* by Dr. David Long.

Virginia and Thomas Greer, for permission to use early material from Amelia Forbes Emerson's *Early History of Naushon Island.*

The Harwich Historical Society for permission to use the story of Katie Baker from *Harwich Men of the Sea.*

The Historical Society of Old Yarmouth, for permission to use excerpts from *Yarmouth's Proud Packets* and *The History of Old Yarmouth.*

The Inquirer and Mirror Press of Nantucket, for permission to use excerpts from Stackpole's *The Loss of the Essex.*

Anne Janerico, for her "labors of Hercules" in preparing the manuscript for photo-ready copy.

Haynes Mahoney of Yarmouth Port, for permission to use excerpts from *Yarmouth's*

Proud Packets, published by the Historical Society of Old Yarmouth.

The Massachusetts Historical Society of Boston, for invaluable information on the opening of the Northwest Territory.

The Nantucket Life-Saving Museum, Maurice Gibbs, President, for excerpts from *Life Saving— Nantucket.*

Dr. Louis A. Norton of Farmington, CT, the Centerville Historical Society, and the National Marine Historical Society, for permission to use the story of Captain Josiah Richardson.

The Peabody Essex Museum of Salem, for invaluable pictures.

The Pilgrim Society of Plymouth for pictorial assistance on the early days of the Plimoth Colony and the loss of *Sparrow Hawk.*

Mrs. William Primavera of East Harwich, and her sisters, daughters of W. Sears Nickerson, for permission to use the works of their father.

William P. Quinn of Orleans, a good and generous friend, for permission to borrow many photographs and to use material from *The Salt Works of Cape Cod, The Grounding of* the Eldia, and his eye-witness account of the sinking of the *Andrea Doria.* And for stepping into the breach and making publication possible.

Arthur R. Railton, an old friend, editor of the *Duke's* County Intelligencer, the journal of the Martha's Vineyard Historical Society, for permission to use a number of articles from the journal.

Nancy Thacher Reid, Dennis Historian, for permission to use material from several of the Dennis Historical Society newsletters, and the Dennis Historical Society for permission to use several of their sources.

The Sturgis Library of Barnstable, for their generous help in researching pictures of many vessels in the Henry C. Kittredge Room.

The United States Coast Guard Historian, Washington, DC, for numerous photographs and information on the sinking of the submarine *U.S.S. S-4* in 1927.

Bernard C. Webber, USCG (Retired) for permission to use material from *Chatham: "The Lifeboatmen."*

And I devoutly hope that I haven't omitted anyone. If I have, I will insert you in the second edition!

Table of Contents

Chapter Nine: Great Seamen

A Foreword

Cape Cod and the islands (Nantucket, Martha's Vineyard, and the Eliza-beth Islands bordering Vineyard Sound) are rich in history. The first settlement in the area occurred eighteen years before the Mayflower landed in what was to become Plymouth harbor. Shortly after 1630 King James I (who blithely assumed that by right of discovery he owned the whole area) granted to the Earl of Stirling "Pemaquid and its dependencies . . . together with Long Island and the adjacent Islands." Then in 1641 the earl sold:

for forty pounds to Thomas Mayhew of Watertown, in Massachusetts, and Thomas Mayhew, his son, the Island of Nantucket, with several small Islands adjacent [Martha's Vineyard and the Elizabeth islands]."

That same year the Mayhews sold most of their interest in Nantucket to ten men led by Tristram Coffin for thirty pounds "and also two bever [sic] hats one for myself and one for my wife." So the Mayhews acquired the Vineyard and Elizabeth islands, as well as a holding on Nantucket, for the net sum of ten pounds! Actual settlement of the islands began a few years later.

Cape Cod's first settlers began arriving in 1639 from Plymouth and Boston and quickly began to organize villages along the shores. By 1800 the population had grown to 10,329 souls. Roads were ruts in the sandy soil, and the fastest way to travel to Boston was by packet; a six-hour trip cost $1.50.

While the Plymouth settlers were literally kept alive by the kindness of the native Americans, the some three dozen Vineyarders (among 3000 natives) struggled to survive, ignored by the inhabitants, who remembered Champlain's battle at Stage Harbor and the kidnappings, often into slavery, of 1614. The Nantucket newcomers were materially helped by the natives. And once the first struggles were over, all of the settlers set to work fishing, farming, raising cattle and sheep, and hunting (game was plentiful at first).

But because Cape Cod and the islands were products of the glaciers, the soil was thin and poor, and soon they took to the sea for a living. Nantucket espe-cially turned to whaling (at first importing a Cape Codder to teach them the skill). At first they caught whales close to shore, as the natives had been doing for centu-ries. Later, in bigger and bigger ships they roamed the world for whale oil— often on two- and three-year voyages. Thomas Jefferson, for instance, reported that from 1771 to 1775 of the 303 Massachusetts whalers 150 were from Nantucket.

But long before these settlements, fishermen from Portugal, France, and other maritime nations were landing their catches along these shores to sun-dry them for the trip home. And some 600 years before the 1602 fort of Bartholomew Gosnold on Cuttyhunk Island, to introduce one aspect of these sea stories there is the Icelandic saga of Freydis, Leif Ericsson's sister.

In about 982 Eric the Red was banished from Iceland for a murder. He moved his goods and family (with others) to the west coast of Greenland (so named by him to attract other settlers). Soon a considerable colony transplanted from Iceland grew up. Later his son Leif decided to follow up on a discovery by Bjarni Herjulfsson of a new land. So gathering supplies for a winter's cruise, he back-tracked on Bjarni's run. The land he found and described had mild weather, and wild grapes grew in profusion; so he called it Vinland (Wineland). Loading his ship with timber (rare indeed in Greenland) and dried grapes, he sailed home, a rich man.

Then Leif's sister Freydis decided to go there in 1014. She sailed her own ship in company with one owned by two brothers, Helgi and Finnbogi. Finding Leif's *bothies* (cabins), they settled in. But soon bad feeling grew between the groups. Freydis, planning to acquire the brothers' ship and goods, complained to her husband that they had molested her. In great anger he roused his crew and attacked and murdered all of the other men. But they would not kill the five women. At that, Freydis screamed, "Hand me an axe!" and killed them.

She tried to bribe her crew, uttering death threats to anyone who told what had happened. Finally even Leif heard the story, but he said he had no heart to punish her. Forever afterward her name was cursed in the sagas, from whence this story comes.

One might be persuaded that the discoveries of Icelandic ruins in New-foundland would put the Freydis saga far from Cape Cod. But there are many mariners who question the exclusion— for good reasons. First, Bjarni's return to Iceland took him ten days of scudding before a strong, often gale-force wind from the south. A Viking longship can easily do seven knots. That comes pretty close to 1700 miles, much farther than from Newfoundland to Greenland. Second the early Greenland map shows a peninsula jutting out into the Atlantic in about the location of Cape Cod, and utterly unlike the Newfoundland coastline. Finally, Leif's cabins were temporary structures, hardly able to survive 900+ years. So why not keep Cape Cod in the running? It seems to fit the sagas very well indeed.

This collection of sea stories is presented with the aim of acquainting you with the world of the seaman and of the history of this area. It was a dangerous world indeed. For instance, Lloyd's of London, the great marine insurer, reported in 1830 that 677 insured vessels were lost at sea; in 1881 the figure was 973.

Aside from a good deal of history, here are, among others, the first English fort on this continent, mutiny, piracy, bravery, a woman navigator or two, clipper ships, dramatic rescues, disasters at sea, rum-running, and cannibalism. You may well marvel at and enjoy these tales, many of them first-hand experiences, and all true.

And for those readers unacquainted with the sea and things maritime, as well as ordinary landlubbers, the appendix depicts much of the jargon of the sea and of whaling. Do feel free to turn to it whenever you need elucidation.

CHAPTER
1

Exploration and Settlement

The First English Settlement

Many explorers (as well as fishermen) sailed these waters, as early as 1511, when Miguel Corte Real left an inscription on a rock in the Taunton River. In 1524 Verrazano, exploring for France, wrote a full description of the area and drew a map. Estevan Gomez, sailing for Spain, also explored this coast as far north as Maine and brought some Native Americans back to Corunna, mapping the coast quite accurately.

But the credit for the first attempt at settling was Bartholomew Gosnold's, in 1602. Sailing from Falmouth, England, on 26 March 1602, his "small Bark of

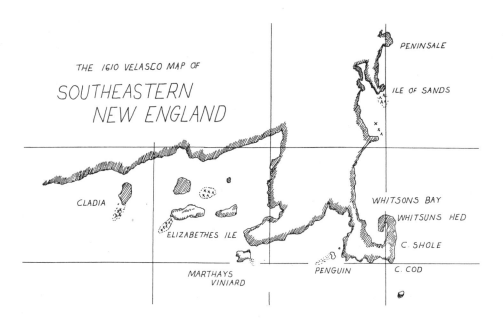

Figure 1-1 Part of Velasco's 1610 map, showing the Elizabeth Islands, Cape Cod and Martha's Vineyard.

Dartmouth, called the Concord," with a crew of thirty-two, aimed for "the North part of Virginia," as John Brereton, one of two diarists, reported.

Driven by contrary winds to the Azores, from there they sailed due west, and forty-nine days later, on 14 May arrived off Cape Cod. At their first anchorage they "took great store of codfish, for which we altered the name (of Shoal Hope), and called it Cape Cod." Finding their way down the outer Cape, they entered Nantucket Sound and anchored off an island (which they called Martha's Vineyard). Ashore, they were delighted to find:

Strawberries, red and white, . . . much bigger than ours; raspberries, goose-berries, whortleberries, and such an incredible store of vines . . .; also many springs of excellent sweet water, and a great standing lake of fresh water. . . Here are also in this Island, great store of deer . . .; as also divers fowls. as cranes, hernshaws [?], bitterns, geese, mallards, teals . . .On the north side of this Island we found many huge bones and ribs of whales.

Figure 1-2 Gosnold's men at Cuttyhunk. From Amelia Forbes Emerson, *Early History of Naushon Island.*

Further exploration of the islands led them to Poocutohhunk-konnoh — which became Cuttyhunk in English— as the best place to establish a settlement. Gabriel Archer describes the location on a pond:

in circuit two miles, on the one side not distant from the sea thirty yards, in the center whereof is a rocky islet, containing near an acre of ground full of wood, on which we began our fort and place of abode.

Gosnold named the island Elizabeth's Isle, in honor of Queen Elizabeth, and on 29 May began to build their fort, intending to leave part of the crew there, as a settlement. A major discovery was a large number of sassafras trees, extremely valuable as medicine in England. These they began to fell, to load aboard the *Comfort* as a return cargo. (Later Elizabeth's name became attached to the entire chain of islands, of which Cuttyhunk is the southernmost.)

They met and were most impressed with the native people. Archer describes them as "tall big boned men, all naked, saving they cover their private parts with a black towed skin, tied about their middle and between their legs behind." Brereton is highly complimentary with his picture of them:

These people as they are exceeding courteous, gentle of disposition, well conditioned, excelling all others that we have seen; . . . of stature much higher than we; of complexion or color much like a dark olive; their eyebrows and hair black, which they wear long, tied up behind in knots.

Much trading went on: furs of beaver, marten, fox, seal, deer, and tobacco offered by the native people for "certain trifles, as knives, points, and such like, which they much esteemed."

On 5 June as they were working on the fort, some fifty "savages . . . stout and lusty men with their bows and arrows," led by their "seignoir" (chief or sachem) landed on the island in canoes. They seemed quite belligerent until Archer

presented my musket with a threatening countenance, thereby to signify unto them, either a choice of peace or war, whereupon he using me with my own sign of peace, I stepped forth and embraced him; his company then all sat down like greyhounds upon their heels, with whom my company fell a bartering.

Captain Gosnold, having arrived, gave the chief a straw hat and two knives. "This our courtesy made them all in love with us."

Two days later the entire entourage arrived again and stayed most of the day. Going to dinner, the ship's company invited the native people to dine with them— quite a feast, including "Scallops, Muscles, Cockles, Crabs, Oisters, and Wilks [whelks]," as well as venison. The only part of the meal that the savages did not like was the hot English mustard; they screwed up their faces mightily at the taste.

During the dinner they stole a "target" [shield], and when told, their chief returned it, fearing retribution from Gosnold, ". . . but seeing our familiarity to continue, they fell afresh to [feasting]."

On the tenth Captain Gosnold sailed to a different island to gather cedar wood, leaving Archer and nine others at the fort with very few supplies. They expected him back soon, but he did not come; so four men went foraging for food on the island. Separating into twos, one group was assaulted by four natives, who wounded one man; the other cut their bow strings and ran off. But on 12 June the ship arrived, much to their relief.

The next few days were spent loading the ship with sassafras and cedar. But some of the men chosen to stay refused to do so, and finally the idea of a settlement was abandoned. On 18 June they set sail for England, and on the way they observed the huge sea of kelp (later known as the Sargasso Sea) within two hundred leagues (600 miles) of Europe. They arrived off Exmouth, England, on 23 July, 1602. The expedition, while it failed, gave an impetus to England to start colonizing.

But Gosnold, thwarted at his first attempt at a colony, along with Gabriel Archer and John Martin (also a member of the *Concord's* crew), joined the ill-fated Jamestown expedition of 1606. After a year a plague hit the colony, the Native Americans attacked, and all three died.

Figure 1-3 Champlain's drawing of the Ile de Sainte Croix settlement. *Permission of the Houghton Library, Harvard University.*

A Death for a Kettle

Long before the founding of Plymouth in 1620, the first recorded confrontation between English and native Americans was recorded in the *Voyages of the Samuel, Sieur de Champlain.* It resulted in the death of a carpenter over the theft of a kettle, much prized by the inhabitants.

In 1604 the French, under Pierre de Monts, built a settlement on the St. Croix river in Maine. Quickly houses, a kitchen, a smithy, and bakery went up, and the company settled in. But the conditions were so bad that during the winter "out of seventy-nine . . . thirty-five died, and more than twenty were on the point of death."

Desperately they decided to go in search of a better site for their settlement. On 18 June 1605, with a crew of twenty men (Champlain along as map-maker) the fifteen-ton barque set out to explore every possible location down to Plymouth harbor. A month later they were sailing along the back side of Cape Cod and anchored off what is now Nauset before finding an opening in the beach and taking refuge inside the bars. While there, Champlain made a map of the area which is valid today, given the changes of almost four hundred years.

The inhabitants' dwellings densely surrounded the anchorage. Quickly a trading pattern grew up: tobacco, bows, and arrows for beads, buttons, and other trinkets. On 21 July Sieur de Monts visited the village and found corn in flower, beans, squash, and tobacco growing in native fields.

Then on the twenty-third a party carrying large kettles went ashore for water. The first man at the spring was the carpenter. After filling his kettle, he had started for the boats. Suddenly a number of natives grabbed the kettle, and when he ran brought him down with arrows and then finished him off with knives.

The others of the party, unarmed, could only cry for help. When the barque responded with gunfire, the raiders retreated into the mainland. The local sachem (chief) sent his representative to the ship to explain that the culprits were not his people but raiders, probably from the area of Barnstable much farther up the Cape. The French accepted his explanation. In Champlain's journal is a graphic drawing of a marauder stabbing the carpenter as the French charge up the beach, firing as they come. Champlain was there, and his musket blew up as he fired it, almost killing him.

The burial of the murdered man occurred shortly, and as the French burial service was read over the body, these nineteen men bowed their heads in tribute to the dead man and erected a wooden cross over his grave.

On 25 June 1605, with a southwest wind, they got underway and headed for St. Croix. They almost grounded on the outer bar off Nauset, but by luck and good seamanship they scraped over and headed for home, leaving the carpenter under the sands of Nauset beach.

The Battle at Stage Harbor

Still searching for a better site for their colony in Maine, the French again sailed southward in 1606 under Baron de Poutrincourt. Again Champlain was aboard as mapmaker, with some twenty crewmen in a fifteen-ton barque. This time Secondon, an Etchemin chief and an enemy of the Cape Cod tribes, was along as interpreter. They set sail on 5 September.

After nearly a month of prospecting along the coasts of Maine and Massachusetts, by October they were crossing Cape Cod Bay. On 1 October they discovered the famous Wellfleet oysters and had a feast of them. That afternoon they rounded the Cape and started down the "backside" during the night. Stopping at Nauset harbor, they paid a visit to the grave of their dead shipmate, the carpenter, who had been killed by the natives two years before.

Continuing down the coast with a fair wind, they anchored near the beach off Chatham. Here they met the Monomoyick, who were able to battle the heavy surf and come out to the vessel. They told the French about a good harbor to the south, and so de Poutrincourt set out the next morning— into that series of dangerous shoals called Mallebarre (Evil bars).

By consummate seamanship they picked their way through, often with only six inches of water under the keel. Rough seas often banged the barque down on the sand, damaging the rudder. Finally they broke free and anchored off Monomoy Point while they rigged some way to steer. Daniel Hay took a boat to explore around Monomoy and found the mouth of Stage Harbor, a totally protected little place up behind Monomoy. Reporting back, he led the barque around and into the harbor. The French named the place Port Fortune (satirically Unlucky Harbor).

Landing, they were allowed by the natives to set up a forge to repair the ironwork of the rudder. They built an oven to replenish their bread supply and set up a tent for a security watch. But nothing was taken. Quickly a trade in native tobacco and bows and arrows for French hatchets and knives grew up. The natives provided the barque with corn, beans, and raisins most hospitably.

Things were going well at first. Repairs on the rudder were almost done and the bread supply was being topped off. Then one of the Monomoyick tried to steal a French hatchet. De Poutrincourt made a tactical error: he did not report the theft to the chief to obtain justice; instead the soldiers fired upon the group of natives where the thief was. The barque had been at Stage Harbor for ten days.

Suddenly the entire encampment of natives disappeared, taking with them their food and goods and moving inland. Hurrying the repairs, de Poutrincourt ordered removal of everything on shore by that night. The cook and two helpers were finishing the baking and were told to be aboard that night.

But they were having a little party of their own, and when the shallop came to pick them up, one refused to go because he could not get drunk on board. The other two joined him, as did two men from the shallop. Giving up, the shallop's crew left them at their carousing. The commander was asleep, and no one told him of the trio's refusal to return; very likely the duty officer was celebrating, too. A dangerous situation indeed.

Before dawn some four hundred Monomoyick were sneaking up on the tent where the five were sleeping off their binge. Aroused by the natives' war cries, they ran toward the water and were cut down by "such a volley of arrows that to rise up was death," reports Grant's *Voyages of Samuel de Champlain.* One man, badly wounded, survived and recovered; another died upon his return to Port Royal.

On the ship, the war cries and screams of the French alerted the crew, and de Poutrincourt, Champlain, and others jumped into the shallop and made for the shore. The boat grounded far from shore, and the rescue party waded in, only to find that the natives had retreated out of range. They could only bury the dead near a cross and rescue the two wounded men.

Immediately the natives returned, dug up the bodies, and started a fire to burn them. When the small cannon on the barque was fired at them, they simply lay prone, and the shot went over their heads. Enraged by the natives' taunting, the shore party again landed, but the natives disappeared again. All they could do was extinguish the fire, rebury the bodies and set up the cross, which the natives had torn down.

Thoroughly demoralized, they set sail to the west on the morning of the sixteenth. Since the head winds were too strong, they returned to Stage Harbor to wait for favorable winds. For three days they waited, and then they tried again, only to give up and return. Conditions aboard were bad. A musket explosion blew off a man's hand; the stench from the wounds of the two survivors of the native attack permeated the ship; medical supplies were almost gone. To go ashore was to court death.

Figure 1-4 The Stage Harbor battle on 15 October 1606. *Permission of the Houghton Library, Harvard University.*

To do something— anything— positive, they decided to revenge themselves on the Monomoyick. A group of the most powerful crew members would go ashore carrying beads over their arms, to gain the natives' confidence and lure them into the boat, if possible. If not, each man should go up to a native with the beads, and, when close enough, grab him and tie him up. If that did not work, the native was to be stabbed to death.

The ruse worked fairly well. Although suspicious, six or seven natives came close enough to be grabbed, but they fought so hard that they were all killed. And Etchemin, their enemy, took all their scalps, as well as one head, which dropped into the water, much to his chagrin.

For a day or two after this massacre, things were quiet. Then the natives in their turn tried to entice the French into an ambush. But the armored men drove them back with musket fire several times. And that was the end of open hostilities. The French had lost four men; beyond the six or seven slain in cold blood, the native losses were unknown; they always took away their dead and wounded.

Finally the wind shifted, and the barque sailed around Monomoy, avoiding the shoals by going far out around them, and anchored off Monomoy. Finally, on 28 October 1606, they left Cape Cod forever, leaving behind such a legacy of treachery that no European could land and live until Governor Bradford made peace in 1622. And the Monomoyicks never really gave their wholehearted allegiance to the settlers until the 1680's.

All the exploring of these waters that they had done came to naught, for they never returned to claim what became New England instead of New France, and history took a new direction within a few brief years with the arrival of the *Mayflower* off these shores.

The First Town Meeting

Probably most of us Americans know something of the voyage of the *Mayflower* to establish the first colony in New England. And a great many of us have seen for ourselves the replica *Mayflower* and its hideously crowded quarters, in which 102 passengers somehow survived a very rough voyage of sixty-five days. Only one person, young William Butten, servant to Samuel Fuller, died on the voyage.

The Puritan passengers ("Saints") were outnumbered by the less religious "Strangers," even though the Saints had organized the expedition. They carried with them a set of instructions from John Robinson, the organizer, which read in part:

Lastly, whereas you are become a body politic, using amongst your selves civill government, . . . let your wisdome and godlines appeare, not only in chusing shuch persons as do entirely love and will promote ye comone good, but also in yeelding unto them all due honour & obedience in their lawful administrations.

These words, and others in his letter of instructions to the the Pilgrims, foreshadow the very first act of the group, once they reached the New World— the *Mayflower Compact.*

The voyage had been a harrowing one. First, westerly winds and the then unknown Gulf Stream had slowed the voyage markedly. One baby had been born and scurvy (lack of vitamin C) was attacking both crew and passengers. Nearing the end of the sixty-five days, water was critically short, and firewood was completely gone, even for cooking. And in mid-November the westerlies held more than a hint of winter for these people without a source of heat.

Then, early in the morning of 11 November (19 November by our calendar), the lookout at the masthead gave the call which brought everyone to the rail. Land was sighted. William Bradford says, "by the break of day we espied the land which we deemed Cape Cod . . . and we were not a little joyfull." As nearly as anyone can reconstruct the landfall, they had arrived off the shore of Eastham, near where the former Coast Guard station is today.

Numerous historians have doubted that Captain Christopher Jones, a most seasoned seaman, hit Cape Cod so accurately, except by chance. But this opinion fails to understand the level of navigation technology of that time. The captain certainly did not know his ship's longitude; there were no chronometers yet. But he did have the tried and true cross-staff and so always knew his latitude. So all he had to do was to hit the forty-second parallel (on which Cape Cod lay) and sail west; all captains knew that.

With a north wind, they decided to head at once for the Hudson River. Accordingly, on a southwest course they sailed down the back shore. Without any warning whatever, suddenly they "fell amongst deangerous shoulds and roring breakers, and they were so farr intangled ther with as they conceived them selves in great danger," says Bradford. And just as suddenly— a miracle, they thought it -- the wind swung around to the south, and they were able to haul around and head north. Prudently, with darkness, the captain kept his ship well offshore, backing and filling until daybreak.

On the twentieth the *Mayflower* struggled against strong currents into the fine harbor that is Provincetown's today. It was there that the first town meeting was held. A tricky situation faced the Saints; they were outnumbered by the Strangers, who "made discontented & mutinous speeches." But the tradition of settling affairs by majority vote prevailed, since they had to form some sort of government in this new land. Every freeman of legal age eventually signed the "combination", as they called it.

And so this document, one of the great pieces of paper in the English-speaking world, like Magna Carta, the Declaration of Independence, and the Constitution, came into being at the New World's first town meeting:

In ye name of God, Amen. We whose names are underwriten, doe by these presents . . . covenant & combine our selves into a body politick . . .to enact,

Figure 1-5 The signing of the Mayflower Compact. *Courtesy of the Pilgrim Society, Plymouth, Mass.*

constitute, and frame such just & equal lawes, ordinances, acts, constitutions, & offices, from time to time, as shall be thought most meete & convenient for ye generall good of ye Colonie. . . .In witness whereof we have hereunder sub- scribed our names at Cap Codd ye Ilth of November. . . Ano: Domini 1620.

Signed and sealed, the Compact next called for election of a governor— John Carver— and the colony, which eventually found its permanent home in Ply- mouth, began its struggle to survive. That winter over half of the signers and the *Mayflower's* crew died of an unknown epidemic, and soon after the captain's re- turn to England he died, still a young man in his thirties, in 1621.

Figure 1-5A This cutaway drawing of *Mayflower* illustrates the crowded conditions aboard during the nine week voyage. The replica, close in size to the original, is 104 feet long, and 102 people lived on *Mayflower I* for the voyage. *Drawing courtesy of The Dicksons, Ply- mouth, Massachusetts.*

Figure 1-6 Model of *Sparrow Hawk. Courtesy of Peabody Essex Museum, Salem, Mass.*

The Loss of the Sparrow Hawk

Governor William Bradford of Plymouth Plantation tells the story of the first recorded wreck on Cape Cod in his *Of Plymouth Plantation*. This series of journals and letters covers the founding of the Puritan church in England, the exile to Holland, and the final arduous voyage to New England in 1620.

In the fall of 1626 the *Sparrow Hawk,* carrying a large number of settlers headed for Virginia, had been six weeks at sea. The vessel's position was unknown, "either by ye insufficiencie of ye maister, or his ilnes; fo he was sick & lame of ye scurvie . . . ; or else ye fear and unrulines of ye passengers . . . "

In addition to not knowing their position, the long voyage had exhausted their supplies. They "had no water, nor beere, nor any woode left, but had burnt up all their emptie casks . . . " Desperately the passengers themselves demanded that the ship steer a course to the west, hoping to hit land somewhere.

By some kind of seaman's luck, at night they somehow crossed the shoals off the east coast of Cape Cod and anchored off a "small blind harbor . . . about ye middle of Manamoyake Bay." When a gale arose they lost their anchor and were driven into the harbor and onto the sand, but the ship had "sprung ye but end of a planke or too, & beat out their occum [oakum, stuffed between planks for water-tightness]."

The next day they were able to "save their lives and goods" and as they were trying to decide their next move, several canoes of native Americans arrived. Fearful, the men stood to their weapons until they were greeted in English, offering to inform the Plymouth colony of their plight. Much relieved, they welcomed the natives and gave them letters telling of the problems of supplies and repairs.

Quickly Governor Bradford himself organized and led a repair party. Wisely, because of the weather, the shallop sailed across Cape Cod Bay into a creek called "Naumskachett" (today the borderline between Brewster and Orleans). There they unloaded and with native help carried food and repair materials across to today's Pleasant Bay and the location of the *Sparrow Hawk*. Repairs completed and food replenished, the governor, while he was there, traded goods for corn and with a full boat sailed home to Plymouth across Cape Cod Bay. The vessel again set sail for Virginia.

But it did not get very far. Apparently they set out "in the teeth of a booming gale," were again driven ashore in almost the same spot and truly wrecked this time. (One does wonder about the competence of their captain!) Miraculously no lives were lost. But their only recourse was "that they might have leave to repair to them [Plymouth] . . . till they could have means to convey them selves to Virginia." The remains of *Sparrow Hawk* lay abandoned on the barrier beach, while the people, their servants, and their goods were taken in until the summer of 1627. Then two barks arrived to carry the colonists to Virginia.

In the interim, however, the two most notable castaways, Messrs. Fells and Sibsie, who owned many servants, asked for land on which to raise corn. A good crop resulted, which Fells and Sibsie sold to Plymouth when they left. But Fells had

Figure 1-7 The recovered "bones" of *Sparrow Hawk* exhibited on Boston Common shortly after their discovery in 1863. *Courtesy of the Pilgrim Society, Plymouth, Mass.*

a maidservant who became pregnant; scandalized, everyone believed she was his concubine, although it could not be proved. Fells, fearing punishment, left the colony with the maid in a small boat, turning up at Cape Ann and then Boston. But he could find no way to return to England and "was forst to come again and submite him selfe; but they pact him away . . . and dismist all the rest . . . being many untoward people amongst them."

But the story of *Sparrow Hawk* is far from over. Buried by shifting sands and later a salt marsh, she lent her name to Old Ship Harbor and was otherwise forgotten. A "tempest" [hurricane] in 1782 rolled back the sand and temporarily revealed her ancient bones. Then she disappeared until 1863, when a powerful storm uncovered her again. With some careful digging, a group of men found the rudder and most of the hull intact. They recognized the history embedded in the *Sparrow Hawk* and had her moved to Boston. There she was reconditioned and later put on exhibit in Boston and Providence; finally she was given to the Pilgrim Society Museum in Plymouth, where she is today-the only relic of the armadas of ships which helped the earliest colonization of what is today the United States.

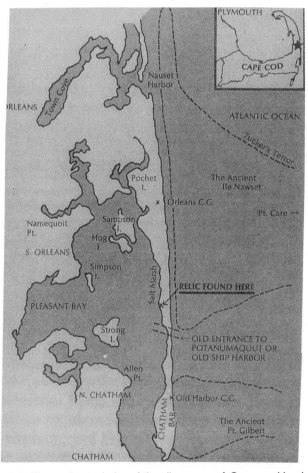

Figure 1-8 The estimated site of the discovery of *Sparrow Hawk. Cour-tesy of the Pilgrim Society, Plymouth, Mass.*

Kendrick and Gray – The Northwest Fur Trade

Captains Jonathan Kendrick and Robert Gray are responsible for not only opening for the United States the incredibly lucrative Northwest fur trade but— much more important— providing the solid basis on which the United States acquired Washington, Oregon, and the northern boundary of the western states. For example, the great Columbia River is named for Captain Gray's ship, in which he discovered the river and sailed far into the interior.

The story has the dimensions of a saga of courage and determination. In two tiny ships (the eighty-foot *Columbia* and the forty-foot *Lady Washington),* they sailed around Cape Horn and up the west coast of the Americas to what became Vancouver Island. Then when they had amassed enough otter and other furs by trading with the native Americans, Captain Kendrick took a cargo of them across the Pacific to Canton, China, in the tiny *Lady Washington.* And that is only the first part of what they accomplished.

And all this was done in the name of private enterprise.

In 1784 the journal of Captain Cook's third voyage along the west coast of North America was published. Its arrival aroused great interest in the possibilities of a fur trade on the northwest coast, mentioned by Cook; sea otter skins sold for about $20 each in China. Joseph Barrett, a prominent merchant, said, "Here is a rich harvest, to be reaped by those who go in first."

Accordingly six well-to-do men subscribed over $50,000 to outfit an expedition. They first bought the ship *Columbia,* which had been built in 1783 on the North River in Scituate, Massachusetts. A full rigged ship, she was eighty-three feet long, measuring 212 tons. With two decks, a square stern, a figurehead, and ten guns, she was a sturdy vessel. Then they acquired the *Lady Washington,* a ninety-ton sloop, about forty feet long, with a shallow draft, excellent for trading.

Figure 1-9 Hobart's Landing, North River, Scituate, Mass., where *Columbia* was built.

As leader and master of *Columbia* they chose Captain Jonathan Kendrick of Harwich on Cape Cod, who commanded several privateers during the Revolutionary War and, some people say, participated in the Boston Tea Party. About forty-five years old, his home was in Wareham, where he had built a large house and fathered six children.

To command the sloop, the owners chose Captain Robert Gray, who had already sailed for two of the owners, Brown and Hatch, with their ship *Pacific*, trading to South Carolina. He had been an officer in the Continental navy and was a friend of Kendrick's. From Tiverton, Rhode Island, he was a descendant of the Plimoth colonists. After his marriage in 1794 he lived in Boston on Salem Street with his family of five children.

Both the federal and state governments issued Sea Letters for the voyage, asking all with whom the ships came in contact to render them every necessary service. In addition, a medal was struck in bronze and pewter, and hundreds of them went aboard to be given to people met on the voyage. Several of them have turned up in the possession of Native Americans, Spaniards, and Hawaiians.

Figure 1-10 Medal (in silver and pewter) struck to commemorate the sailing of the two ships.

The vessels carried full cargoes of necessary stores, a plentiful supply of tools, and trading trinkets— buttons, beads, necklaces, toys, jew's harps, earrings, combs, snuff, and snuff boxes. The officers were carefully chosen: Simon Woodruff as first mate, who had been an officer of Captain Cook's; as second mate Joseph Ingraham, who later played a large part in the fur trade; and Robert Haswell, son of a British naval officer, who made a meticulous record of the expedition. And other officers included a clerk, a surgeon, an astronomer, and a furrier.

The owners' instructions were quite detailed and specific. They read in part:

Sir:The ship Columbia *and the sloop* Washington *being completely equipped for a voyage to the Pacific-ocean and China, we place such confidence in you as to give you the entire command of this enterprise. . . . [It is] our wish and expectation that the most inviolable harmony . . . may be cultivated between you and the natives, and that no advantage be taken of them, in trading.*

If you make any fort . . . be sure you purchase the soil of the natives; and it would not be amiss if you purchased some advantageous tracts of land, in the name of the owners. . . . You are strictly enjoined not to touch at any part of the Spanish dominions . . . unless driven there by some unavoidable accident. . . yet we depend you will suffer insult and injury from none, without showing that spirit which will ever become A FREE AND INDEPENDENT AMERICAN.

On 1 October 1787, the two vessels left Boston and had a good run across the Atlantic to the Cape Verde Islands, off Africa. There, for some unknown reason, Captain Kendrick dawdled for two months; two of the officers left the ship in disgust. Then on they went to the Falkland Islands, off the tip of South America, where they found plenty of wildfowl but no firewood. They stayed there so long that Kendrick wanted to stay over for the next season, but he was persuaded to go on, and on 28 February 1788 they sailed for the Pacific.

Running into dreadful westerly weather rounding Cape Horn, they struggled

AFTER AN OLD DRAWING BY DAVIDSON.

At the Falkland Islands.

Figure 1-11 Captain Gray (holding chart) talking with an officer in the Falkland Islands.

for a month to pass that ominous series of islands and were indeed lucky to have survived. On 1 April in a hurricane they lost sight of each other, and it was two weeks later that the weather broke. Sailing separately, Captain Gray on 2 August spotted Cape Mendocino, north of San Francisco, sailed on up the coast, and anchored near Cape Lookout. There they had their first fight with the natives. The cabin boy had his cutlass stolen, and when he tried to retrieve it the natives stabbed him to death, despite the best efforts of the rest of the landing party. With only three men aboard *Lady Washington,* if the boat crew had been taken the sloop might well have been captured. They named the bay Murderers' Harbor, probably Tillamook Bay, some fifty miles south of the mouth of the Columbia River.

Columbia had suffered so much damage in the hurricane that Captain Kendrick put into the San Juan Fernando Islands (Spanish territory) to refit. The governor, Don Blas Gonzales, gave them everything they needed— and for that generosity he was cashiered by the Viceroy of Peru. After a refit of seventeen days, it was a smooth run up the coast. But word of *Columbia's* coming preceded them, so that the governor of San Francisco ordered the captain of the Presidio (the fortress) to seize the vessel and crew if she came into the harbor.

Finally, on 16 August 1788, *Lady Washington* arrived at the rendezvous in Nootka Sound, on Vancouver Island. They found two friendly English snows (small vessels) in the harbor whose captains welcomed them. A week later *Columbia* appeared, with her crew mostly so sick with scurvy that they could not handle the sails.

In fact little did Kendrick know just what a whirlpool of international competition he and Gray were sailing into. The Spanish were trying to extend their sovereignty farther north above California, and the Russians were trying to extend their territory farther south from Alaska. And the English had commissioned a study and map of the entire coastline. They were all looking for the fabled Northwest Passage, to save the terrible trip around Cape Horn.

Captain George Vancouver's commission was to survey the coast from the 35th parallel (just above Los Angeles) to the 60th parallel (where the main part of Alaska begins today) and try to find the Northwest passage and the Strait of San Juan de Fuca (behind Vancouver Island). He failed in the last two of these endeavors. In fact it was Captain Kendrick who discovered in 1789 that Vancouver was an island, sailing all the way behind it and into Queen Charlotte Sound above it. Vancouver thought that it was part of the mainland. Meanwhile the Spanish were claiming it, arresting two English vessels, *Argonaut* and *Northwest America,* and their crews. The Russians were also prospecting southward.

But Kendrick's and Gray's job was to collect otter skins. At one place a fleet of canoes came out, offering a skin for a chisel. They bought the whole two hundred, worth up to $8000. This was their best bargain: usually the price was one skin for a blanket, four for a pistol, and six for a musket. After further exploring and with a full cargo, Kendrick and Gray exchanged commands, and on 30 July 1789

Figure 1-12 Captain Gray at Whampoa, China, planning the Columbia River search in 1790. *Drawn by George Davidson of Charlestown, Mass.,the ship's artist.*

Gray in *Columbia* set out for Canton, China, with the fur, stopping at the Hawaiian Islands for supplies and getting involved in a dynastic war.

The sea otter skin market was poor; Gray lost money, but he loaded up with tea and sailed home around the Cape of Good Hope (the "round voyage," seamen called it), arriving in Boston on 10 August 1790, having logged some 50,000 miles. Meanwhile Kendrick in *Washington,* with five hundred skins, anchored in Macao (the Portuguese island colony off China) on 26 January 1790. The sloop was in such bad shape that he spent four months repairing and rerigging her as a brig.

Captain Gray in *Columbia* soon again set out and arrived on the northwest coast in seven months instead of eleven. On 12 August 1791 three of his men were massacred by the natives; one body, Caswell's, was recovered and buried. On another occasion Kendrick was trading in *Washington,* being very careful to allow only two natives on deck at once. Going below, he heard a native laugh on deck and, charging up, he found a whole row of them along the rail; the arms chest key was in possession of one of the intruders. When he demanded the key, the native said, "The key is mine and the ship is mine too!" The captain promptly heaved the man overboard, and all the rest dived after him.

Near here, too, Captain Kendrick's son, Solomon, was killed by the natives. Finding his son's scalp of curly red hair, he demanded custody of the murderer, but then wisely he returned the man to the chief for punishment, thinking of the future safety of white men in the area.

During this time Kendrick, with great ceremony, bought a number of tracts of land from various chiefs. The deeds were similar in form:

AFTER AN OLD DRAWING BY DAVIDSON.

In the Straits of Juan de Fuca.

Figure 1-13 *Columbia* in the straits of San Juan de Fuca, firing on native canoes trying to take the ship. *Drawn by George Davidson.*

In consideration of six muskets, a boat's sail, a quantity of powder, and an American flag . . . we do bargain, grant, and sell unto Johh Kendrick of Boston a certain harbor . . . with all the lands, mines, minerals, bays, harbors, sounds, creeks, and all islands . . . with all the produce of land and sea . . . being a territorial distance of eighteen miles square . . . to have and to hold.

This was the deal made with Norry-Youk. Macquinnah sold him nine miles square; Wickananish, chief of the Clyoquet, sold him eighteen miles square for even less; Tarassom let his eighteen miles go for only two muskets and powder; Caarshucornook of Nootka Sound sold his nine miles for two muskets and powder. If one calculates the actual size of the purchases on Vancouver Island, one finds that Kendrick had bought some *two hundred forty square miles!* The deeds, legal at that time, are in the State Department archives.

And this was Jonathan Kendrick's greatest achievement. These deeds, supported by many affidavits of captains as to their validity, and the discovery and exploration of the Columbia River. When the United States and England finally drew their mutual western boundary in 1846, the United States won Washington and Oregon as well as the northern tier of our states.

With all the ship traffic along that coast, one would have thought that the Columbia River would have been found much sooner. But it was Robert Gray who claimed the river for the United States. On 29 April 1792 he took *Columbia* on a cruise to the south. Meeting Vancouver, he exchanged information. Vancouver said that he had passed a river but thought it not worth his attention. Gray had tried for nine days to enter a river in latitude 46° 10' and was going to try again. On 11

May he sighted the river's mouth and ran in through the breakers, anchoring in ten fathoms in a river three or four miles wide, a huge river. On the fourteenth he sailed fifteen miles upriver until blocked by narrow channels. Finding no way to go farther, he sailed back down to the mouth and formally named the river "Columbia", planting coins under a pine tree, and thus claiming it for the United States.

Leaving the river, Gray sailed north again to Nootka, where, having run upon a rock, he asked for help from the Spanish governor, Don Quadra. He received such hospitality and help that he named his first son Robert Don Quadra Gray. From there he left with his furs for China, arriving at Macao on 7 December 1792. Selling his furs, he took on a cargo of tea, sugar, chinaware, and curios. On 3 February 1793 he sailed for Boston, arriving on 29 July 1793 to a hero's welcome.

Captain Kendrick never returned to America. In the Hawaiian Islands he developed a lucrative trade in sandalwood with China, still in *Lady Washington*. In 1793, six years after leaving Boston, he was killed in Karakakua Bay on "Owyhee" (Hawaii) on New Year's Day. *Washington* and an English ship were exchanging salutes. Carelessly the gunner on the English ship had a shot in the cannon (instead of a blank) and aimed it too accurately, killing Kendrick outright. Captain Gray went on to command several other ships but died in 1806 in Charleston, S.C.

For years the Kendrick and Gray families, as well as those of the owners of the original ships, tried to obtain some recompense for the vast lands which Captain Kendrick had acquired— without success. They were trying for some $7000, in addition to the cost of the ships and outfit, with interest. The committee of Congress eventually reported out a bill, giving

to the widow of Captain Gray, and to the children of Captain Kendrick, and to each of the owners of the two exploring vessels, five sections of land . . . [which] may yet afford a solace . . . that time has not obliterated from the memory of their country the worth and the services of their departed relatives.

But the adventure was a magnificent one, having major consequences for the history of the United States. May this report, even though the bill never was passed, remind us all of what we owe these two intrepid captains and their achievements in the tiny *Columbia* and the even tinier *Lady Washington*.

As a bonus, this sailor's chantey telling of a harrowing near-disaster was unearthed. It comes from the Doane family, formerly of Nova Scotia. Captain Benjamin Doane, born in 1823, learned it as a small boy from his father, Nehemiah, born in 1776, who knew Captain Kendrick's father, and Captain Kendrick himself. Omissions are the result of faulty remembering.

Come all ye Nor'west men who plow the raging main,
And listen to my story while I relate the same.
'Tis of the "Lady Washington", decoyed as she lay
At Queen Charlotty's Island, Northwest Americay.

'Twas on the fourteenth day of June in the year of '91,
The savages in great numbers on board our ship did come;
Then for to buy the furs our captain did begin—
Mark well what they attempted ere 'fore long time had been.
'Twas aft upon the quarterdeck two arms-chests there did stand,
And in them were left the keys by our gunner's careless hand.
No sooner did they perceive them, of them they made a prize,
Thinking we had no other arms for to defend our lives.

"Our captain then spoke in Coyah and thus to him did say,
'If you'll deliver up the keys 'tis for the same i'll pay.'
No sooner had he spoken than they all drew out their knives,
Crying, 'The ship, she's ours! We intend to have your lives.'

"Then aft upon the quarterdeck Kendrick was forced to stand,
Confronting twelve cross savages with knives all in their hands,
Pointing toward his body, ready to pierce him through
If he offered to stir or move— Poor man, what could he do?

"The captain then perceiving the ship was in their power,
He called for his seamen, likewise his officers.
"Go down in yonder cabin; a few firearms prepare.
See that they are well loaded; be sure they don't misfire."

(Three lines were lost from memory)
"And the sign that I will give you, brave boys, is 'Follow me!

"Then down into the cabin his 'brave boys' did retire,
And to our grave misfortune we found but few small arms there:
Only one gun, two pistols, and one or two small swords.

(Five lines lost from memory.)
"And then it was agreed upon, 'Blow up the ship, my boys!

"We got our powder in readiness, in open gun-room laid,
And committed our souls to God, for a watery grave prepared,
When one of those cross savages making a spring below,
Our captain cries out, 'Follow me!' and after him we go.

"With what few firearms then we had we rushed on deck amain
And by means of being resolute the quarterdeck did gain.
Oh, when we got to our arms chests, what slaughter then made we;

In less than fifteen minutes our decks from them were free.
(Two lines lost from memory.)
"Threw their bodies overboard and upon their town did play*
'Til they delivered up the keys they stole from us that day.

(Two lines lost from memory)
"Here's health unto bold Kendrick! Safe voyages may he go.
Prosperity attend him, and death befall his foe!"

* *With their guns.*

Figure 1-14 This foundered wreck illustrates vividly the dangers, especially to sailing ships, of trying to navigate the mouth of the Columbia River between Washington and Oregon in rough weather. Today, the U.S. Coast Guard maintains its surfboat training school there because of the incredibly tall surf at the river's mouth. *Courtesy of William P. Quinn.*

CHAPTER
2

War

A Puzzling Pair of Pirates

Few of us Americans remember from our history classes that New England had a revolution long before 1775—the "Glorious Revolution" of 1689. During the confusion of that time two well-established Englishmen (one a cartographer and pilot in the British navy, the other well connected by marriage) went on a rampage in Vineyard Sound. Men were killed, vessels were seized, and goods stolen. And when the fourteen pirates were caught and tried, only one of the fourteen was hanged. A most strange story indeed.

It had its origins in England, four years earlier. James, Duke of York, became King James II, a strong Catholic, with close ties to Martha's Vineyard. Thomas Mayhew, owner and perpetual governor (nearly the dictator) of the island, had named Edgartown for the king's son. At least half of the inhabitants wanted to move from New York's control to that of Puritan Massachusetts, but the king detested the Puritan rule and refused.

James wasted no time in reorganizing the colonies. In 1686 he established the Dominion of New England, covering Massachusetts, New Hampshire, Maine, Connecticut, New York, and New Jersey. And to make his intentions quite plain, he sent three companies of British troops to Boston in the frigate *Rose*. Soon the new governor, Sir Edmund Andros, arrived and began to issue royal decrees: he abolished the town meeting, made Boston's South Church the first Anglican church in New England, and claimed that all lands in the Dominion still belonged to the King. This of course made all native American deeds "no more worth than a scratch with a bear's paw," as he put it.

Two years later, on 23 December 1688, the king was forced by Parliament to abdicate, and he fled to France. Elected king and queen were Protestant Prince William of Orange and Princess Mary, a sister of King James. Word of the great change arrived with John Winslow early in April 1689, and on 18 April the pent-up anger of the Puritans boiled over. By the end of the day Governor Andros was a prisoner, and the frigate, two British-manned forts, and the redcoats all had surrendered—a truly bloodless revolution. But on 3 August Andros escaped from Castle Island and fled to Newport.

Somehow this seemed a good time for our two pirates, Captain Thomas Pound, who was pilot of *Rose,* and Thomas Hawkins, who owned a small vessel, to move. They recruited a crew of British deserters and former privateers and sailed out of Boston hunting for victims. Their first victim on 9 August was the ketch *Mary,* from which they took sixty pounds' worth of supplies.

A few days later, in Cape Cod Bay, they simply took over the *Good Speed* and put her crew aboard their old boat. Much larger, and with weapons and ammunition stolen from *Rose,* their new pirate vessel was large enough to impress their victims.

Having heard about this new threat, Governor Simon Bradstreet ordered the sloop *Resolution,* with a crew of forty, to find and seize the pirates. But Captain Joseph Thaxter never found them, for they had slipped out of Cape Cod Bay and into Vineyard Sound. In Holmes' Hole, (Vineyard Haven today), they attacked the brigantine *Merrimack* and at gunpoint took ten barrels of flour, sugar, rum, three guns, and 100 pounds of tobacco. Sailing away, they found themselves driven by adverse winds to Virginia, where they kidnapped an African-American slave.

Once back in the sound, they anchored in Naushon Island's Tarpaulin Cove near a Salem barque. Since there was too large a crew for the pirates to tackle, they resorted to diplomacy. They bought an anchor for 200 pounds of their stolen sugar and sold the slave to the captain.

From there they sailed across the sound to Edgartown, chasing a ketch right into the harbor. But when a fleet of small boats manned by angry citizens surrounded them, they departed for Cape Cod. There Captain Hawkins deserted (probably he had had his fill of privacy) and Thomas Pound took over. Back at Holmes' Hole, they boarded a sloop and pretty well cleaned out the larder; then they returned to Tarpaulin Cove. In all their depredations so far, no ammunition had been spent and no one had been harmed— at least physically.

But their time was running out. Having received word of the *Good Speed*'s location, on Governor Bradstreet's orders Captain Pease headed for Naushon in the armed sloop *Mary,* and on 4 October they heard that the pirates were anchored in Tarpaulin Cove, where *Mary* found them.

The story of the defeat of the pirates is told in great detail by one of the crew:

. . . our Sloop Sailing so very well we quickly came within Shot and our Captain ordered a great Gun to be fired thwart her fore foot. . . . our Captain commanded us to fire on them which accordingly we did, and also called to them to strike [or surrender] Captain Pounds . . . said, come aboard ye Doggs, and I will strike you presently . . . wee many times called to them telling them, if they would yield to us we would give them good quarter . . . [As the fire fight continued] our Captain was much wounded. . . . The Lieutenant quickly after ordered us to get all ready to board, which was readily done, we layd then on

board presently. . . . At last we queld them, killing foure, and wounding twelve, two remaining pretty well.

Mary returned to Boston with her fourteen prisoners. They sat in Boston's brand-new stone jail together with Thomas Hawkins, who had been captured on Cape Cod, until their trial in early January 1690. Hawkins was found guilty of piracy; the others also were found guilty of murder, for Captain Pease had died of his wounds. But only one man was hanged; the others were all pardoned. And here is the puzzle. Why?

On 27 January, execution day, Judge Samuel Sewell and the Reverend Cotton Mather visited the prisoners. There is no record of what was said, but Hawkins was the brother-in-law of Wait Winthrop, a prominent Bostonian. In any event, only five were ordered to be executed. Only one, Thomas Johnson, actually paid for their crimes, a scapegoat, who may have had a criminal record earlier.

But Thomas Hawkins' luck ran out. He and Pound were put aboard the frigate *Rose* to be taken to England. On the voyage they met a French frigate. In the battle that followed Hawkins was killed. History loses sight of Pound at this point.

There are really two puzzles here. First, why were fourteen out of fifteen pirates let off from certain death for their crimes? At least seven men had died, they had stolen a vessel and large quantities of supplies. Too many leaders of Boston were involved for there to be coincidence involved. Second, why the piracy at all? Hawkins moved in the top of Boston society and Pound was a pilot and cartographer in the Royal Navy. There have been guesses over the years, but no answers.

Two French Gentlemen

The story of Elizabeth Vickery and the French privateers is the stuff of oral tradition on Cape Cod. Daughter of the Reverend Jonathan Vickery, Chatham's first minister, she had spent months earning the money for her wedding gown, since she was about to be married to young Jonathan Collins. Now she was about to leave on the packet to find the finest dress in Boston.

Queen Anne's War, so-called, between England and France over who should inherit the throne of Spain, had drawn in the colonies. There were bloody native massacres on the frontiers and plundering of vessels on the high seas. Going to sea was a definitely risky business. But she had to have that dress.

So on a threatening September morning in 1704 she booked passage on a small coaster and with the wind astern they scudded northwest. Before noon they could see the harbor islands and a single sail on its way into Boston. Soon it was clear to the captain that she would cross their bow. This was no ordinary trader but an armed French privateer, gun ports open and *fleur-de-lis* at the masthead.

It was obvious that the Frenchman could outsail him. What to do? Thinking fast, he jibed and, on the other tack, headed for the shoals at Cohasset. But the nimble enemy foresaw the maneuver and with a couple of shots through the rigging forced him to heave to and surrender.

A prize crew came aboard, made the crew and passengers take to their boats, and in a half-hour set sail for their stronghold, Louisbourg, with the captured sloop. Meanwhile Elizabeth had hidden in the sloop's bows. Hearing a boat pull away, she emerged from her hiding-place only to find herself on a sloop full of Frenchmen— a dapper French officer in charge. The surprise was mutual; the officer had not planned on having a twenty-year-old Cape Cod girl to deal with. But a storm was upon them; all he could do was to get underway. Since Elizabeth was shivering, he threw his cloak around her shoulders.

This was a real nor'easter. Despite all that the crew could do, two days later the little sloop, dismasted, water-logged, crashed on Sable Island off the coast of Maine. As the sloop broke up, the captain lashed Elizabeth to the rigging, with himself and the one remaining crewman. Finally a huge wave tossed them far up the beach. Battered, barely alive, they knelt and thanked God for the rescue.

Somehow word leaked out that the packet had never reached Louisbourg. Elizabeth's fiancé sailed to Boston and enlisted in the first warship leaving to fight the French. Then one bright December day, three months after the wreck, his ship was passing Sable Island. The masthead lookout yelled down that he had seen a distress flag on the beach. Jonathan Collins was coxswain of the boat crew sent to investigate. Suddenly he saw his Elizabeth, thin and drawn, dressed in sailcloth, along with the two other survivors. Scarcely believing his eyes, he jumped from the boat and took her in his arms.

Once aboard ship, she was able to tell the whole story. The two men had built a hut with a separate room for her from the wreckage. They used the flints from their pistols to make fire and dug shellfish and trapped wild pigs to stay alive. And not once had these Frenchmen treated her otherwise than with kindness and respect. She begged that they be treated as gentlemen, despite their being prisoners of war. We have no record of what happened to them.

Elizabeth's story has a happy ending, recorded in the old town records of Eastham: "Jonathan Collens and Elisabeth vickerie were married at Easthem by mr. Samll Treat the 27th day of Januarie 1704/ 1705." One can still see the watermark of the lion and the unicorn in the paper. A short ten years later she was dead, very likely on account of the hardships on Sable Island. But her story was told and retold to her children, and their children, and so on through the generations since her time.

Figure 2-1A New England's coasts are littered with the bones of thousands of ships of all types. This might be the remains of the French privateer in which our bride-to-be was imprisoned, after their shipwreck. It was from the flotsam of the wreck that the two French officers built the cabin in which they survived the Maine winter. *Courtesy of William P. Quinn.*

Falmouth and British Privateers

Even before the start of hostilities in April 1775, the Cape and island towns were suffering from raids by the British privateers and warships. Naushon Island, sparsely settled, was the object of a series of raids which denuded it of its livestock several times over. First Captain Lindsey of *Faulkland* (the first British warship built here) hit the island on 5 May 1775. He landed soldiers, who took the livestock of the innkeeper at Tarpaulin Cove, Elisha Nye, later a captain of militia. In response the Massachusetts Committee of Safety ordered the stationing of one hundred men there to protect the cove and the inhabitants.

This was only the first of five such raids by various men-of-war; on 6 December 1776 a flotilla including *H.M.S. Harlem, H.M.S Sphynx,* and four smaller vessels landed troops. They spread out across the width of the island and drove all the livestock they could find to a pen, from which they loaded them aboard ship. There were three more such forays during the war.

Meanwhile, just up the bay in Woods Hole and Falmouth, in May 1775 Falmouth town meeting voted to prepare for future food shortages and defense by acquiring a thousand bushels of bread corn and a good supply of firearms for the company of Minute Men to be raised. Two shillings per day was the pay authorized, and Major Joseph Dimmick (later Brigadier General) became commander. The militia was to train on Falmouth Green. After the colonial troops were removed from Naushon, British depredations became worse, with almost constant presence at Tarpaulin Cove on Naushon, thus bottling up Vineyard Sound.

Joseph Dimmick was the leading figure here. A schooner had been sent to Connecticut for corn; when she entered Vineyard Sound she was taken by the British. The captain, however, escaped by boat and rowed to Woods Hole, rousing Dimmick at midnight. Calling his brother, Lot, he found twenty volunteers and with three whaleboats sailed to Tarpalin Cove, arriving just before sunrise. Landing, they lit a fire in a hollow to keep warm, and then they rowed silently out and boarded the captured schooner. Under fire, they took back the schooner and got underway.

But the privateer chased them so closely that they decided to beach the schooner on the Vineyard. Ashore, they were able to repel the Britisher, which could not come too near because of low tide. Later Dimmick took advantage of the rising tide, refloated the schooner, and brought the cargo of corn to Woods Hole.

Later on Major Dimmick pulled off an even greater feat against the British. He heard of two privateers and a captured schooner at Holmes's Hole on Martha's Vineyard. In a small sloop with twenty five men he arrived before dawn, only to find a British man-of-war also at anchor. "In for a penny, in for a pound," they sneaked in behind the outer privateer and boarded the other one. The surprise was complete; the man-of-war was slow in rousing, and Dimmick was able to escape with both his own and the captured privateer. He sent thirty-three prisoners to Boston for internment in the hulks.

The major became a colonel in 1790, and a brigadier general in 1794; he was at the taking of Fort Ticonderoga. After the war he was high sheriff of Barnstable County for twenty-five years and also state senator just before the War of 1812.

The last British raid on Naushon in April 1779 was part of a larger attempt at Falmouth; their purpose was to burn the town. On 2 April some British officers were at a "frolic" at the home of a well-known Tory, John Slocomb, on Pasque Island. Of course they discussed their plans, and Slocomb decided that his feelings had changed. Secretly he told his son to row to Woods Hole and alert the defenses there.

Warned by the boy that ten or twelve vessels were on the way to burn the town, Major Dimmick promptly sent to Sandwich and Barnstable asking their militia to help repel the fleet. Colonel Nathaniel Freeman and two Sandwich companies arrived by the next morning.

Some of the fleet appeared off Woods Hole, and militia marched there. Colonel Freeman posted some fifty men at a trench along the beach and another thirty farther along at likely landing sites. Just before noon two schooners and eight sloops lined up opposite the landing sites and opened fire. Cannon bails, double-headed shot, grape shot, and musket fire poured into the beach. Then some ten boats with perhaps 220 men tried to land, while the shelling continued from noon to past 5:00 P.M. But the two position held firm and began to return fire, forcing the British to retire. At Woods Hole the boats were driven off and instead landed on Nonamesset Island, close by, where they stole a pig and half a cow before retreating to the ships. Off they sailed to Holmes's Hole.

The next day (5 September) the British were back and again tried to land—to no avail. One sloop sent in a boat to Nonamesset to retrieve the pig and cow that they had killed, but again they were driven off and almost captured by the militia. And that ended the siege of Falmouth.

Figure 2-1 Captain Elijah Cobb of Brewster, whose wits often got him out of trouble during the French Revolution.

Captain Elijah Cobb and Citizen Robespierre

Elijah Cobb, born in Harwich (now Brewster) on 4 July 1768, grew up like most Cape Cod boys of the times: he went to sea. He kept a journal which records his profit from his first voyage:

By my first voyage to sea I gained $20 and a suit of clothing placing in my mother's hands this sum— the largest she had received since she became a widow. . . . After about a year was promoted to . . . mate and served in that capacity for six or seven years. After making several voyages [as captain of a brig] *I went to the Cape and was married. I was then 25 years old.*

In 1794 his owners sent the brig on a voyage to Spain. But he never got there; a French frigate captured the brig, and a prize crew took it to Brest. The French Revolution was in full cry. Captain Cobb lost his vessel and his papers, and his cargo was confiscated to feed the "half-starved populace." And without papers he could not claim his ship.

After six weeks two officers called on him to tell him that the government would buy his load of food. He put his crew aboard and sent her off home in ballast while he went to Paris to get the paperwork done. After a non-stop dash of 684 miles, with twelve mounted men as guards, they arrived safely.

As he was trying to figure out what to do next, a Frenchman in the next room came by and suggested that he write Robespierre, who liked Americans, directly. This he did:

35

An American citizen, captured by a French frigate on the high seas, requests a personal interview and to lay his grievances before the citizen Robespierre.
Very Resp'y
Elijah Cobb

In about an hour he received a reply from the virtual dictator of France: "I will grant citizen Cobb an interview tomorrow at 1 0 A.M. Robespierre." At a cordial meeting (speaking English), Robespierre said:

Go to [the Rue de St. Honoré] *and tell citizen F.T. that you came from Robespierre, and if he does not produce your papers . . . he will hear from me aqain in a way not pleasing to him.*

By the next day he had his papers and was on his way to Hamburg in Germany to collect on his bills of credit. When he arrived home, he was lionized as the man who talked with Robespierre. As a result he was in great demand, and received a new ship, the *Monsoon,* with valuable cargo, headed for Europe.

A considerable quantity of Newburyport rum might have a good market in Ireland, but he could not get permission. However, word had gotten out, and off the Scilly Islands he dropped eight hogsheads of rum overboard and received a bag containing sixty-four English guineas— actual rum-running before 1800! The rest of the cargo sold well in Hamburg. He stayed there all winter and heard of the illness of his wife and the death of his brother, and he was severely ill and lost his hair.

Figure 2-2 The ship *Monsoon*, Captain Cobb's rum-runner.

Soon the *Monsoon* was sold, and he took command of the new brig *Sally and Mary* with another Hamburg cargo. But the French were blockading Hamburg, and he decided that Copenhagen, Denmark, would be a likely port. Home again, he received orders for Malaga, Spain, where he arrived in January 1808.

That day the British order prohibiting return cargoes went into effect. Quickly finding a return load, in eight days he was ready to sail. Off Gibraltar the wind died, and he was boarded by a frigate's boat. With a Spanish cargo, he told them the truth: that he was headed for Gibraltar for a British clearance— and got away with it; they let him go. Fortunately some money changed hands. How he managed to do this was a matter of much conjecture in Boston— and his reputation grew.

Next came the ship *William Tell,* in which again he outwitted the British embargo against all shipping to Europe. He had had word from Mr. Randolph in Congress: "What you do must be done quickly, for the embargo will be upon you at 10 a.m. on Sunday." So beginning on Friday afternoon he rounded up everyone in the "lazy corner," as he called it, and got his crew aboard. With the extra help he loaded 3,050 barrels of flour and had the ship ready for sea an hour before the deadline for custom house clearance. Two hours before the embargo he was underway. But he was becalmed in Hampton Roads, and a customs boat was fast approaching to stop him. "Well," he said to his mate, "I fear we are gone." Just then a breeze came up, just enough to help outdistance the boat.

On he went to Cadiz, Spain, bringing first news of the embargo, a British plan to weaken the new United States during the War of 1812. With a fresh cargo he left Cadiz of 25 July 1812 and was almost to Boston when he saw an armed British schooner bearing down on him. Most politely the British captain asked him to stand by for a boarding. A further polite conversation in which the other captain offered to let him go for $4000 cash— which Elijah Cobb did not have aboard. As a result the ship was taken, and he and his crew were interned in Sant John, Newfoundland. There were already twenty-seven American vessels there as prizes.

But within a week the Americans were exchanged for the officers and crew of a captured British frigate, and all 246 of them sailed for New York in the *Alert.* Arriving home at midnight, he knocked on his wife's bedroom window. He writes:

The doors flew open, and the greetings of affection and consanguinity multiplied upon me rapidly. Thus in a moment was I transported to the greatest earthly bliss man can enjoy, viz.:to the enjoyment of the happy family circle.

General Elijah Cobb's journal, written in 1848, ends here. He was unable for health reasons to complete it. Until 1816 he stayed at home. Then he took *Paragon*, built for him, to Europe several times, and in 1819-1820 he made two trips to Africa in the ship *Ten Brothers,* taking along his son Freeman. On the second trip so many crewmen fell sick of an unknown disease that the ship was sunk at the wharf in Boston to prevent an epidemic.

Retiring in 1820 at age fifty-two, He became active in state and local affairs as town clerk, treasurer, inspector general, representative and senator to the General Court (legislature), justice of the peace, and brigadier general in the militia.

Here was a man who performed brilliantly as a captain, using his native wits to carry out his duties. Then when he retired he continued to serve his town and Commonwealth. He was the highest type of Yankee mariner.

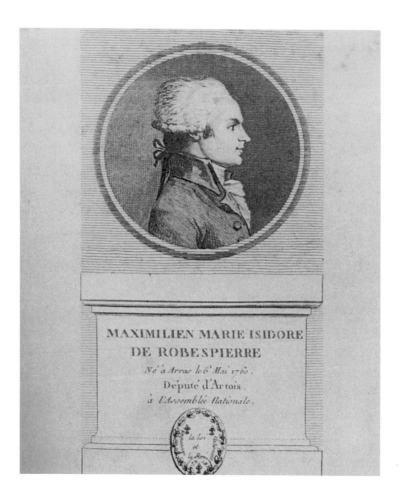

Figure 2-2A "Maximilien Marie Isidore de Robespierre. Born at Arras 6 May 1760 – deputy from Artois to the National Assembly." From the National Library, Paris.

The British Raid Martha's Vineyard

The Revolutionary war was in its third year when the people of Martha's Vineyard even more directly experienced the conflict. Cut off from their usual supply lines to the mainland by British privateers and warships, they were barely "making do" by tightening their belts considerably. The three companies of troops from the Massachusetts colony had been withdrawn by March 1777; their maintenance on the island had cost £2625 by September 1776, and the legislature decided that the colony could no longer carry that cost.

That same month on 11 March the town of Tisbury petitioned Massachusetts for some sort of protection, saying:

We therefore Humbly & earnestly Request your Honors to send us some Assistance under our exposed situation To defend us aganst a force that may be Expected to Attack this Place. . . . We therefore Pray . . . [you] Grant us such Relief as you in your wisdom shall Think necessary. . . .

The reply of the General Court was a resolution basically abandoning the island to its fate.

To that many Vineyarders responded by joining regiments on the mainland; others went privateering; those who stayed home organized the island's defenses as best they could. Elisha Nye on Naushon received supplies from the departing troops and promised that with his "Cannon" he would be able to keep the British out of "Tarpoland Cove." Cornelius Marchant shipped on the *Marlborough,* and reported that in six months she had destroyed British property in Africa, captured two ships, one a slaver, and a large brig loaded with ivory. On the way home they took two more ships, one laden with British army supplies. A pretty good few months' work. Individuals were waging the war, but the island was for all practical purposes defenseless.

We know how desperate was the rebel struggle. But less well known is the British situation in 1778. France, with whom Britain had been warring off and on for centuries, had signed a treaty of alliance with the thirteen states and was preparing to intervene decisively in the war. British leadership was inept; a French fleet was already in Newport, Rhode Island; and the British badly needed a victory.

The solution arrived at was to send a strong force to ravage the accessible ports between New York and Nova Scotia, destroying vessels, wharfs, stores and material for shipbuilding. This policy of revenge perhaps revealed the British sense that they had already lost their colonies. Accordingly an armada under the command of General Sir Charles Grey was organized on Long Island. It consisted of eleven warships and some twenty transports carrying 4333 grenadiers, infantry, artillery, and dismounted cavalry.

General Grey had had a distinguished career. Now fifty, he had arrived here in 1776 and had defeated "Mad Anthony" Wayne and had a brigade command at Germantown. After the war he continued his career, eventually becoming Earl Grey in 1806. His adjutant-general was even more interesting: Major John André (later caught by the Americans and executed as a spy). From his journal we have the details of this raid.

The first port attacked was New Bedford. The fleet anchored late on 5 September 1778 and quickly landed six companies of troops to destroy the waterfront. Taken totally by surprise, Captain Cushing of the Massachusetts Artillery, with only fifteen men, had to abandon his supplies and equipment and retreat out of town. He kept hoping for reinforcements, but none came. His lieutenant and a soldier were killed.

The British, now nine companies strong, marched up the waterfront destroying everything in their path. Then, six miles up the river, they crossed to Fairhaven and marched back, wreaking havoc there. By noon the next day, reported General Grey, they were all back aboard and ready for their next victim, Martha's Vineyard. The smoke from the fires was visible for two days in Newport, twenty miles or so away. Casualties were small. The British lost one killed, four wounded, and sixteen deserters. The Americans' losses were Lieutenant Metcalf and Abraham Russell killed and two men wounded.

To General Clinton, Grey reported the destruction of seventy vessels, large numbers of whaleboats and small craft, and " . . . 26 warehouses at [New] Bedford and Fairhaven; these were filled with . . . rum, sugar, molasses, coffee, tobacco, cotton, tea, medicines, gunpowder, sailcloth, cordage, etc. Two large ropewalks."

On 8 September General Grey's fleet set sail for the Vineyard, and on the tenth sailed up Vineyard Sound, the flagship, *Carysfort,* anchoring off Holmes's Hole (Vineyard Haven), while the transports went into the harbor. Grey wanted Captain Fanshawe of *Carysfort,* with troops, to sail for Nantucket, but the island was saved because of contrary winds.

Dumbstruck, a committee under Colonel Beriah Norton went out to find out what the British were up to. This is the colonel's report:

General Gray, Commanding a detachment of his Majesty's army, arrived at Martha's Vineyard Sep'r 10, 1778, when I waited on him . . . & agreed to deliver him 10,000 Sheep & 300 head of Cattle the Stock to be brought to the landing the next day.

The general also required all the arms of the militia, and the moneys in the town treasuries. The livestock would be paid for, and milk cows would not be taken, he announced. Failure would incur an invasion of the island.

Desperately livestock from all over the island were rounded up and driven to the harbor. One panicky woman drove her cow up into her attic to hide it.

Meanwhile 150 men landed and camped in the center of town to strengthen the threat, which now included hay for the cattle. Twenty transports from Rhode Island arrived to load the livestock.

By the fourteenth 10,574 sheep and 315 oxen had been delivered, as well as fifty-two tons of hay. The militia had coughed up 388 stands of flintlocks with their equipment, and about £1,000 of town moneys had been surrendered by town treasurers at the point of a sword.

That day the troops spent "destroying some Salt Works, in burning or taking in the Inlets, what vessels and boats could be found," reported General Grey. These amounted to six vessels and some thirty boats, mainly whaleboats. The fleet sailed that evening.

A similar raid had been planned for Falmouth, close by, but, as Brigadier Joseph Otis, commanding the Falmouth militia, reported:

The enemy fleet began to sail westward . . . to the number of Twenty Six Ships besides small craft; . . . [The British] told the Inhabitants [of the Vineyard] . . . that we was as they term'd us a pack of dam'd Rebels and five thousand strong with a plenty of artillery [actually 600 men and one cannon].

But the general had accomplished his purpose: creating havoc in two ports and providing the British garrison of 10,000 men at Newport with a good deal of meat. The fleet returned to Whitestone, Long Island, on 17 September. As for applying to the British in New York for payment (as promised), the Vineyarders were to find themselves out of luck— but not for want of trying, as we shall see. Within a short time the three villages on the island had compiled lists of personal losses; when the livestock was taken, no assignment of owners was made.

Again the good colonel stepped forward and addressed a petition to the Massachusetts legislature asking for quick relief:

. . . the last step of the British troops . . . Depriving them of their stock has rendered the case of many persons with large families Truly deplorable. In particular near the Harbour of Holmes Hole . . . [people] are not only Deprived of every article & necessary of life . . . and unless immediately assisted must unavoidably suffer extremely or perish. . .

The petition was tabled.

Next, since Grey had promised payment, George Washington granted permission for someone to travel to New York and collect. Colonel Norton was chosen, along with William Mayhew of the island's ruling family. Meanwhile twice more the British stopped by for supplies, with payment promised. On 14 December 1798 the colonel wrote General Clinton, commander-in-chief, in New York a long explanation of the situation. On the eighteenth, aide-de-camp Major André wrote back:

The Commander in Chief knows of no Engagement entered into by Gen. Grey respecting the Cattle, etc., taken from Martha's Vineyard, and does not see fit to make any enquiry into the matter at present.

But Beriah Norton persisted over the new few years, making at least two trips to London as he tried to make the British live up to their promises. At one point Grey claimed that the islanders "took a very active part in the Rebellion [and] that the [raid] was intended to punish them for their past bad behavior." This blatant lie so infuriated Norton that he wrote a very strong rebuttal which he sent to General Sir Guy Carleton, now British commander. The reply so impressed the general that he set up a board of inquiry, which recommended compensation of £7923, with a first payment of £3000.

Then peace was signed in September 1783; the British would be most unlikely to complete the deal. So the Vineyard turned again to the Massachusetts legislature, and on 15 October 1783 in a long memorandum they asked for forgiveness of all state and county taxes after 1777. In due course the General Court (legislature) on 31 January 1785:

exempted from paying any part of the several species of taxes . . . which have been required of them . . . the said towns shall be held severally to pay . . . the arrearages of taxes due before the first day of January 1778.

Back to London went the colonel in 1784, still trying for the nearly £5000 due to the Vineyard. He stayed three years and became a well-known figure, this Vineyard farmer moving in the highest society, as he tried to raise sympathy for his cause— to no avail. Incidentally, not much was left of the original £3000 by the time he came home in 1787.

But before he died in 1820, aged eighty-six, he had served his island and his country well, as state senator and representative, selectman and constable of Edgartown, commander of the island militia, and Edgartown's first postmaster. And, alas, of the nine children born to the Nortons, none had sons to carry on the name of Norton. Beriah's long life had been devoted to public service.

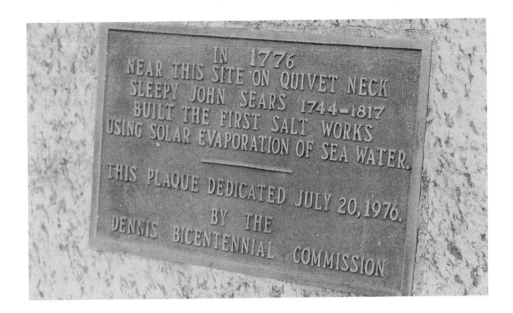

Figure 3-1 This plaque, near the site of the first solar evaporation works on Cape Cod, commemorates the invention. *Photo by William P. Quinn.*

CHAPTER
3

Entrepreneurs

Salt Works:
A Brilliant Invention

     Cape Codders were known for their ingenuity, finding ways of making a living that fit their environment and made life easier for them. To begin with, subsistence farming was their way of life, with each homestead essentially self-sufficient. For clothes, for instance, they raised sheep, spun the wool into yarn, and created their own garments; they had to. Their food came from their own backyards.

     It was Captain John Sears of Dennis— "Sleepy John," they called him for his tendency to just sit and think for long periods of time— who produced a real breakthrough in the economy of Cape Cod. A fifth-generation descendant of Richard Sears, one of the founders of Yarmouth, he was born on 20 July 1744 and died in Dennis on 9 July 1817. The eastern part of the original Yarmouth had become a separate town, Dennis, named for the first minister, Josiah Dennis, whose manse is owned by the Dennis Historical Society.

Figure 3-2 A view of an early Cape Cod salt works. Buildings are probably a drying room and a warehouse. From Deyo's *History of Barnstable County.*

The idea of solar evaporation of sea water to produce the salt so desperately needed by fishermen and the entire economy while the British were blockading New England soon became reality. In 1776, on Sesuit Harbor in East Dennis, he built "a large trough ten feet wide and a hundred feet long with a series of shutters to cover the vats when it rained."

The first major problem was that the trough leaked (until in good seamanlike fashion, he calked it) and after weeks of hard work hauling the water bucket by bucket to fill the trough, he produced only eight bushels of salts. His neighbors called the experiment "Sears's Folly." But in the summer of 1777 his vat provided him with thirty bushels of salt.

How to reduce the labor? In 1778 the British ship-of-the-line *Somerset* (the battleship of the 18th century) stranded on Peaked Hill Bars at the tip of the Cape. The lower Cape "wreckers" managed to strip almost everything of value from the hull, and Captain Sears acquired one of the ship's bilge pumps. This eliminated the "bucket brigade," but to work the pump was still hard work, and the salt cost more to produce than it was worth. More improvements had to follow.

A few years later Major John Freeman of Harwich proposed using windmills (called "salt mills") to pump the seawater into the vats. For piping they bored out pine logs, with the joints sealed with white lead. Captain Sears quickly built salt mills and pumps raised off the ground a few feet— and the system was now self-filling on demand.

Other improvements followed. Hattil Kelley of Dennis changed the vat dimensions to square and built swinging covers that could protect two vats set corner to corner. He later patented this approach. In 1793 Reuben Sears of Harwich devised a simple sliding square roof on rollers made of oak. The Reverend Ephraim Briggs of Chatham was an amateur chemist who helped with the problem of separating out the different salts in the water.

Very early government realized the value of salt-making. The General Court (legislature) of Massachusetts passed a law which specified that:

to encourage the manufacture of salt, a bounty of three shillings per bushel be paid by the state treasury for salt manufactured within the state and produced from salt water.

Salt making took place from March until October, when the sun was higher in the sky, and the vats were covered during the night and whenever rain was likely. In fact, often children were let out of school to help shift the covers. Normally one bushel of salt required 350 gallons of salt water, and the entire process took some three weeks to complete.

Receiving a patent for his process in 1799, Captain Sears was helped by several other East Dennis captains: William and Christopher Crowell and Edward Sears. But the most important role that John Sears played was as the creator of a new and desperately needed industry. And once the technology was developed, the industry quickly spread. All over Cape Cod the distinctive profiles of the vats, windmills, and drying rooms arose on the uplands near the water.

The earliest vats cost about $100 to build one hundred square feet, and since profits ranged from 25% to 30%, it was no wonder that soon the entire peninsula was making salt. And Cape Cod's water contained more salt, since it was far from large freshwater rivers, which would dilute the salt content.

Some rather clever methods were developed to separate out the various salts in sea water. It contains about 3.5% solids, of which sodium chloride contributes 2.68%. The remaining .82% is a mixture of five different different sulphates and bromides, as well as traces of some forty elements, even including gold.

The vats were ten to sixteen feet square and about a foot deep, and built in groups of three usually. The first vat was called the "water room," where plant and animal material was eliminated. Then came the "pickle room," where the carbonates (lime) were removed. The last vat was the "salt room," where the sodium chloride was gathered and later dried. Very little was wasted. The detritus of the first vat made fine fertilizer. And after the common salt was taken out, further treatment yielded Glauber and Epsom salts.

Effort involved, once the vats were up and running, was minimal. The salt mills did the pumping, the sun did the heating, gravity fed the water from one vat to the next. About all that was needed was someone to shovel the salt up and take it to the drying room. The usual workers were old men and boys, since the mature adult men were either fishing or farming.

The industry grew and grew— and small wonder. By 1827 there were 881 salt works on Cape Cod, with about one and a half million square feet of vats. Production of salts reached over 250,000 bushels annually, and over $2,000,000 was invested.

This growth was reflected in the growth of the fishing fleet, since the only way to preserve the fish was to salt it. In addition a lusty export trade in salt developed, trading to the West Indies for such goods as sugar, rum, cotton, and molasses.

The Revolutionary War and British blockades and depredations closed the industry, but soon after peace the fleets were rebuilt and needed salt as before. Of especial interest, too, was the ripple effect of this new means of making a dollar (or many, often). As mentioned, the fishing industry grew literally as the supply of salt grew. And the many ancillary industries and trades servicing the fishermen also increased dramatically. In short, what happened was a gradual change from a subsistence economy, relying on the land alone, to a mixed economy of coastwise and foreign trade, ship building, and various industries. One might say that Cape Cod's prosperity had been generated by the salt works. Many of the former fishing captains graduated to the world-spanning clipper ship trade. Carl Cutler in *Greyhounds of the Sea* says: "In the matter of men no similar area produced more deep sea masters of outstanding ability than Cape Cod." Many of the tales in this book illustrate in detail just how right he was.

Figure 3-3 An 1849 map of East Dennis village. The checkerboard areas represent salt works, located close to salt water. The road across the bottom of the map is today's Route 6A, then the King's Highway.

Figure 3-4 The house in East Dennis in which Osborn Howes was born.

Osborn Howes:
Cabin Boy, Supercargo, Captain, Shipowner

Osborn Howes was born in Dennis, Cape Cod, in 1806. His father and mother were both descendants of Thomas Howes, who with his wife and three sons had come from England and was one of the three first settlers of Yarmouth. All Cape Cod Howeses today are descendants of this couple.

His father, Elisha, was a seafarer, so that his mother had to manage affairs when he was gone. During the War of 1812 Elisha was twice captured by the British; once he was exchanged; the other time he and his crew retook their schooner from the prize crew and delivered them to Portland and prison.

It was a hard life for a woman. The family bought cotton and wool from Boston, but then his mother, Deborah, turned the raw materials into cloth on her loom, making all the clothes for the five children, including suits each year for the two boys. Since her children were very young, she milked the cow, fed the pigs, fetched water, made breakfast, and sent the children off to school. And with all that she kept her sense of humor.

When Osborn was twelve, they moved to Dedham, where he worked for a farmer for the next four years at forty cents a day. In the winter he went to school for two or three months, where, he says, "[I] am under the impression that I learned little or nothing during that time." That was all the schooling he had.

Next he worked in a large general store which carried just about everything a family might need, as well as all kinds of wine and liquor. In fact, a hogshead of rum lasted only about ten days. He also had to work in the owner's nail factory, weighing and marking casks of nails. Some three thousand pounds a day were shipped to Boston. His pay started as $6 per month; the next year it rose to $7.

His father, disliking Osborn's closeness to so much liquor, arranged a berth for him as cabin boy on the brig *Cypher*, sailing to Elsinor in Denmark. Deathly seasick the whole way, and homesick, he wished himself back in the store. But this was the beginning of a career at sea. After visiting several cities, *Cypher* sailed for home, arriving just after Osborn had turned nineteen. A good Yankee, he had invested his $100 from the store in tobacco, snuff, and cigars, which he sold in Prussia, bought cloth goods there, and arrived home with $300 in his pocket.

A year later, after a stint in a counting-house, the *Cypher's* owners sent him back to Europe, to Königsberg in Prussia, as their agent in Europe to buy and sell the cargoes of *Cypher* and other vessels. This twenty-year-old was to receive one percent of the value of cargoes sold and one percent of the cargoes bought. And he did very well, meanwhile enjoying the winter sports of sleighing, skating, and visiting when the harbors were closed by ice. All was not work f or Osborn. On a trip to London he was aghast at the constant demands for *pourboires* for the least service.

Returning to New York in the ship *Coroo,* he experienced a furious storm, and a whirlwind broke off two masts and almost carried off the second officer. This was followed by two days more of gales, before they were able to jury-rig sails. The ship had been so tossed about that their water and provisions were partly destroyed, so that they lived on short rations for the next thirty-two days: three pints of water, a half-pound of bread, and a half-pound of salt beef per day. Finally, on 2 April, having been at sea since 15 January, a brig saw their distress signals and resupplied them. Two days later they were in Boston.

Business was very dull, says Osborn, so bad that when *Cypher* was loaded for Brazil, the owner told him that he could not afford both a supercargo and a captain. He would have to serve both roles, at the age of twenty-two with no experience. A fourth of the cargo was his. He had learned navigation, but he was uncertain as to managing the brig. But the voyage was a success, and his cargo of flour went for good prices in Bahia. Next off to Gibraltar he went with a load of sugar; finding prices poor there, he went on to Marseilles, where the price was better. With a load of wine, he sailed for Philadelphia, where he sold it and with another cargo sailed for Boston.

This paragraph illustrates vividly how merchant skippers of those days had to operate: entirely on their own judgment, trying to make each leg of a voyage profitable, rather than to lose money on an empty hold.

When his father returned from the Rio Grande in *Hebe*, Osborn bought a half-interest in her and loaded for a trip to Smyrna, in Turkey. In the Mediterranean they sighted Mount Etna, 125 miles away, and a cloud of smoke. After sunset, he writes,

Streams of fire shot up many thousands of feet into the sky, continuing for two or three minutes, [then dark], *until another burst of light. . . . I therefore concluded that a new volcano had made its appearance. . . . At daylight the next morning the atmosphere was thick and hazy, and the water filled with pumice-*

stone [which floats]. [The volcano, sixty miles northwest of Malta] *soon rose to a height of 180 feet . . . but in fifteen or twenty days the island sank into the sea.*

Selling the cargo, he took on a load of figs for Genoa, and then loaded up with oranges and lemons in Palermo. When the brig returned to New York, however, Asiatic cholera, brought from England, was raging for the first time, killing hundreds. Doctors advised eating no fruit; so the whole cargo was a total loss.

After a busy flurry of further trips to the Near East and elsewhere, he stayed ashore toward the end of 1834— for a very good reason. He had met and wooed Hannah Crowell of Yarmouth (somehow, between trips), and on 22 January 1835 they were married and settled in Yarmouth. A happy four months followed, until his next voyage to Rio de Janeiro and Antwerp.

In Rio the brig began to leak badly, and even though they careened her and recaulked the hull, it continued. Nevertheless, they made it to Antwerp, where Osborn discovered that a six-inch square of planking at the stern had lost all caulking; the leak was taken care of within half an hour. Back in Boston on 8 February 1836, as he and his father started for Yarmouth in a sleigh, his father told him that Hannah had died during the previous November. He writes:

The family of my dear Hannah received me with great kindness, and from them I learned the full particulars of her sickness and death. . . . The ship was loaded for New Orleans, but I remained at home. My last voyage as a sailor had been made.

They had had four months of happiness. He was twenty-nine years old. In June he and Captain Joseph Nickerson (a descendant of the William Nickerson who had settled Chatham on Cape Cod) went to see about possible western land purchases. They traveled by rail, canal boat, stage coaches, and river steamer. Going down the Ohio River to the Mississippi, they then went up-river to St. Louis, "a very important point, with the prospect that it would become a large city. It then contained nine thousand inhabitants." Finally they settled on 560 acres of woodland on the Illinois River, from which the steamboat people cut all the wood, "and did not even thank us for it." After some fifteen years they sold it for about what it cost.

On the way to Peoria, Illinois, by steamboat, at about midnight, the boat and another collided. His boat sank in about a minute with some 150 people aboard. Still dressed, he jumped overboard and swam ashore. Since the water was only about twelve feet deep, the ladies' cabins on the upper deck were unharmed. Swimming to the other boat, he found it leaking so badly that it was run ashore. But after shifting cargo aft the crew decided to continue down-river. They put the passengers they had rescued back on the sunken boat, left them some bread, and departed. Only seven or eight people drowned. A small steamer came along and took everyone aboard, and a day later they were in Peoria.

On to Chicago they went, then a small town of about 2000 inhabitants. The center of Chicago was completely flooded, so they did not stay long. Across Lake Michigan by boat they traveled, and then to Detroit, and by steamboat to Buffalo, canal boat on the Erie Canal, and railroad to Albany and back to Boston. The trip had taken two and a half months.

Now that Capt. Osborn was no longer going to sea, with his uncle, William Howes, he started a ship chandlery (ship stores, groceries, etc.) on Commercial Street in Boston. Capitalization was $7000, most of it his. With his connections the store did very well.

On 7 August 1837 (thirty-one years old), he married his wife's sister, Abba Crowell, a happy marriage that lasted twenty-eight years. Eventually they bought a house in South Boston.

Parting company with his uncle, he began to acquire ships, by either buying them or having them built. Thus he and his brother-in-law acquired the bark *Leda*, the brig *Josephine,* the ships *George Hallett* and *Newton.* This was the start of a wide-ranging commercial shipping business in which many Cape Cod people invested.

When Captain Howes moved to Boston in 1825, he found a small city of some 60,000. Transportation was by sail or by horse or oxen, so that the city drew only on the surrounding area for foodstuffs. But in the early 1830's the railroad boom began, and what was a thriving coastal trade began to disappear with the coming of the network of rails that soon spread across the country. Then in 1844 Samuel F.B. Morse introduced the telegraph, providing extremely rapid communication. For example, Isaac Small of Truro was stationed at Highland Light to identify passing ships and telegraph their owners in Boston of their imminent arrival.

Moving to a new house in 1844 he and Abba began to raise a family: there were Osborne, Nelly, Fanny, Frank, Anna, and Edith. His mother, Deborah, lived with them until her death in 1848 of quinsy (a severe inflammation of the throat). The noted physician, Dr. Warren, had been called in, and she said to him:

Now, doctor . . . tell me just what you think of my case. It will not alarm me in the least, for I made the needed preparations for death a long time ago.

He did not offer an opinion, and she died a day later.

In June 1859, his wife having been ill for several years, Captain Howes decided on a trip to Europe. They sailed on the steamer *Canada* and landed in Liverpool in ten days. Crossings of thirty or more days were fast disappearing. And the record of the clipper *Red Jacket* (seventeen days) was routinely bested by steamers. Visiting friends and conducting business, they went to Antwerp, Amsterdam, Hanover, Berlin, Konigsberg, and Cologne, before returning to England for the trip home.

Here ends the lively, vivid autobiography of Captain Osborn Howes, with its pictures of the country, its developing transportation, the way people lived in those days. He was fifty-three years old, and he had a good thirty years in which to carry out his plans. The rest of his story is told by his children, who published the autobiography soon after his death in 1893.

Meanwhile, with the California gold discovery in 1848, the Australian gold rush in 1851, and the general rise in world trade, the firm of Howes and Crowell widened its vision. They built or bought a number of clipper ships, the "greyhounds of the sea," according to Carl Cutler, and abandoned the coastwise trade. Captain Howes's judgment and honesty were so well known that the company flourished.

But he was not prepared to accept the rapid changes in business practices. He would not borrow money, and if his name were on a note he was uncomfortable, even though he had plenty to back it up. Against his better judgment he agreed to build and manage a fleet of ocean-going steamships sailing to Liverpool. But the effort soon proved quite unprofitable, and as the responsible party he had to try to dispose of the fleet to minimize the losses. This effort weighed on him, and he aged a great deal.

Captain Howes finally decided to retire in 1874 (at age 68) and sold his partnership to Nathan Crowell, with whom he had worked for thirty-four years. Off to Europe with his wife, Anna, and daughter, Edith, he went for over a year. When he returned, he found that his investments in world shipping were in trouble, reflecting the decline of the trade. So as quickly as he could he "unloaded" and went into other types of property. But the divestiture was a long and trying one, taxing his skill and judgment to the utmost until he was nearly seventy-five.

In his later years he listed for his children the vessels which he partly or wholly owned during his long career: It may be of interest to show them here:

Brigs: —*Josephine, Globe.*
Barks:— *Leda, Ubermes, Flora, Autoleon, Kilby.*
Ships:— *George Hallett, Newton, Kedron, Isaiah Crowell, Austra-Revere, Hamlet, J.Q. Adams, Hortensia, Climax, Ringleader, Robin Hood, Rival, Winged Arrow, Lizzie Oakford, Ellen Foster, John Tucker, Regent, Audubon, Ericsson, Ringleader II, Carrolton, Comet, Garibaldi, Helicon, Importer, Fleetwing, Osborn Howes, Edith Rose, Manlius, Swallow.*
Steamers:— *Concordia, Kensington, St. Louis, Ontario, Erie.*

His was a strong stance against slavery before the Civil War, and unlike many ship owners he refused to transfer his fleet to foreign flags of convenience. He felt that as long as his country was in danger his ships should fly the colors of his country.

His children write that when they asked Captain Howes to continue writing about the rest of his life, he would say, "The children know it as well as I do." A deeply religious man, he had participated in the great religious revival of 1842 in

Figure 3-5 The ship Osborn Howes, one of many owned by the captain.

Boston and, as he says:

It was on the 18th of March, 1842, that I felt that the Lord had forgiven my sins and owned me as His child, and . . . I still pray that I may be forgiven and may at last attain to everlasting happiness.

Abba's health had been improved by the 1859 visit to Europe, but it began to fail again in 1862. In 1864 she went to Philadelphia, hoping that the milder climate would help. But there was little change, and after her return to Boston she failed more rapidly and died in December 1865. She and the captain had had twenty-eight years together.

Multiple marriages were common in those days; physicians still knew very little about the human body; as a result death from ordinary diseases was common. So Captain Howes remarried in 1867: Mrs. Alma Curtis, a longtime friend of the family, related by marriage. The oldest daughter, Hannah, died in 1870, and five of the siblings were married and gone; only the oldest and youngest daughters lived at home for the last seven years of their father's life.

These last years were serene, happy ones for Osborn Howes. The trustees of the Second National Bank kept electing him president, after some forty years of association. Pleased, he would say, "They ought to have a younger man." His many friends visited often, and he maintained to the end his deep interest in political affairs.

Looking back on his life, he saw many things that he might have changed, but he was aware that he had always dealt honorably with others. Sometimes he would say, "I might have made more money and have been a richer man, but I have no remembrance of having deceived or defrauded any man. " His religion was a mainstay and so he did not fear death, being sure of another life. He died on Saturday, 23 December 1893, eighty-eight years old. His children wrote this epitaph, which sums up a quietly great man— great in the eyes of his friends and family:

He has left to his children that noblest of all legacies, an honorable life. He loved punctuality and order, all the qualities that go with a character bent on doing its duty in life. He was serious and home loving, caring little for general society. . . .He had about him a shyness and modesty that made him dread to be conspicuous. . . . With all this seriousness, he loved a good story, [and told to us not a few of his own stories], *and his hearty laugh would always reward any person who told one.*

Figure 3-6 Captain Howes during the thirty-four years that he and Nathan Howes Crowell were partners.

Figure 3-7 On Shiverick Road in East Dennis, above the harbor, is this low-relief plaque indicating the site and layout of the shipyard. *Courtesy of Craig Studio.*

Cape Cod's Clipper Ships

The thirty years between about 1830 and 1860 saw a nearly miraculous change in world trade— produced by a powerful shift in the concepts of shipbuilding. The bluff bows and heavy underwater bodies of 17th century ships, gave way gradually over time to sharp bows and sterns that slipped through the water instead of thrusting it aside. Instead of three or four square sails on a mast, first five and then six sails rose up towering masts.

Designers such as Samuel Hartt Pook appeared. At the age of twenty he designed the first iron-hulled, propeller-driven steam ocean-going tug; he went on to be responsible for such great clipper ships as *Red Jacket,* holding the record of thirteen days and one hour from New York to Liverpool; *Surprise,* on her maiden circumnavigation paying for herself, all expenses, and netting $50,000;*Gamecock; Northern Light; Telegraph;* and many more. And builders like Donald McKay, in East Boston, produced the ships, including the great *Flying Cloud.*

The results on world trade were dramatic. People and goods were being moved at faster and faster speeds; later the huge British tea trade was essentially stolen from the British by these ships. To illustrate: when a famous American clipper was in drydock in Britain, the Admiralty made a point of "taking off her lines" (copying the hull shape and sail plan of the ship.)

And here on Cape Cod shipbuilding was an essential part of earning a living. In almost every possible stream a small yard would spring up, producing the sloops and schooners needed for the fishing industry, the mainstay of Cape Cod's economy, since the land was too poor for farming on a large scale.

One such yard was started on Sesuit Creek in East Dennis by Asa Shiverick, descendant of Falmouth's first minister. Beginning in 1815 his yard turned out sturdy schooners and brigs. As his three sons, Asa, Jr., David, and Paul, grew up they learned the art of shipbuilding and helped their father. Between 1835 and 1838 the yard produced five vessels instead of the earlier one a year. But the boys had bigger ideas: they had seen and worked on these new designs, and when Asa, Sr., retired and returned to Falmouth, they moved the yard a half -mile closer to the bay and began to "think big." They were to build the ships; Captains Christopher Hall, Prince S. Crowell, and Levi Howes financed the venture (although most of the village also owned shares); and nearly all of the officers, including "ship's cousins" (boys of ten and up), came from East Dennis.

And the times were right. The China tea trade was already booming. *Sea Witch* roared into Boston, seventy-four days from Canton, China, the record trip. The Liverpool packets offered fast, comfortable, reliable service. And East Dennis was ready.

Then on 19 September 1848 the *Washington Union* announced the news of gold in California:

But the most extraordinary intelligence . . . is about the real EL DORADO, the gold region in California. . . . [The] extraordinary richness of the gold surface, and the excitement it has produced . . . are confirmed by letters from Commodore Jones.
The danger in California is from want of food. . . . Would not some of our merchants find it profitable speculation to send cargoes . . . around to the Pacific Coast?

East Dennis thought so.

In 1850 *Revenue,* a medium clipper of only 546 tons, was finally launched after first breaking down the ways. A consistent earner under Captains Seth Crowell and David Seabury Sears, twelve years old, she fetched an offer of $20,000 in Genoa. Captain Sears declined and sailed her home. Later she was sold in New York.

Next came *Hippogriffe* in 1852, somewhat larger. She was 156 feet long, with a beam of thirty-one feet. Captain Anthony Howes took command as she hit the water, to sail jury-rigged to Boston for rigging. Her first few trips were: Boston

Figure 3-8 An oil portrait of *Belle of the West*. Asa Shiverick wanted a portrait of this most beautiful of the yard's ships. He asked Captain Thomas Frederick Howes, her former master, to give the artist minute details of her lines and rigging. This was the result: a truly authentic painting. *Courtesy of Mary Shiverick Fisher.*

to San Francisco and return around the globe; to Callao, Peru; and back to Boston.

His logs (which I have read) show good passages. But *Hippogriffe*'s main claim to fame was discovery — the hard way— of an uncharted reef in the Java Sea in 1858. Skillfully he got her off and went into Hong Kong for repairs.

After scarfing in new planking in her bow, he set out for London and ran into a terrible storm, the worst he had ever seen. The sails all tore away, the jib boom and foremast broke, the mainmast was sprung, and even the hull was strained— among other major damage reported by a survey when they reached London. With desperate hard work the crew managed to set some sails and limped into London, just glad to have survived.

On went *Hippogriffe* for another five years. Then, in 1863, with Confederate raiders hunting Yankee ships, Captain John H. Addy sold this eleven-year-old ship in Calcutta for 70,000 rupees, more than she cost to build.

Next in 1853 came *Belle of the West*, designed by the great Samuel Hartt Pook, called by Captain Thomas Franklin Hall "the Praxiteles of his time." She was just plain beautiful! Just under 1000 tons, 167 feet long, she carried more sail than McKay's *Flying Cloud*, which was sixty-three feet longer and had almost twice *Belle*'s tonnage.

Captain Hall, who grew up in her, said:

She at last became my sweetheart, my idol, a graven image before which, for years, I daily bowed and worshipped, and although she has been lying at the bottom of the Bay of Bengal for sixty years, I would delight . . . to erect a marble shaft over the spot where her sacred bones are resting.

This love of a man for his ship is by no means rare— especially at this time of the greatest maritime beauty that sailors had ever seen. And so much of his self, his very soul was embodied in his ship that remarks like this are characteristic.

Under Captain William Frederick Howes she shuttled all over the world for the first six years. Then his brother Captain Allison took over. In 1863 he met another brother Captain Levi of *Starlight* in Calcutta. Levi challenged Allison to a race home to Boston. They started down the river twelve hours apart, sighted each other three times, and arrived twelve hours apart— a 17,000 mile dead heat!

Eleven years old, she was sold to Mowjee Huny Doss in Calcutta and renamed *Fiery Cross,* a most prophetic name; in 1868 she burned while en route to Muscat, Arabia, with a cargo of rice.

Kit Carson came down the ways in 1854, just over 1000 tons, with Captain Seth Crowell in command. Then owner Captain Prince S. Crowell chose Captain John Dillingham of Brewster as master. Now, Prince Crowell trusted his captains completely, but on one occasion he wrote Dillingham:

To go to Calcutta . . . and take a cargo from there in the height of the monsoon at a rate equal to $8.50 a ton . . . exceeds by far all miscalculations I ever had anything to do with any ships.

Figure 3-9 An oil portrait of *Wild Hunter.* The captain's daughter often rode her pony on deck for exercise. *Courtesy of Minerva Crowell Wexler.*

Dillingham was soon relieved by Captain Josiah Gorham of Yarmouth, and then by Captain Anthony Howes from *Hippogriffe.* Next came Captain Prince F. Crowell, son of the owner. His logs of three years show: Boston to San Francisco; to Callao, Peru; to Falmouth, England; to Montevideo, Uruguay; to Moulmein, Burma; and back to New York.

But while *Kit Carson* had evaded the Confederate cruisers all through the Civil War, she landed in the middle of a savage little South American war, was commandeered, and was sunk to block the harbor of Rio de Janeiro, Brazil.

Then world trade began to slacken, leading to a depression in the mid-1870's. The bonanzas of the California and Australian gold rushes were over; the biggest single trade route left was the British tea trade, largely captured by American clippers. There was a mad race to see who could deliver the first tea cargoes to England each season; they fetched the highest prices.

But East Dennis still believed in clipper ships, despite their high building costs, relatively small hold capacity, and high overheads. Designers ultimately realized that hull shapes could be much more full-bodied— large boxes, in fact, if the bows and sterns were very sharp. *Red Jacket,* with a full-bodied hull, on her record run to Liverpool covered 413 miles in twenty-four hours, at 17.2 knots (or almost twenty miles per hour).

So the Shivericks started their largest ship yet. She was *Wild Hunter,* almost 1100 tons, drawing 22½ feet. Command went to Captain Joshua Sears, a real driver. Earlier he had had *Orissa,* not a clipper, in which he often beat clipper ships. And fifteen year old Thomas Franklin Hall was aboard as a "ship's cousin. " On her second trip to California, he and Heman Kelly ran away to the gold fields. Captain Josh's comment was: "It is the custom here for everyone to leave their ships, and they don't want to be behind the times."

Impatient, meticulous— and seasick most of the time— Captain Josh when bedeviled by lack of wind would let off steam in his logs:

Oh for a cot in some vast wildreness where I shall never see a ship again. If ever one poor fellow was tired of anything, it is I, Josh Sears, that is sick and tired of going to sea.

Once, sailing for Singapore in ballast (with no paying cargo), his log records the composition of his crew: "two half-way sailors, white; eight boys; one shoemaker; four Manila men; three Malays and three Kanakas"— twenty-one men to handle that huge spread of canvas, and eight of them were boys.

A shrewd businessman, he roamed the world for four years, with a salary of $200 a month— a good deal of money then. After the worldwide depression of 1857 hit world trade, he retired to his beautiful three-story house in East Dennis. But *Wild Hunter* sailed on, to a fiery death in 1873 on a voyage from Boston to Revel, Russia. The schooner *Gloucester* saved the crew.

Webfoot, a medium clipper came next, with Captain Milton P. Hedge in command of the fastest of the Shiverick ships. She holds two records: eighty-five days Calcutta-New York, and second-fastest San Francisco-Liverpool passage (around Africa) of 115 days. In 1864, after a grounding off Dunkirk, France, Captain Hedge sold her to the British for £2882 rather than pay twice that for repairs. She too sailed on until 1886, when she burned at sea, a venerable thirty-year-old.

After Captain Christopher Hall, a major financier of the ships, died in 1857, the next ship was named for him. About the size of *Revenue* (the first ship), she had an active ten-year career across the world before her complete loss on an uncharted reef off Apia Island in the Pacific. All hands (including Mrs. Addy, the captain's wife) escaped and were carried to England at what Captain Addy considered an exorbitant price of "60 pounds a piece [sic]."

After a considerable hiatus, the last of the Shiverick ships was *Ellen Sears,* built for their own account. She was sold on the ways to Captain Joseph Henry Sears of Brewster for more than the $70,000 she had cost. Her career was the shortest; she disappeared in 1867— as thousands of ships had before her, and since— somewhere between San Francisco and Liverpool.

Stripped of men by the Civil War, East Dennis was unable to continue building the ships. So the ways were dismantled, and the various shops were moved and recycled into houses and barns— a common Cape Cod usage. Asa, Jr., became manager of the Pacific Guano Company in Woods Hole, founded in 1859 by Captain Prince S. Crowell; Paul went south, working for Pacific Guano, and then to work for Thomas Franklin Hall, who in 1866 had trekked out to Omaha and opened the first machine shop/foundry on the territory.

Captain Prince S. Crowell, whose home had been a station on the anti-slavery Underground Railroad, turned to his other interests. He was a moving force in bringing the railroad to Cape Cod; the first section reached Sandwich in 1848. He also experimented with making paper from Spartina (marsh) grass, unsuccessfully.

In retrospect the East Dennis clippers were extremely successful. Although *Webfoot* was the only record-holder, they all performed most profitably. The captains, the Howeses, Crowells, Halls, Searses, were skillful seamen, "free, self-reliant, frugal, and indomitable," according to Simeon Deyo's history. And only one, *Christopher Hall,* was lost under East Dennis command.

Today the village still remembers. The captains' descendants live in the captains' houses, and East Dennis looks very much as it did in the heyday of the Shiverick ships.

Captain Thomas Franklin Hall, who lived with his beloved ships, spoke at the 1925 unveiling of the bas-relief plaque that marks the yard's location, saying, in part:

When, therefore, it is realized that [these ships] *were not only equal, but in some technical respects, superior to any in the American fleet, it is more than grati-*

fying to local pride; . . .

It was a masterful undertaking . . . to establish such an enterprise in such a quiet spot, on the banks of such a small stream. . . . Those were great years; great events; great men.

THE BELLE OF THE WEST — BUILT AT SHIVERICK SHIPYARD 1853
EAST DENNIS • MASSACHUSETTS

Figure 3-9A *Belle of the West* was designed by the Great Samuel Hartt Pook, who was responsible for a number of great clipper ships – *Red Jacket, Gamecock, Herald of the Morning, Northern Light,* to mention some. Pride of the Shiverick fleet, she excited even blasé Boston with her beauty. She was never outsailed at sea, according to Dr. Henry Kittredge in *Shipmasters of Cape Cod. Courtesy of the artist, Dorothy Ellen.*

Figure 3-10 The Shiverick clipper ship *Hippogriffe*, 678 tons, built in East Dennis in 1852, was the second of the eight clipper ships built there. *Courtesy of the artist, Donn Devita of Worden Hall, East Dennis.*

The Hippogriffe Puzzle

Anyone researching Cape Cod history must beware of booby traps and mine fields. Over the years so much has been written about the truths and legends of the area by so many people that to separate fact from fiction can be most difficult. So it was with the grounding of *Hippogriffe* in 1858.

Just who was in command, where it happened, and even what it was that the ship hit have had many different answers over the years. For example, Howe and Matthews, in *American Clipper Ships I*, imply that David Seabury Sears was in command— and they are authorities on the era— and that the grounding was in the China Sea. As a result, Atwood, Crosby and others ascribe the grounding to Sears.

But Dr. Kittredge, in *Shipmasters of Cape Cod,* refutes these claims: Captain Anthony Howes was in charge, and it happened in the Java Sea. And he was right. In going over the same ground, the evidence in the posession of Mrs. Minerva Wexler, a granddaughter of Captain Prince S. Crowell, includes the originals of:
(1) the warrant for a survey, signed by Robert Campbell, U.S.Consul to the Port of London;
(2) the survey by three captains of the condition of *Hippogriffe* on her arrival in London;
(3) the certificate of seaworthiness issued by the London Surveyor of Shipping on completion of repairs.

Anthony Howes is named as master, and the Java Sea is the location of the grounding.

The type of shoal is even in question. Daniel Willis Howes, the first mate, claims that it was just a sand bank, and not a rock at all. But the *Hippogriffe's* log says that a piece of the rock broke off and filled most of the hole stove in the bow; it was probably coral.

We have direct evidence of the shoal. In 1866 *H.M.S. Swallow* found the shoal and described it in detail, in *The China Sea Directory* of 1867:

HIPPOGRIFFE SHOAL.— Mr. Wilds . . . found it in lat. 3 33' 36" S., long. 106 54' 30" E. It is a dangerous boulder rock with only 3 feet of water at low water, of circular shape, and about 150 feet in diameter, having large branches of coral upon it. It was not seen until close to . . .; the weather being fine and clear. . . . Regular soundings of 8 fathoms, sand and shell, were found around it, and the water in that depth was of a pale color.

This would seem to solve the problem of location.

Further evidence came over a hundred years later. A former student of mine at the Massachusetts Maritime Academy, sailing in tankers, wrote me from Singapore that he had passed by Hippogriffe Shoal and had located it by loran. He commented that those British seamen certainly knew their stuff, because his position and theirs of 1867 differed by only a couple of miles.

So now we know the historical truth: Captain Anthony Howes was in command; the shoal is in the Java Sea and it is quite likely that a piece of coral did break off and fill most of the hole punched in the bow of *Hippogriffe.*

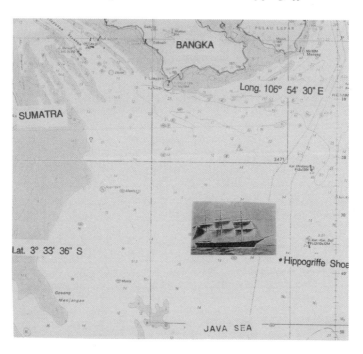

Figure 3-11 A portion of the chart of the Java Sea, showing the location of Hippogriffe Shoal. This is a current chart. *Courtesy of Jim Carr of Dennis.*

But the sea was not done with Captain Anthony Howes. After scarfing in (replacing) new planking, he ran into the worst storm (probably a hurricane) of his career. The jib boom and foremast went over the side; the mainmast was sprung; the hull was badly strained. The crew went to work, fished (wrapped) the mainmast with chains, rigged her as best they could, and limped into London, very glad they had made it.

On 23 February 1859 three well-known captains, at the request of the American consul, surveyed the ship. This is their report in brief:

Jib boom badly broken, Fore topmast & Topgallant Mast carried away, Fore Yard & upper Topsail yard badly sprung, Main Mast badly sprung and fished with spare spars & chains, . . . Main top gallant Mast & Yard broken, Mizen [sic] Mast broken, the foremost house on deck, window frames & sashes smashed in by the Sea, Stays & rigging fore and aft much chafed, ship generally strained, . . . & nearly a whole suit of Sails were split & torn, and running rigging much cut and lost when the masts were carried away, & a number of Blocks lost. Recommend that . . . the ship be placed in drydock, . . . Main & Mizen Masts taken out, the whole of standing rigging be taken out & refitted, and the Foremast examined.

With the Civil War raging, and the Confederate cruisers hunting Yankee ships everywhere, Captain John Addy sold her in Calcutta to the British for 70,000 rupees— more than she had cost to build eleven years earlier, in 1852.

Figure 3-12 Dow Baker (as he was called) at nineteen in 1859. *Courtesy of Captain Reuben Rich Baker, Jr.*

Captain Lorenzo Dow Baker
Cape Entrepreneur

"Dow," as his friends called him, was Wellfleet-born-and-bred, with all that that implies. In fact he was named after a popular itinerant Methodist preacher. In passing through he had aroused such a fervor that Methodist campgrounds sprang up in Eastham, Wellfleet, and Yarmouth Port. Wellfleet fishermen, it was said, refused to fish on Sunday, or even work the vessel. They would "lay off to windward praying and singing hymns," while they drifted through the fleet, fouling the other boats' gear. And, as we shall see, he carried his faith aboard ship all his life.

Born in March 1840, like his peers he grew up learning the ways of the sea— arduous, sometimes fatal, rarely profitable. His education ceased with the primary grades; yet he became a well-educated man. At ten he was a cook's helper/cabin boy, and at twenty he had his own vessel, the *Robert D. Rhodes*. The next year he married Martha Hopkins (of an old Wellfleet family) and eventually sired four children. Fishing in the summer and sailing coastwise in the winter became his accustomed round, throughout the Civil War and until the 1870's, when an inspiration changed his life.

With a load of mining equipment for Venezuela, he set out in *Telegraph* in the spring of 1870. Coming home, he stopped at Port Morant, Jamaica, looking for a return cargo. There he decided to take a load of bananas back to Boston, and

Figure 3-13 The old schooner *Telegraph*, thirty four years old, when Captain Dow Baker took his first cargo of bananas north in 1871. *Courtesy of the Peabody Essex Museum, Salem, Mass.*

when he arrived he found that even though many bunches had spoiled, he made money. Each bunch had cost him twenty-five cents; those he was able to sell went for $2.50 to $3.00.

The return voyage in his tired little schooner was difficult. Marginally seaworthy, she kept the crew (and even Captain Baker) at the pumps continually. But she made it, and early on 29 May 1871 she tied up at Long Wharf to discharge 35,220 coconuts and some four hundred bunches of bananas. This was the historic first appearance in Boston of bananas and the small seed from which the massive Caribbean fruit trade grew.

For the rest of the nineteenth century his idea blossomed into the L.D. Baker and Company, and eventually into the United Fruit Company in 1899. But he worked slowly at mastering (and inventing) the techniques of preserving such a perishable fruit. With only three or four weeks from field to market, he developed great skill at lengthening the life of his cargo. And he diversified, providing coconuts, pineapples, citrus fruit, and tropical logwood. Eventually he decided to drop fishing and coasting and concentrate on the fruit trade.

Acquiring larger and faster vessels, by 1880 he moved the whole family— his wife Martha, son Loren, then sixteen, and the younger ones, Joshua, Martha Alberta, and Reuben— to Jamaica to expedite the whole enterprise.

And he chose just the right time to change careers. Close to American markets, with abundant fruit and cheap labor, Jamaica was a British colony where slavery had been abolished. The Island had seen the old sugar plantation economy die, and the peasants were eager for a new way of making a living. Having made arrangements with the peasants, when he needed a cargo he would let it be known. The peasants would go into the mountains to harvest the wild fruit.

As the bunches arrived, he would inspect and buy only the best of the green fruit and load the bunches at once onto his ship. He would reward careful stevedores, knowing that any bruise of the fruit meant less value. In fact, he prized employees who were loyal and honest. And since he did not use alcohol, he preferred to hire non-drinkers. As a result, his supervisors and clerks were mostly Cape Codders of his persuasion.

L.D. Baker and Company was not the only banana exporting firm on the island; there was considerable competition. But he was deeply convinced that God's hand was over him and that with guidance from the Bible he would win out. By 1888 Dow's company was doing 42% of the fruit export trade. Even on the old *Telegraph* he carried a hand-pump organ and a crewman who could play hymns for the Sunday services aboard.

Captain Baker quickly understood the need for reliable shipping, and over the years he made various arrangements to use steamships, for their faster travel. First he arranged with the British Atlas Steamship Company for unused space in return for becoming their agent in Jamaica. Thus he got direct, fast access to the New York market. Then he allied himself with Jesse Freeman, a longtime fishing associate from Wellfleet, and a highly respected businessman.

Together they formed the Standard Steam Navigation Company with capital from a group of Massachusetts enterpreneurs. They built two ships specifically designed for the banana trade, to Baker's design. In 1883 and 1884 *Jesse H. Freeman* and *Lorenzo Dow Baker* became the first true "banana boats," able to handle 12,000 bunches of bananas in ventilated holds.

Thanks to Freeman, the Baker enterprise survived the recession of 1884. They formed the Boston Fruit Company, and even though prices dropped from $1.50 to $.35 per bunch, they weathered the storm. Baker wrote son Loren that "The banana business is flat here. The whole country is full of fruit . . . there is [sic]

Figure 3-14 The wooden steamer *Lorenzo Dow Baker*, 190 feet long, one of the first ships designed by Captain Baker specifically for the banana trade. She burned on 15 July 1889 near Nantucket Shoals. *Courtesy of Captain Reuben Baker, Jr.*

bananas, bananas, bananas. Today bananas is the cheapest thing on the market." And one company owing him $9000 went bankrupt.

To survive, Freeman suggested a two-way split of responsibilities: Freeman would handle marketing and distribution; Baker would deal with production. This appealed to Baker, who felt that he spent too much time away from Jamaica on selling to his customers. And the next few years proved the correctness of their decision. In Jamaica dilapidated sugar plantations became Boston Fruit's banana plantations, ensuring a much more regular supply of first-grade fruit. By 1889 Boston Fruit was the most effective banana enterprise on the island.

In February 1888 Andrew Preston joined the partnership to handle marketing, and the heydays of the company began. But Preston had much larger ideas, and eventually Baker was forced out when the United Fruit Company was formed. Then Jesse Freeman, upon whom Dow had leaned for support, died— a great loss.

A power play began, as the company considered incorporation, about which Dow knew nothing. Ultimately he was named president, in charge of the Tropical Division; Preston handled the Boston Division. Since Dow insisted on staying in Jamaica, his impact as president was minimal; in addition he had lost control of what he always thought of as *his company.* Preston thought in terms of widening the field to include other Caribbean areas such as Cuba and the Dominican Republic.

Figure 3-15 The *U.S.S. Montgomery* anchored at Port Antonio, Jamaica, in front of a hotel built by Captain Dow Baker, during the Spanish-American War. *Courtesy of Captain Reuben Baker, Jr.*

When the Spanish American War ended in 1899, the company was already expanding its resources; Dow had become a figurehead president.

Then Preston proposed a merger with a rival, Minor Cooper Keith, with a strong position in Central America and New Orleans. Left out of the decision, although he bitterly opposed it, Dow realized that he was now an outsider in the enterprise he had built. And, ironically, he had contrived his own displacement by insisting on staying in Jamaica, far from the center of the business. He wrote:

These seems [sic] to be two ways open to us, the one that we are now following, steadily plodding and safe, or the formation of a mighty trust combination that may or may not lead us into great prosperity. On the one hand, we have few allurements or temptations, and plenty of hard work; on the other hand, the temptations are great.

And so, despite Dow's urgings, the merger happened. The Boston Fruit Company became the United Fruit Company. Its president: Andrew Woodbury Preston, who was to lead this giant monopoly for the next twenty years.

Times had changed, and Lorenzo Dow Baker could not change with them. Although on the board of directors until he died, Dow was on the outside looking in. The new *shibboleth* was marketing, not production, and Dow had no desire to become a cog in an industrial machine. He had always been a self-propelled entrepreneur.

But he did not relapse into his rocking chair. Still active in Jamaica, he was honored in 1905 for his leadership in the island's highly prosperous fruit trade. He traveled frequently, often with his daughter Mattie, since his wife of forty-two years died in 1903. But the effect of the years of tropical living began to be felt. At sixty-eight he developed a lung problem, for which his doctors urged a higher degree of treatment than was available in Jamaica. So he took passage on a company steamer for Boston. Soon after his arrival, on 21 June 1908 he died at the Parker House.

Figure 3-16 Captain Lorenzo Dow Baker (1840-1908) about 1905. *Courtesy of Captain Reuben Baker, Jr.*

How to sum up this Cape Codder? Clearly it was his character and his religion that gave him his success. Hard-working, honest as everyone who knew him would state, ambitious, he knew instinctively how to lead men. In addition, his intelligent approach to the manifold problems of his business, leading to highly successful technological solutions, ensured his success. Further, his ability as a communicator convinced strangers of his total honesty. Ultimately, however, it was his family and his friends who made possible his success. His frail wife, Martha, his two sons Loren and Joshua— Loren especially gave up his youth to support his father— gave him the utmost in support throughout his life. His Wellfleet friends, Elisha Hopkins, his brother-in-law, and Jesse H. Freeman, a friend from his youth, contributed mightily to the cause.

Figure 3-17 Captain Lorenzo Dow Baker's leaky old *Telegraph* was quite similar to this portrait of the schooner *Polly*, built in Amesbury, Massachusetts, in 1805. Finally, in 1918 – 113 years after her launching – her owners laid her up, abandoned. *From* Maritime Sketches *by Paul C. Morris, with permission from the author.*

Figure 4-1 House of Refuge built by the Humane Society of Boston.

CHAPTER
4

Wrecks and Life-Saving

Cape Cod Houses of Refuge

The Humane Society of Boston, founded in the mid-1700's by ship owners and captains, very early expressed concern for the many shipwrecked crews on Cape Cod. Accordingly, on 4 October 1802, we find the following entry in their minutes of the meeting:

A Gentleman (Dr. James Freeman of Wellfleet) *who was requested by the Trustees to contract for a number of Huts . . . for the preservation of shipwrecked seamen, made the following report.* It was Voted— *That the Treasurer be requested to have two thousand Copies of said Report printed, and cause the same to be dispersed among the several Custom-Houses and Insurance Offices in this Commonwealth.*
A true Extract from the Minutes.
Attest. JOHN AVERY, Secretary

The report is a detailed fifteen-page description of the entire back shore of Cape Cod, locating the six Houses of Refuge established by Dr. Freeman. At the end of the report he describes the huts, which were all of the same design. On piles in the sand, each hut was eight feet long, eight feet wide, and seven feet high (at the peak of the roof). There was a sliding door on the south, a sliding shutter on the west, and a fifteen-foot pole at the ridge. Inside, the shipwrecked mariner would find either straw or hay and a bench.

Dr. Freeman must have walked the entire coastline from Race Point to Monomoy, such is the detail he presents. The first hut was located on a ridge halfway between Race Point and Stout's Creek, a mile from Peaked Hill, "a landmark well known to seamen." There were also fishing huts at Race Point that were available for shelter.

A second hut was built at the head of Stout's Creek. But it was not well designed: the winds scoured the sand from its foundation, and its chimney (the only one so equipped) pulled it to the ground. This happened about six weeks before the *Brutus* came ashore; had the hut been there, "the whole crew would have been saved." A new hut nearby (where beach grass stabilized the sand) was under the care of Dr. Thaddeus Brown and Captain Thomas Smalley of Provincetown, who kept it supplied and in good order.

Describing the coast down to the "Clay Pounds," where Highland Light was built in 1797 on a cliff over 130 feet tall, Dr. Freeman comments:

The shore . . . is unquestionably the part of the coast the most exposed to shipwrecks. A north east storm . . . blows directly on the land: a strong current sets along added to which ships . . . endeavor to work to the northward. . . . Should they be unable to weather Race a shipwreck is inevitable. Huts therefore, placed within a mile of each other have been thought necessary by persons.

He says that if the society has funds, it plans to provide those additional huts.

Then comes a long description of the many "hollows" or valleys: Dyer's, Harding's, Head of Pamet, Brush Valley, Newcomb's, Pearce's, Cahoon's, Fresh Brook, and Plum Valley. These all run perpendicularly to the shoreline, and there are often dwellings in which shelter may be had.

On Nauset Beach, a mile and a half north of "Nauset Harbour", was the third hut. Notable landmarks are given to help the mariner find it. Two Eastham men agreed to maintain this hut. From the harbor mouth to Chatham runs a beach with a ridge behind it. About halfway between Nauset and Chatham harbors was the fourth hut. Again several landmarks (a windmill to the northeast, a hill with two crests) are given. Timothy Bascom, Esq., of Orleans was the inspector.

A mile north of the mouth of Chatham harbor was the fifth hut, opposite the town. Dr. Freeman suggests a location for another house, north of the fourth hut, east of the middle of Pochet Island.

The sixth hut was on the beach of Cape Mallebarre (Champlain's angry name for Monomoy Point because of the dangerous shoals to the east). Beginning in 1849 three lightships were stationed in various locations— as the shoals shifted— east of Monomoy. The hut was two hundred yards from the ocean, southeast of Wreck Cove, which is on the west side of Monomoy. It was six miles to Chatham up the beach. Richard Sears, Esq., of Chatham was the inspector for these last two houses of refuge.

Dr. Freeman ends his description with some extremely valuable, practical advice to seamen as to how to cope with strandings on Cape Cod:

The whole of the coast . . . is sandy, and free of rocks. Along the shore, at the distance of a half of a mile, is a bar; which is called the outer bar. . . . Large, heavy ships strike on the outer bar, even at high water; and their fragments only reach the shore. But smaller vessels pass over it at full sea. . . and soon come to land. If a vessel is cast away at low water, it ought to be left as soon as possible; . . . because the vessel is generally broken to pieces with the rising flood. But seamen, shipwrecked at full sea, ought to remain on board till near low water; for then the vessel does not break to pieces. On this subject there is one opinion only among judicious mariners.

Over the next years the information in this little pamphlet was responsible for saving innumerable lives. And as time passed the Humane Society became the precursor of the Life-Saving Service, as it built more houses of refuge and small life-saving stations equipped with a sturdy lifeboat, lifejackets, and other equipment that would be needed for a rescue from shore— by volunteers. As we will see later, volunteers made some of the most daring rescues from this time until the establishment of the Life-Saving Service in 1872, using Humane Society equipment.

The Thirty Two Hour Rescue

The Nantucket *Inquirer and Mirror* of 6 April 1879 reported in great detail on the storm of that week and the many vessels caught in it:

Of the many severe gales which have visited us during the past winter, none have proved more disastrous than that which broke upon us on Monday morning last. . . . During the entire day and night the storm raged, . . . while sleet and snow added nothing to the comfort . . . [of] especially the unfortunate mariners on the coast. . . . There were wrecks or disabled vessels to be seen on all sides.

Learning that four vessels were in trouble off the west end of the island, Captain Thomas F. Sandsbury gathered a volunteer crew and headed for the west-end. In a dory the eight men managed to cross to Tuckernuck Island in the raging seas. There they pulled out the big Boston Humane Society life boat, launched it, and struck out for the schooner *Emma G. Edwards,* on Tuckernuck Shoal. All day she had been fighting the storm and, having passed Chatham, she was driven back into Nantucket Sound and all the way to Martha's Vineyard. Captain Bryant anchored her off Tuckernuck Shoal, but her cable let go and she was driven onto the shoal, and onto her beam ends (her side).

After a long exhausting pull, the rescuers reached *Edwards.* Only two sailors had survived the wreck, and only Thomas Brown was alive. It was the

Figure 4-2 Nantucket's Old South Tower, for many years used as a lookout post.

heroism of George Coffin, in swimming from the lifeboat to the schooner to secure a mooring line that saved Brown.

Now the gale was so strong that the lifeboat could not make headway back to Tuckernuck. So, after an eleven-mile row in that storm, they reached town and unloaded their icy cargo. But Captain Sandsbury would not rest; he knew that there were other crews in terror this night. Hauling a whaleboat on a cart, he and his men hauled it to the west end of the island. As they waited for dawn, they huddled under the overturned boat.

Pushing their boat through the breakers, they rowed out to the schooner *J.W. Hall* and took the crew off. Then on they went to the schooner *Emma*, removing that crew. Finally, at 3:00 P.M. on Tuesday, 3 April 1879, the whaleboat, dangerously overloaded with the nine-man crew and survivors from two vessels, reached a safe haven. They had been out in that hellish storm for thirty-two hours.

Another Tuckernuck crew of volunteers led by Isaac P. Dunham had also been active. He and four men went to the rescue of two other wrecked schooners, *Andrew H. Edwards* and *Convey*, and pulled off both crews, bringing them back to Tuckernuck. These men all received Humane Society Silver Medals and $25 each.

Many other vessels were in trouble during that storm. The brig *Manzanilla*, with lumber aboard, began leaking so badly that Captain John Rich ran her ashore. Since the surf was still too high to launch a boat, fishermen on shore rigged up a bos'n's chair and saved the crew. The schooner *Cargill* lost her main boom and all her sails but managed to anchor after cutting away her masts to keep her afloat. Another Humane Society boat, hauled five miles by volunteers, tried to get out to her but could not. In any case, mastless she rode out the storm with the crew aboard. Later the steamer *Island Home* took her in tow.

And the list goes on. The *Jefferson Borden* and *American Chief* went aground on Muskeget Island, but the crews stayed aboard, and *Alice Oaks* and

Figure 4-3 Model of a surfboat and carriage (hauled by the brew of a life-saving station to the scene of a wreck). *Courtesy of the Peabody Essex Museum, Salem, MA.*

Daniel Brittain dragged their anchors and stranded on Great Point, near the lighthouse. Later they were refloated.

The Sandsbury crew, who had endured so much, was rewarded. Congress awarded Captain Sandsbury a Gold Medal and his crew Silver Medals, and the Humane Society awarded them all $25 each. Treasury Secretary John Sherman in presenting the medals wrote to each man:

The entire adventure occupied thirty-two hours. Its humanity and the courage and constancy with which it was conducted, merit the highest praise, and it is with sincere pleasure that I transmit to you the medal which at once recognizes and commemorates an action altogether worthy.

Of course, what is striking about this series of events is, quite simply, that every one of these men was a volunteer, with thoughts only for his "Brethren of the Sea," the forty men saved.

Figure 4-3A A typical duty of the Life-Saving Service was to make every human effort to save crews of stranded ships. Note the crewmen gathered in the bow of this brigantine and the reefed sails of the lifeboat. *Courtesy of William P. Quinn.*

STATION OF MASSACHUSETTS HUMANE SOCIETY.
FROM WHICH THE LIFE SAVERS STARTED.

Figure 4-4 Mass. Humane Society Station No. 43 on Cuttyhunk. *Courtesy of the Cuttyhunk Historical Society.*

Life-Saving on Cuttyhunk

Cuttyhunk— the best the English could do with the Wampanoag name Pocutohhunkkunnah— is the small island at the southern end of the Elizabeth Islands on the eastern side of Buzzards Bay. Captain Bartholomew Gosnold built a fort there in 1602. Thomas Mayhew bought it as part of his purchase of the islands for £40 in 1641. Fifty years later a Quaker named Peleg Slocum bought the island for £335 — nearly ten times what Mayhew paid for all the islands! Never heavily populated, forty to fifty families lived there in 1880.

Despite the small number of people there, Cuttyhunk looms large in the lore of life-saving, a necessary task in view of the underwater dangers to ships. Ledges called Sow and Pigs run out from the island, and to the northwest are the dreaded Hen and Chickens; to the south is "The Graveyard." The shores of the islands are strewn with the bones of vessels, and there are hundreds of unmarked graves of lost mariners.

But since most men on the island made their living from the sea, they were great volunteer life-savers. The Massachusetts Humane Society, founded in 1786, was, able by 1847 to build a series of stations— two on Cuttyhunk and one on Nashawena, the northern-most island. These buildings held supplies such as life vests and flares as well as lifeboats, which were manned by island volunteers. And wrecks there were a-plenty, enough to keep both the Humane Society volunteers and the United States Lifesaving Service (organized in 1872) busy. Here are some examples.

The rescue of the schooner *Rob and Harry's* crew on 11 March 1892 best illustrates the way in which both life-saving teams worked. Coming out of Vineyard Haven, she was hit by gale-force winds, so strong that both masts fell overboard, crunching the ship's boat. Barely missing Sow and Pigs, she fetched up on the west end of Cuttyhunk, a hundred yards from shore.

When A.J. Eisner, the lighthouse keeper, saw her two hours later, he quickly organized a volunteer crew and set out in the Humane Society lifeboat. Meanwhile the USLSS crew under Keeper David Bosworth (the first keeper of the station) hitched up the station's mules and left with the beach apparatus, a two-hour trip. The volunteers, in the teeth of a gale, reached the schooner and rescued the master and mate. But a huge wave swept the boat half way up the beach, and a piece of wreckage stove it in. As they were about to launch another boat, the USLSS crew arrived. Three shots from the Lyle gun (used to fire a line out to a stricken vessel) put lines aboard, but the wrecked crew could not find them in the dark.

Bosworth launched his smaller boat but was driven ashore twice, and the boat was wrecked. They repaired the larger boat with a canvas patch, and the USLSS crew took it out, Bosworth in command. With the surf down, they reached

Figure 4-5 The Cuttyhunk Life Saving Station crew in the 1890's: L to R: standing, Captain Weeks, Jo Tilton, Humphrey Jamieson, Willard Church, (?) Peterson. Above: Tom Jones ("The Hero of Cuttyhunk") and Wall Allen. *Courtesy of the Cuttyhunk Historical Society.*

the schooner and took off the one remaining survivor; the steward had died of exposure. So reported the USLSS Report of 1892.

One of the members of the USLSS boat crew that night was Tom Jones, who became known as "the Hero of Cuttyhunk" for the number of rescues he made. His is quite a story. In May 1888 the schooner *Onrust,* in ballast, came ashore on the island, and all of the crew were rescued by the Humane Society volunteers. The second mate, Tom Jones, looked around and decided to stay, instead of leaving with the others.

He had run away to sea at twelve to get away from a sadistic stepfather in South Boston and had literally seen the world. In Rio de Janeiro he caught smallpox and almost died. Now, "liking the looks of Cuttyhunk," his first job was helper on David Bosworth's fishing boat; then when Bosworth became keeper of the USLSS station in 1889, he chose Tom for the crew. The record shows that Tom was among the few who had helped save the most seamen.

And he was content. For the first time in his life he had a home, money in the bank, and a loving wife, Jane, who eked out their livelihood by keeping a shop and making pottery.

A considerable part of the lifesaver's duties was to patrol the shoreline all night, alert for danger. Each man carried a lantern, Coston flares, and rockets. One night, on patrol, Tom saw quite close in both a red and a green light. This meant that a ship was headed directly toward him, and in deadly danger. He fired his Coston flare, and the ship, a large passenger steamer, turned sharply and, with a hoarse "Thank you" of the whistle, she anchored safely.

Figure 4-6 The first Cuttyhunk Life Saving Station. (Note the two boats in the open area and the lookout tower, as well as the two-masted schhoner offshore). *Courtesy of the Cuttyhunk Historical Society.*

For a while patrolling was done on horseback. One night he was riding close to the edge of a bluff when the horse missed the path, and horse and Tom went over. Forty feet down he fetched up against a boulder, but the horse fell to the bottom, where he was found next day so badly injured that he was shot. Lucky Tom worked his way back up and staggered to the patrol shelter, where his relief found him three hours later, bruised and with several broken ribs.

In 1905 a reporter asked him what his feelings were, starting out in a gale to row to a rescue. Tom said,

Why, I don't rightly know. I never gave much attention to it. Of course we know it's dangerous, but it's got to be done, so what's the use of fretting about it? We know we've got a tough boat . . . and beyond that it's only a case of keeping your wits about you and of pulling hard enough to overcome the sea. Once you've started you don't have time to think about the danger, and before you know it, you're back safe and sound.

On 2 February 1891, in thick fog, the schooner *Gardner Deering* grounded close to shore. With their breeches buoy (a seat hanging from a pulley that can be hauled from shore to ship and back) the lifesavers rescued thirteen men— a routine affair. But just after they had returned to the station, they saw new distress signals (usually the national ensign flown upside down). From almost the same spot they saved five crewmen from the *George Francis.*

Figure 4-7 The schooner *Douglas Dearborn* ashore. *Courtesy of the Cuttyhunk Historical Society.*

Perhaps the strangest rescue occurred in the winter of 1897, when a West Indian schooner hit North Ledge in Buzzards Bay. On a bitterly cold night the lifesavers had a row of three hours to reach the wreck. Six men were loaded into the lifeboat. But they refused to leave unless their valuable cargo was saved: several monkeys and two wild bears. To lasso them, tie them securely, and then to get them into the lifeboat, heavily overloading it, was a singular achievement. Then to locate them so that they could not claw the men's legs was even more skillful. The whole boatload - seven lifesavers, six rescued men, the monkeys, and the two bears - somehow landed safely on Cuttyhunk.

In 1905 Tom Jones retired from the Lifesaving Service. Immediately he was hired by William M. Wood, who bought most of the island in 1921 from the Cuttyhunk Fishing Club. The newspapers gave him the title of " General Marine Adviser." Summering on the island, Tom acted as manager of the Wood properties. And when Mr. Wood was on the island, he would often be seen playing cribbage with Tom. Tom Jones had found his home.

But the sea, ruthless with ships and their men, was not always kind to the rescuers. In February 1893 the brig *Aquatic* was lost on Sow and Pigs Reef soon after an arduous, ice-covered rescue of the crew of the *Douglass Dearborn*. One by one the lifesavers hauled the half-frozen crew off by breeches buoy. With little rest, the volunteers responded to the cry of "Brig ashore!" Captain Tim Akin, Jr., quickly found five volunteers for a boat crew, despite dire warnings that "No boat can live in such a sea."

Hauling their gear and boat to the west end of the island, they launched into the fearsome combers breaking on the reef. Captain Akins, as he skillfully steered into the breakers, shouted, "Come on, boys—, ain't this fun!" Outside the first line of breakers, they pulled for the brig. But close by it a giant of a wave swallowed the boat and crew, and the shipwrecked men saw their rescuers, clinging to the boat, swept away. Josiah Tilton (an old island family name, that) floated toward the brig's stern, and the brig's crew saved him by throwing him a line.

Surprisingly, the *Aquatic* did not break up as expected, and by noon the next day all (including Tilton) were saved from the foretop; there they had huddled, wrapped in the topsails.

Cuttyhunk mourned their five sons. Some $30,000 was raised and with $1000 from the Canadian government was divided among the families of the lost men— $8000 per family, hardly an adequate recompense for the lives of these men who went out, time after time, to save the lives of others, with no other reward than the sense of a duty to others rightly performed.

The Wreck of the Witherspoon

Sunday, 10 January 1886, was a day that lives long in the memory of Nantucketers who watched as man after man lost his hold on the rigging and fell to his death from the hulk of the three-masted schooner *T.B. Witherspoon*.

It seemed like a mild winter at first, but on 8 January a nor'east blizzard hit the island, followed by a nor'wester. The thermometer was well below freezing. Even the side-wheeler *Island Home* was forced to turn back from her trip across the sound; the gale was just too strong.

The schooner, Captain Albert Anderson in command, had a cargo of cocoa, spices, molasses, and pickled limes from Surinam aboard as she neared the coast. The mate, Burdick Berry, had his wife and son, seven-year-old Sidney, with him. There was a seven-man crew. In a nor'east gale, well offshore, they were blown off course. Thinking himself some twenty miles off Montauk Point, Long Island, the captain decided to run with the wind and perhaps make Sandy Hook, New Jersey. But then the wind went nor'west and the rigging and sails became encased in ice.

At 3:00 A.M. on the tenth, Mate Berry saw a light on the starboard bow which Captain Anderson timed through the snow as Montauk Point. So they set a westerly course. But the light was Sankaty Head, on Natucket's east coast, and about a half-hour later *Witherspoon* was pounding through several shoals until she hit hard about one hundred yards from the beach.

Nobody could stay on deck; the waves were breaking right over her. So they all took refuge below. Hundreds of people ignored the bitter cold and drove to the beach to watch helplessly as the vessel became an icy tomb from the wind-driven spray. Soon the seas smashed in the cabin skylight, flooding all areas below deck. As a last resort the crew climbed into the icy rigging.

In the flooded cabin Burdick Berry stayed with his wife and son, putting them up as high as possible on furniture. As he waded about, trying to block portholes, the freezing cold and rising water took their toll, and his wife Sarah died in his arms. Later son Sidney died as well.

Quickly the crew of the Surfside Life-Saving Station used their Lyle gun to shoot two lines over the schooner, preparatory to setting up their breeches buoy. But the crew in the rigging could not reach the first line over the schooner's stern. A second shot landed amidships, and John Mattis grabbed it and hauled in the tailblock. As he was trying to secure it, the line parted, and, trying to keep his balance on the rail, he fell into the frigid water and died.

There was a huge ground swell, too powerful to launch a lifeboat. But a life-raft might have a chance. Nine men, Life Savers and volunteers from the crowd on the beach, launched it and tried to pull the raft to the vessel on the leader line. But halfway there the line, under terrible stress from the seas, parted. Two men fell into the water but were pulled back aboard, and the crew ashore pulled the raft back in.

By now it was after noon, and the watchers had seen Captain Anderson and a sailor lose their grip on the rigging and fall to their deaths. Two men were left alive and active: Mate Berry and a sailor, Charles Wulff. The Life Savers fired another line aboard, and Wulff managed to secure the heavy line on which the breeches buoy would ride.

Joseph Folger, Jr., volunteered to pull himself out to the schooner, but the line on the vessel had fouled and they could not free it at first. Finally, in darkness, they heard a hail and, pulling carefully, they brought Berry ashore. Back went the buoy and returned, with Wulff, who was barely able to gasp that he was the last survivor.

Nevertheless, the crew stood by all night, and daylight revealed a complete wreck. That afternoon they were able to get aboard and found the ship's boy, Nicholas, frozen to the shrouds. Over the next several days the bodies of six of the seven aboard, including Mary Burdick and young Sidney, came ashore and were found.

The annual report of the Life Saving Service of 1868 praised the work of the Surfside Station thus:

No better work under the circumstances could have been done than Veeder [Surfside commander] and his crew did that memorable day; and when it is related that a vessel was wrecked near the Surfside Station and seven out of nine of her crew perished, it will also be told that the lifesaving crew did their whole duty.

This desperate rescue, carried out under the worst possible conditions, was only one of the more or less routine assignments of that station.

Bernard Webber and the CG-36500

Thirty-six men in a thirty-six-foot boat in a howling nor'east blizzard. What man would carry out such an assignment? Boatswain's Mate First Class Bernard Webber of the Chatham Coast Guard Station would, on the night of 18 February 1952.

The other protagonist in this saga of skill and bravery is the *CG-36500,* one of the standard Coast Guard motor lifeboats from the 1920's until the 1960's. Self-righting, self-bailing, with the engine amidships, she was built in 1946 and today is still a treasured relic of an older time. She performed magnificently for BM1 Bernard Webber on that awful night.

Son of a Baptist minister in Boston, at fifteen he had seen three older brothers go off to World War II. School was far down on his list of priorities; kicked out of Mount Hermon School in Greenfield, he itched to get into action of some kind. So when he turned sixteen his father agreed to his entering the Maritime Service. After his boot camp at Sheepshead Bay, he found himself a seaman aboard a T-2 tanker delivering gasoline from Aruba to the South Pacific. In February 1946 he enlisted in the Coast Guard, and after boot camp he became one of the keepers at Highland Light in North Truro briefly. Then for the next three years he was at Gay Head Light and aboard a cutter on weather patrol.

Having served briefly at Chatham Station, he was glad to be reassigned there in 1949. He served at the loran unit and the Monomoy Lookout Station before returning to the Lifeboat Station. And he writes fondly of the comradeship and discipline of this small unit:

We really were a family at Chatham Lifeboat Station. There were formalities. For example, at mealtimes the crew would stand until the man-in-charge, Alvin Newcomb, arrived, [and] *the others sat along the table according to rank. There was respect and protocol, and our lives were disciplined. The system not only kept us organized, it provided security and stabilization in our young lives.*

Chatham Station has always been a busy place. With a large fleet of fishing vessels, there are numerous recipes for disaster. Then there are many ships passing along this dangerous shore, where the captain of the *Mayflower* ran into such shoals that he aborted his goal of Virginia, turned around, and settled for Provincetown harbor and finally Plymouth.

During Bernie's first three years at Chatham he shared in a number of rescues before that fateful night. A Naval Reserve destroyer ran up on Bearse's Shoal, opposite Monomoy Light. Luckily, while Chatham's lifeboat stood by all night in case of need, and served to run the heavy hawsers out of shoal water to the tugs, there was little harm done, and at a high tide the *Livermore* floated off.

On 7 April 1950 a different situation faced the station. The captain of the fisherman *William J. Landry* radioed that they were sinking and would try to reach the Pollock Rip Lightship, off Monomoy Point. A wild nor' easter with snow, sleet and heavy seas was blowing. It was necessary to use the 36383 in Stage Harbor to reach the fisherman. That meant a long haul around Monomoy and a hard row to the boat's mooring. First the boat capsized; on the second try the seas were so strong that the oars broke. Meanwhile *Landry* had reached the lightship but had been damaged by smashing into the steel hull of the lightship and was sinking fast. Shortly the lightship radioed that *Landry* had gone down with all hands. A Coast Guard inquiry cleared the station of liability.

Fishing out of Chatham was and is a dangerous, life-threatening business. Getting over the bar at the harbor mouth is often a real gamble when the huge seas are running. So it was with *Cachalot* on 30 October 1950. A huge wave picked up the forty-foot Novi boat of Archie Nickerson and Elroy Larkin, coming in, and pitchpoled it (picked up the stern and turned it upside down) over the bar. Only Elroy Larkin's body was found. *Cachalot* was repaired and went fishing for another fifteen years.

On 18 February 1952 Cape Cod was being blasted by a seventy mile-an-hour northeast blizzard. Seas offshore were forty to sixty feet high by 10:00 A.M.

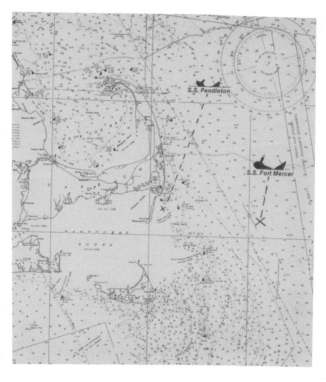

Figure 4-8 C&GS chart no. 1107, showing the locations of the two tankers which broke in half and then drifted as shown. *Courtesy of Bernard Webber.*

Figure 4-9 This is the sort of weather that Webber and his three-man crew faced in their struggle to reach *Pendleton*.

Chatham Station had word of a ship in distress; the tanker *Fort Mercer* had broken in half forty miles at sea. And the fishing fleet in the harbor needed help; their moorings were not holding. Bernie was told to take *CG-36500* and help the fishermen. By afternoon all was secure, and, cold and wet, the crew returned to the station. Chief Bangs in *36383* had gone off to try to help the tanker; Bernie did not believe that they would return. Then word came of the breaking apart of another tanker, the *Pendleton*, closer inshore. Meanwhile Bangs had found the bow of *Pendleton* and seen one man aboard.

Bos'n Cluff decided that *CG-36500* had to find the stern. He turned to Bernie and said, "Webber, pick yourself a crew, Y'all got to take the 36500 over the bar and assist that ship, ya-heah?" Three of his shipmates volunteered: Engineman Andrew Fitzgerald, Seaman Richard Ivesey, and Seaman Irving Maske. Rowing out to the lifeboat in the harbor, they were underway by 5:55; it was already dark.

Near the bar, the ocean's roar was intimidating; without foul weather gear, they were already soaked through. And where was the tanker they were supposed to find? With no radar and only a compass, how could they do it? Would they survive? Well, it was their job, Bernie decided; so he opened the throttle on the 90 h.p. gas engine and drove for the bar.

The first sea tossed the boat onto its side. The next shattered the cockpit windshield and ripped the compass from its mount. Then the engine stopped, and Fitzgerald crawled into the compartment and restarted it; this happened several times as the engine lost its prime when the boat was thrown about.

Once they were outside the bar, the waves became higher but farther apart, as they headed blindly into the seas. Up a wave and then tobogganing down the back side, they went on for what seemed like forever. Suddenly Bernie saw the huge opening of the broken hull, and as they went down the ship's port side, they saw lights high above them; a man was waving his arms.

Down dropped a Jacob's ladder over the side, and men began climbing down. Timing his move, Bernie put the boat where the men could jump onto the foredeck; there the two seamen would grab them and put them into the forward cabin. Men kept coming and coming. Some five missed, and Livesey and Maske somehow pulled them aboard, while trying to maintain their footing.

Still some men were on the tanker, and the lifeboat was already heavily overloaded. But somehow Webber just could not leave them, and so shortly thirty-two tankermen were aboard. The last man jumped too soon but managed to catch hold of a propeller blade of the tanker. Still trying to rescue him, Webber eased forward with the boat. But a wave picked her up and smashed against three-hundred-pound George (Tiny) Myers, who disappeared.

The situation was desperate: a badly overloaded boat, no idea of where they were, no compass. Calling the station by radio, Bernie reported the situation. Suddenly the airwaves were filled with questions from a nearby cutter and others, trying to decide what orders to give Bernie.

So he shut down the radio and told everyone that he would ride the waves toward shore, and they would have to hit somewhere. All agreed, and they started in. Steering totally blind for what seemed like forever, Bernie finally spotted a red blinking light ahead, and discovered with his searchlight (which surprisingly functioned throughout the ordeal) that he had slipped over the dreaded bar and was looking at the buoy marking the turn to Chatham Old Harbor and safety. They had made it! He called in for help with the survivors when they docked.

At the Fish Pier a large crowd of neighbors and friends, their wives and children too, was waiting to help in any way they could. Then, of course reaction set in, as Bernie realized what blind chance had permitted him to do. He wrote:

I stood at the stern of this little lifeboat, her name only CG-36500 *and realized she had carried us out into the unknown on a mission of mercy. We had come from, I didn't know where, to the safety of Chatham Harbor, crossing the bar, I didn't know how. . . . With my crewman Irving Maske, beside me I unashamedly cried in the near solitude and gave thanks to God for guiding us through the unknown.*

Then all hell broke loose among the media as the word got out as to the rescue. But the four heroes soon went upstairs to bed.

Bernie Webber's rescue was a small part— but the most dramatic part— of the Coast Guard's operations that day. For example, Chief Bangs's *36383* fought her way around Monomoy to get to the bow of *Pendleton*, where he found no one

Figure 4-10 This airview shows what Webber found. Note the Jacob's ladder hanging over the side, down which the tanker's crew climbed to the dubious safety of the *CG-36500. Courtesy of Kelsey-Kinnard Studio, Chatham, Mass.*

Figure 4-11 Shown are about half of the thirty-two men saved, as they arrived at the Chatham Fish Pier. *Courtesy of Kelsey-Kinnard Studio, Chatham, Mass.*

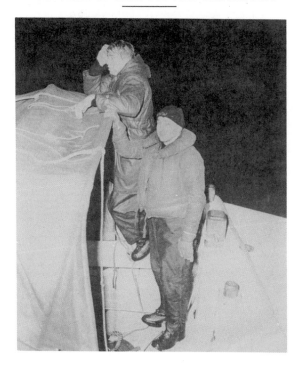

Figure 4-12 Seaman Irving Maske (foreground) and Boatswain's Mate First Class Bernard Webber, drained by their ordeal. *Courtesy of Kelsey-Kinnard Studio, Chatham, Mass.*

Figure 4-13 Coast Guard Commandant Vice Admiral Merlin O'Neill congratulates Webber on his Gold Lifesaving Medal, the Coast Guard's highest award. *Courtesy of William P. Quinn.*

alive after long circling and searching. They were out twenty-two hours, soaked through, with no food. The *36524*, from Nantucket, under Chief Ormsby, was out for eighteen hours.

The *CGC Yakutat* arrived at the Fort Mercer's bow and with a whaleboat under Ensign W.R. Kiely, USCGR, managed to rescue two of the four men on the bow, while nearly stoving in the boat. The other two were rescued by drifting a rubber raft downwind for them to jump into.

The *CGC Eastwind* was at the stern of the *Fort Mercer* but could not get close enough for a rescue. But the small tug *Acushnet,* more maneuverable, was able to ease alongside so that survivors could jump aboard. Thirty tankermen made the jump safely. Thirteen men stayed aboard, and salvage tugs towed this half of the tanker to Newport and then to New York.

At the decoration ceremony for the twenty-one Coast Guardsmen the Comandant, Vice Admiral Merlin O'Neill noted that a total of seventy men "were snatched from the elements and deliverd [sic] safely ashore." In fact *only one man* (from the *Pendleton*) was lost during the whole complex operation. And Bernard Webber and the trusty *CG-36500* brought back thirty-two of the seventy rescued!

Admiral O'Neill summed up the effort thus:

I am proud to say that it was the teamwork of all Coast Guard units involved that made possible the exceptional exploits that we note here today. . . . In reality these men faced four separate rescue operations. . . . The operations were unique in Coast Guard history, and called for the skillful use of all types of rescue equipment . . . of cutters and small lifeboats, of an airplane, a sea-going tug; of rubber life rafts, radar, scramble nets and exposure suits.

BM1 Webber and his crew received the Coast Guard's highest award, the Gold Lifesaving Medal, as did Ensign Kiely, USCGR, for his rescue from *Fort Mercer.* Four men received the Silver Life Saving Medal, and fifteen others received the Coast Guard Commendation Ribbon for their work.

And what of *CG-36500?* Replaced in 1968 by the faster 44-foot, steel-hulled lifeboats, she went to the Cape Cod National Seashore to be part of a life-saving museum; the project never developed. So she sat out in the weather until 1981.

That October the Orleans Historical Society took custody and began the arduous task of restoring this thirty-five-year old wooden boat. News stories ran nationally, and over $10,000 in cash and donated materials came in. Hundreds of hours of volunteer labor produced a totally new-seeming boat. In June 1982 a grand relaunching took place at Rock Harbor in Orleans, and today (2000) she is still a showpiece, moored in Orleans during the summer.

And what of Bernie Webber? His career continued. On promotion to Chief he left Chatham, spending five years at various stations. Then he returned as

Officer-in-Charge of Chatham, always an active location. In 1963 he left Chatham for command of *Point Banks* out of Woods Hole. Then came a tour of duty in Viet Nam, soon after which he retired as Warrant Boatswain.

As a civilian he found that he had to make a living for his family of four. Naturally he went into maritime-related work, holding many different positions before moving to Florida and working for a towing company for some time. Now he frequently returns to Chatham to renew old friendships and to see his beloved *CG-36500.*

Figure 4-13A This airview shows the other major rescue occurring at the same time that Webber and *CG-36500* were saving 32 crewmen from the *Fort Mercer.* Shown here are the Coast Guard Cutter *Yakutat* and the stern of the *Pendleton,* the other tanker that broke in two in the storm. *Courtesy of William P. Quinn.*

Figure 4-14 High and dry at high tide. *Aerial photo by William P. Quinn*

The Loss of the Eldia

Since long before the *Sparrow Hawk* stranded on Nauset Beach in 1626 ships have come ashore along the Cape's "back side" as it is called. Why? The prevailing northeast winter storms roar down on the fifty miles of north-south shore-line. In addition ships collide, catch fire and run aground, or are destroyed by pure human error.

In this case, however, it was the weather. On 29 March 1984 a powerful circular storm caused by the collision of warm and cold masses developed south of New Jersey and moved toward us. Over the ocean the storm became a hurricane. And the freighter *Eldia*, from Valletta, Malta, in ballast after unloading sugar in St. John, New Brunswick, headed south, found herself off that back shore.

High in the water, this 471' ship was barely under control because of the wind and sea. Pushed obliquely toward shore, she soon was only five hundred yards off the beach. Trying to save his ship, the captain dropped both anchors, but the winds were so strong that she lifted over the outer bar and fetched up on Nauset Beach, bow-on.

The Cape Codders could see that the ship was in real trouble, and quickly at least a hundred people were standing on the beach, watching to see what would happen. A call had gone out for rescue apparatus, and the Orleans Fire Department was already on the scene. An H-3 Coast Guard helicopter was on its way, and the Chatham Coast Guard crew was there, Chief Boatswain's Mate Tom Pezzi in charge.

The classic method for rescuing men from a stranded vessel, the breeches buoy, had been withdrawn from Coast Guard service twenty-four years before. But the Orleans Historical Society had preserved it, and there it was, ready for use if needed.

However, the Coast Guard helicopter was able to hover over the *Eldia* and hoist the ship's crew of twenty-three aboard in their rescue basket. Making several trips to the Coast Guard parking lot, below the lighthouse, the helo crew delivered everyone safely and without injuries. Rescue ambulances then took them to the Orleans Fire Station for check-ups, and later several local motels housed them.

The storm blew itself up to Canada by Sunday, 31 March, and a constant stream of hundreds of people (and their cars) choked the Nauset Beach lot and overflowed up Lighthouse Road, leading to the beach. Then they faced a long walk through the sand to reach *Eldia*. She was now so close to and parallel to the beach that at low tide one could walk to her side. Meanwhile a sand bar, built up by each tide, was rising on the seaward side of the ship. This would make salvage even more difficult.

But the first priority was an ecological one: to remove the 140,000 gallons of bunker oil as quickly as possible. Another March storm might well damage her single hull and spill all that viscous oil along the beautiful beaches all alongshore, even down to Monomoy.

Called upon to handle the job was Clean Harbors, Inc., of Kingston, just a little way off the Cape. They laid 1400 feet of large hose lines from the ship's tanks onto the shore and, with their own pumping equipment, siphoned the oil into tank trucks for storage ashore. A clean job it was, accomplished quickly. Next came the problem of moving that ship off the beach. The owners, Thenamaris, Inc. of Athens, Greece, chose two organizations to do the job: Don John Marine, of New Jersey, and McAllister Towing and Salvage, of Montreal, they announced the choices on 23 April, almost a month after the grounding. Meanwhile tourists from all over the East came to see this stranded whale. And Orleans and Eastham enjoyed a second major tourist season that year.

Work started at once. Deep in the holds welders secured heavy I-beams against the starboard side, weakened when she pounded onto the beach. The heavy-

Figure 4-15 Parking became a real problem if you wanted to look at the ship. *Aerial photo by William P. Quinn.*

lift barge *Century* arrived in Provincetown with a ten-yard front-end loader to help to remove the sand piled up around *Eldia*. Moored offshore, *Century* was ready to pull *Eldia* off the beach. At low tide the loader and a bulldozer worked at scraping away the sand on both sides of the ship. A tug carried both of her anchors out into deep water, and two heavy cables led from the barge.

At midnight high tide the pulling started, from the ship and from the barge, By morning she was perpendicular to the beach. But other leaks were found and more pumping out took place. In addition a containment boom around the ship could catch any further spilled oil.

Again at high tide on the third night, the final effort began and was successful. *Eldia* was free. Taken in tow, she left the scene of her troubles at about 4:00 P.M. on 17 May, seven weeks after it happened. The tug *Merion* towed her through the Cape Cod Canal and to Newport, Rhode Island, to be drydocked at the Direktor Shipyard.

Cape Codders and visitors rarely get a chance to see a stranding like this. In 1960 the *Monica Smith* came ashore at New Beach in Provincetown but was freed a week later by a large tug. In that time thousands of people visited the site, giving the town a mini-tourist season in February.

Another notable stranding in December 1976 was that of the Liberian tanker, *Argo Merchant,* on Nantucket Shoal. Luckily she was carrying light oil— seven and a half million gallons— which dissipated far out to sea, endangering no shorelines.

Figure 4-16 Workmen in the number four hold preparing to weld I-beams to reinforce the weakened hull. *Photo by William P. Quinn.*

Figure 4-17 At low tide bulldozers dig sand from around the hull. Offshore the heavy lift barge Century from New York waits to haul the ship off. *Photo by WIlliam P. Quinn.*

Figure 4-18 A media event: *Eldia* is ready to be refloated. Channels 4 and 7 covered the action live the entire three days of the final move. *Photo by William P. Quinn.*

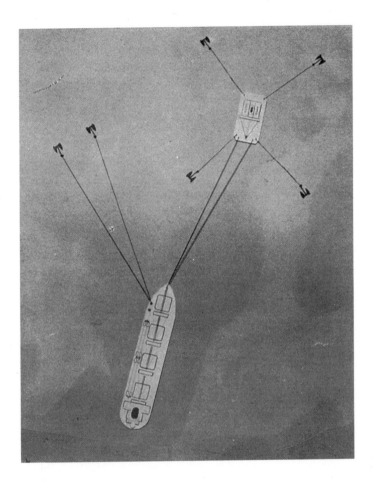

Figure 4-19 And this is how they did it. With anchors out the ship is turned seaward. Then both ship and barge haul away and draw the ship into deeper water. *Drawing courtesy of William P. Quinn.*

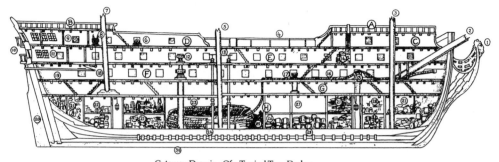

Cutaway Drawing Of a Typical Two-Decker

A. Forecastle deck B. Poop deck C. Forecastle D. Quarter deck E. Upper deck F. Lower Deck G. Orlop deck H. Hold

1. Figure head 2. Bowsprit 3. Fore mast 4. Hammock rail 5. Main mast 6. Gun port 7. Mizzen mast 8. Wheel 9. Upper cabin 10. Stern Galleries 11. Lower cabins 12. Main capstan 13. Pumps 14. Galley 15. Bitts 16. Cable 17. Forward capstan 18. Tiller 19. Warrant officers' quarters 20. Rudder 21. Stores 22. After magazine 23. Cable tier 24. Pump well 25. Shot lockers 26. Water casks 27. Cockpit 28. Forward Magazine 29. Keelson 30. Keel (From "Ships And Seamen Of The American Revolution" by Jack Coggins. Used with Permission of Stackpole Books.)

Figure 5-1 Cutaway drawing of a typical two-decker. **A**. Forecastle Deck **B**. Poop Deck **C**. Forecastle **D**. Quarter deck **E**. Upper Deck **F**. Lower Deck **G**. Orlop Deck **H**. Hold **1**. Figure Head **2**. Bowsprit **3**. Fore Mast **4**. Hammock Rail **5**. Main Mast **6**. Gun Port **7**. Mizzen Mast **8**. Wheel **9**. Upper Cabin **10**. Stern Galleries **11**. Lower Cabins **12**. Main Capsters **13**. Pumps **14**. Galley **15**. Bitts **16**. Cable **17**. Forward Capstan **18**. Tiller **19**. Warrant Officers' Quarters **20**. Rudder **21**. Stores **22**. After Magazine **23**. Cable Tier **24**. Pump Well **25**. Shot Lockers **26**. Water Casks **27**. Cockpit **28**. Forward Magazine **29**. Keelson **30**. Keel. *Permission of Stackpole Books.*

CHAPTER

5

Disasters

The Capture of H.M.S. Somerset

    H.M.S. Somerset was a British ship-of-the-line— the battleships of the seventeenth century. She actually changed the course of the American Revolution in the opening battles (Lexington, Concord, and Bunker Hill) and eventually stranded on the tip of Cape Cod. Many myths exist on Cape Cod right up until today about her, most of which are quite different from the facts.

    Her keel was laid down on 5 May 1746 in Chatham, England, at the Royal Dockyard, originally established by Henry VIII. She was one of five ships built to the same plans, which were drawn by master shipwrights and approved by the Admiralty. Generally speaking, some two hundred trees were used for such a ship. The keel was of elm, for its water resistance, and oak was the wood of choice for general construction.

After seasoning for a year the wood began to shape the hull. Once the keel and frames were in place, another year of seasoning was usual. Then the double-planked hull, a foot thick, was fitted to the frames with wooden trunnels (or tree-nails) of oak, driven into holes to hold the planking together. After more seasoning the two decks were added. Then began the final steps of fitting masts, spars, ratlines, stays, armament, sails, equipment, and supplies for a crew of some 480— a long, slow process. After some seven years as a guard ship, she finally went to sea in 1755.

Guns were rated as to the weight of the cannon balls which they fired. *Somerset* probably had twenty-six 32-pounders, twenty six 18-pounders, and twelve 9-pounders. These last had a range of about 1700 yards; the larger guns reached up to two miles. There were also swivel guns, and guns of three and four-pound weight. In addition there were plenty of muskets, pistols, and blunderbusses, as well as cutlasses, dirks, boarding axes and pikes.

The complement of *Somerset* consisted of a captain, Captain Francis Geary, four lieutenants, a sailing master (responsible for navigation and maneuvers), some twelve midshipmen (officers in training, often about twelve years old), a boatswain (responsible for sails, rigging, small boats, anchors, etc.), a chaplain, a surgeon, a purser (responsible for all stores), a gunner, a carpenter, cook, some sixty marines (the ship's soldiers), the able and ordinary seamen, and— often— women, espe-cially in port but also frequently at sea and in combat, where they helped carry the powder to the guns. John Nichol, whose memoirs have been published, relates:

I was much indebted to the gunner's wife, who gave her husband and me a drink of wine now and then [in the heat of battle] *which lessened our fatigue much. There were some of the women wounded and one woman died of her wounds, and was buried on a small island. . . .One woman bore a son in the heat of action; she belonged to Edinburgh.*

The term "son-of-a-gun" may well derive from the conditions under which a male child was born aboard ship!

Somerset's first mission was as part of a large fleet sent to America to prevent the French from expanding their territories. On 18 June 1755 the fleet began a blockade of the French fortress, Louisbourg, Nova Scotia. And men began dying from scurvy in alarming numbers. But bad weather and fog allowed the French to evade the fleet and land reinforcements, and so the fleet in October returned to England. The fleet had lost some two thousand men not to battle but to scurvy and fevers. In addition General Braddock and been killed and his army destroyed.

The next year was spent losing more men to scurvy, impressing men from captured ships to replace those lost, and taking prizes. After every tour of duty *Somerset* had to have extensive work done in shipyard; those wooden hulls worked and leaked all the time. In fact the costs of rebuilding her during the Seven Years War a mounted to £37,600.

For the rest of that war she was either operating with the fleet or independently (when she wasn't in drydock, that is) capturing French vessels. A seven-week battle for Louisbourg in 1758 ended with taking of the fortress by Wolfe and destruction of the French fleet. During the night of 26 July, for example, six hundred men from *Somerset* and other ships rowed into the harbor and captured *Bienfaisant* and *Prudent*, burning the latter and towing away the former, a 64-gun ship. The garrison surrendered.

The British goal for 1759 was capture of Quebec, and a formidable armada gathered: twenty-two warships, with frigates and transports. Among them was *Somerset,* flagship of Admiral Holmes. The squadron sailed south to the African coast, stopped at the Madeiras, was off Sandy Hook (Long Island) on 26 April, and finally anchored in Halifax, Nova Scotia, on 15 May— a rather roundabout route.

The French at Quebec underestimated the British skill in navigating a tricky passage in the St. Lawrence River and soon found the fleet in front of the city. And, believing that no one could scale the rocky cliffs on which the city lay, although they built elaborate defenses they were utterly surprised when 150 men of General Wolfe's army scaled the cliffs. The British forces had landed by night, and after a fierce battle in which both Wolfe and Montcalm, (the French general), were killed, the French had to surrender on 18 September.

A month later the fleet started home, only to be met by the first of the winter gales of the North Atlantic: rain, sleet, gales, and squalls requiring these unwieldy square-rigged ships to work the sails frequently. Rodgers, in *Wooden Worlds,* describes the difficulties well:

In the winter of 1759, with the sea frozen sixty miles offshore, many men in the North American squadron died from frostbite. It was generally reckoned very difficult to keep square-rigged ships at sea in Canadian waters in winter.: The running ropes freeze in the blocks, the sails are stiff like sheets of tin, and the men cannot expose their hands long enough to the cold to do their duty aloft, so that topsails are not easily handled.

In 1760 the French control of Canada expired with the surrender of Montreal and other posts in Canada. *Somerset,* in Portsmouth drydock, received a new copper-sheathed bottom and was rerigged. On 12 May the crew received their pay, but only to 30 June 1760— almost a year behind. Soon she went to sea, hunting prizes in the Mediterranean, returning to Gibraltar on 27 November.

The next years were spent similarly, broken only by frequent stays in dock-yard. 1762 was spent operating out of Gibraltar in the Mediterranean. Captain's log entries from that period reveal somewhat of the ship's duties:

1-10 Jan. Moored at Gibralter cleaning and victualling.

9 Feb. Punished Jno. Cravens marine 12 lashes for selling his clothes contrary to the order of the captain.

19 Feb. Read Articles of War Abstract of the late Act of Parliament and declaration of war against Spain to the ship's company.

28 Feb.-9 Mar. Watering and hogging ship. New rigged the foretopmast, top gallant mast fore and aft. Scraped sides and and masts. Received water. Hulled and scrubbed sides.

17 May. Still in Gibraltar Bay. Adm. [admiral] made the signal for 2 boats manned and armed to attend the punishment of 2 men for sodomy who received 18 lashes each alongside each ship in the Bay in part of their punish-ment of 1000 lashes each by sentence of a court martial.

5 July. Executed a man aboard the THUNDERER for desertion.

27 Sept. CAME ON BOARD CAPT. WILLIAM PARRY WHO SUPER-CEDED [sic] CAPT. EDWARD HUGHES and hoisted a white distinguishing pendant per order of Sir Thos. Saunders.

10 Oct. Saluted the Moorish Ambassador with 15 guns at his going on shore.

28 December. Gibraltar. CAPT. JOHN CLARK TOOK OVER FROM CAPT. WILLIAM PARRY.

In the next year the Treaty of Paris ended the Seven Years' War. Spain lost Florida and France confirmed her loss of Canada. And *Somerset* was in such bad shape that by the time she had been made fit for sea, the cost of repairs was £35,758—only a little less than her building cost. Inactivity led to harsher discipline. In two months Captain Clark ordered twenty-eight men to be flogged. On comple-tion in 1771, Captain Edward Hughes received orders to command and took her to the Channel as a guardship.

One hardly needs to review the many sources of friction that led to 18 April 1775 ("Hardly a man is now alive," wrote Longfellow) : the Stamp Act, the Quar-tering Act, the Townshend Act, the colonies' boycott of British goods, stationing of four regiments in Boston, the "Boston Tea Party". In April 1773 four ships with 450 officers and men sailed for Boston with their women, children, and animals. In March 1774 Parliament closed the port of Boston and in October General (and Governor) Gage fortified Boston Neck (the whole town was on a peninsula then) and seized all military stores. The Massachusetts Assembly had been dissolved by Gage, but they met again as the Provincial Congress and voted to equip 12,000 men, a fourth of them to be Minutemen, ready for instant action when called upon.

Finally realizing that the situation was serious, the king sent *Somerset* and other ships with 600 marines and 4000 troops to quell the unrest. Sailing on 19 October 1774, the convoy drove into a series of winter gales and took two months to reach Boston. After further major work on her hull, *Somerset* was positioned between Boston and Charlestown.

During the night of 18 April a large number of British troops (Grenadiers and Light Infantry) were ferried across to Phipp's farm in Cambridge. Meanwhile Dawes and Revere were ready to ride to "spread the alarm/ To every Middlesex village and town" (Longfellow). As a result, when the footsore, wet troops arrived in Lexington at 5:00 A.M., the Minute Company under Captain John Parker was ready for them. Both leaders had their troops hold their fire, but someone on the edge of the green fired a pistol, and the British fired a volley, killing eight and wounding ten Americans. One British soldier was wounded.

Leaving their casualties, the British marched on to Concord to destroy the military stores there, arriving at about 8:00 A.M. Meeting the Minutemen at the North Bridge, the British tried to disperse the Americans but lost two soldiers and four officers killed before they retreated to Lexington. After a brief rest the 1500 exhausted soldiers started their retreat to Boston at about 3:15 P.M. Luckily the Americans were short of ammunition; nevertheless 73 British were killed and 174 wounded; the Americans lost 49 killed and 41 wounded.

Figure 5-2 A view of Boston. Ink and watercolor drawing. **1.** Mistic River **2.** Charlestown Pt. Where the British troops landed 17 June **3.** Redoubt of the Rebels **4.** Noodles Island (now East Boston) **5.** Hog Island **6.** Boston Harbour **7.** The Dykes **8.** Boston North **9.** Kops Hill and battery which played on the Rebels redoubt on Bunkers Hill the 17th of June. **10.** Beacon Hill **11.** The *Somerset.* *Courtesy of the Library of Congress.*

And luckily the British chose to return via Charlestown, under the guns of *Somerset,* rather than via Cambridge, where hundreds of fresh American troops were lying in wait for them. All the British ships' boats ferried the troops back to Boston. Admiral Graves sent this message to the Admiralty:

BUT IT WAS THE SOMERSET ALONE THAT PRESERVED THE DETACHMENT FROM RUIN. [SHE] SO INTIMIDATED THE INHABITANTS THAT THEY THOUGH RELUCTANTLY SUFFERED THE KING'S TROOPS TO COME IN AND PASS OVER TO BOSTON, WHO WOULD OTHERWISE BEEN UNDOUBTEDLY ATTACKED . . . FOR, HAD THE CHARLESTOWN PEOPLE MASSACRED THOSE POOR HARASSED SOLDIERS . . . THEY WOULD HAVE IMMEDIATELY CROSSED OVER TO BOSTON WHERE THEY WERE CERTAIN TO FIND 19 OUT OF 20 WILLING AND READY TO ASSIST THEM IN FINISHING THEIR WORK.

From then on there were frequent skirmishes around Boston, Charlestown, and Cambridge, as the British moved to strengthen their defenses, including Bunker Hill and Dorchester Heights. But the Americans moved first and on the night of 16 June began building a redoubt 160 feet long and 130 feet wide on Bunker (or Breed's hill), By daylight more than 1000 men had created a strong position, seen and reported by the British lookout on *H.M.S. Lively.* Soon the British ships began firing at the fort, and by 2:00 P.M. "Redcoats" were in Charlestown and began to set fire to the town. *Somerset* had been moved to deeper water.

At 3:15 the battle began. The British were carrying 125-pound packs and

Figure 5-3 The attack on Bunker (Breed's) Hill. Note the rocket fire from the Boston side of the harbor. *Courtesy of the Library of Congress.*

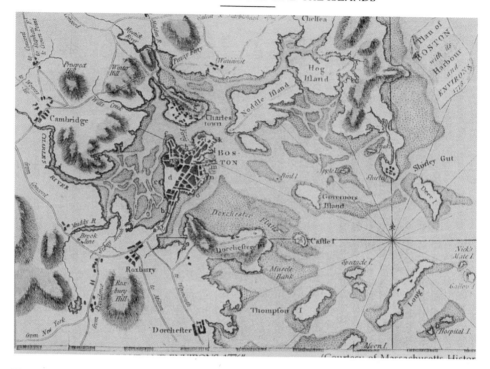

Figure 5-4 "Plan of Boston with its Harbour and Environs 1776" **A.** Advance Entrench-ments **B.** A battery of 8 24-pounders on Boston Neck **C.** A redoubt and 4 brass 12-pound-ers on the small island at the bottom of the Common **E.** A redoubt with 2 12-pounders on Beacon Hill **F.** Barter's Point **G.** Bunkers Hill **H.** Mill Pond **I.** A battery of 8 24-pounders on Copps Hill **K.** N. Battery **L.** Clark's Wharf **M.** Long Wharf **N.** S. battery **O.** Wind-mill Point *Courtesy of Massachusetts Historical Society.*

wearing their heavy woolen uniforms. As they marched in lines up the hill, the Americans held their fire until the British lines were within yards of the fort; the withering fire drove the British back. Their guns were useless, too; the wrong size shot had been provided, and the guns bogged down in mud. The second attempt up the hill was as deadly as the first, only on the third charge were the defenders, out of ammunition and exhausted, driven out. Only thirty-five were captured; those re-maining alive retreated to Cambridge.

It was a costly battle. Of the 2400 British, some 226 died and 828 were wounded; about ninety officers were killed or wounded. The 2000 Americans lost 140 killed and 271 wounded.

Somerset despite her recent repairs was leaking so badly that in August she sailed for Halifax for more work. Her log shows:

28 Aug.-30 Sept. Removed guns, shot, stores, booms. Cleared hold, removed ballast and cleaned ship. Careened [tipped the ship on her side for repairs]. Found garboard streaks [seams along the keel] very open. Part of the main mast was found to be rotten and was removed. Overhauled the main rigging,

Figure 5-5 Adm. Howe's fleet sailing from Sandy Hook, N.J., to Philadelphia Bay and the Delaware River in July 1777 with 14,000 British and Hessian troops on board. *Courtesy of the Mariner's Museum, Newport News, VA.*

Returned supplies, guns, coals on board and hove the ship away from the wharf; anchored in 13 fathoms [78 feet]- Stowed and tarred the booms. Flogged 10 men.

For the rest of the year she acted as a guard ship against any rebel attack on Halifax. Then early in 1776 she was ordered to England; after a terrible voyage, on which three seamen drowned falling off the main top yard when it broke in a storm, she came into Torbay. On 19 February "1/2 past noon Captain Ourry came on board and superceded [sic] Captain LeCras." During that year at least fourteen men were flogged, four drowned, and one was executed.

In April 1777 *Somerset* left England for the last time. For the rest of that year and the next she operated with the fleet supporting the army's campaigns in New York, Pennsylvania, and Rhode Island, where they tried to come to grips with the French fleet. Her log ends on 10 October, at anchor in New York. The last crucial days before her loss can be told through other sources. On the 19th she sailed from Sandy Hook for Boston, and on 1 and 2 November in a violent storm "THE SOMERSET WENT AGROUND AT PEAKED HILL BARS OFF TRURO, CAPE COD, AND WAS WRECKED DURING THE STORM." H.M.S. *Cornwall* (74 guns) was also lost, and *Bedford* was dismasted and towed into New York.

Because of her heavy construction only twenty-one men were lost; about 480 others got ashore when she rode over the bars and close in. They were made prisoners of war by the Provincetown militia, and in a body were marched from town to town toward Boston and imprisonment. Captain Ourry and others went to Providence. But when the crew arrived there were only 314 accounted for. The others had simply disappeared en route and were not recovered, despite strong British efforts to recapture them.

In March 1779 Captain Ourry underwent a court-martial for the loss of his ship. After much testimony from officers and crew, The court's verdict:

The Court . . . having deliberately and maturely Considered the Account Given by Captain Ourry and His Officers, . . . are of Opinion . . . that every care and Attention was used . . . In Consequence of which we do in the fullest manner acquit Captain Ourry, the Officers . . . of the Somerset *of her Loss; and they are hereby acquitted accordingly.*

Cape Codders promptly moved aboard after the wreck and began to salvage just about everything removable, storing it well before the Massachusetts authorities could arrive with six small ships to unload the "goodies." One John Greenough received £1500 as superintendent of the wreck, and a vast quantity of material, the guns, shot, powder, small arms, and so forth was salvaged.

The Maritime Court gave 66% of the auction proceeds to the state (later reduced to 50%) and the rest to groups of salvagers. The proceeds amounted to £32,510, and the salvagers received half. Simeon Spencer of Provincetown and three others received about £5335; Silvanus Snow of Truro and ninety-eight others, £2670; and Seth Nickerson of Truro and ninety-eight others, £8001. It seems as if nearly the entire male population of Truro was involved!

In the more than two hundred years since 2 November 1779, many myths have grown up about *Somerset,* to be repeated *ad nauseam* by writers. Marjorie Gibson, author of *H.M.S. Somerset,* has debunked many of them. A partial list includes:

Somerset *was a frigate.* She was much larger, with 64 guns.

Figure 5-6 Periodically the "bones" of *Somerset* appear above the sands. A photo taken in 1883 and one taken over two hundred years after the wreck in 1776 show almost the same amount of wreckage. *Photo by William P. Quinn.*

She was stationed in Provincetown. Never, although she visited.

A third of her crew drowned. Only twenty-one did.

She left Provincetown to find the French fleet. Not true.

Captain Ourry, with a huge black beard, was used to frighten children. Probably this is a confusion with Sam Bellamy, the pirate, whose ship *Whydah* had been wrecked here in 1717.

Cape Cod girls were courted by the Somerset *crew.* No decent girl would have been allowed to consort with the enemy.

Provincetown men guarded the prisoners all the way to Boston where they stayed for the duration. Neither myth is true.

This accident deeply affected Cape Cod, whose inhabitants had suffered severely during the war, when shipping (their main livelihood) was at a standstill because of the British. Small wonder, then, that the men of the lower Cape helped themselves as much as they could to the property of the hated enemy.

The Sailor's Nightmare
Fire at Sea

A newspaper account begins this tale of the worst nightmare of going to sea in a wooden ship, a moving tinder box of tar and wood and canvas, all highly inflammable:

The bark Burlington, Captain Hallett of Boston, left New Orleans, Saturday, February 15, 1840, for [Le] Havre, with cotton, and a crew of 16 hands, including two officers, cook and steward . . . when in the latitude of 37 N and longitude 54.40 W, . . . on Tuesday, March 10, she was struck by lightning which came down the larboard [port] main topsail sheet, knocked down the second officer and all the starboard watch, with the exception of the man at the wheel.

Captain Bangs Hallett was a Yarmouth man, born in 1807. He was a seventh generation descendant of Andrew Hallett, one of twenty-eight men who founded the town in 1639. One of his ships was the brig *Pilgrim,* believed to have been the source of Richard Henry Dana's *Two Years Before the Mast."*

A skillful navigator, he commanded a succession of vessels. In 1837, in the ship *Nantasket* he made a round-trip voyage from Boston to Liverpool in thirty-nine days, a very fast trip. In 1846, in *Faneuil Hall*, he sailed to Calcutta with a most diverse cargo, illustrating what was valued in India: "100 mahogany logs, 12 bales of corks, 130 boxes of tobacco, turpentine, 5 barrels of flour, 625 tons of ice (The ice, a most desirable cargo, was owned by Henry Tudor, the "Ice King," who made a fortune shipping it to India and the West Indies), 192 packages of missionary goods, 1 box of spice, 1 hay cutter, 1,000,000 shingles, and 10,000 feet of lumber." *Vancouver, Burlington, Cato, Herbert,* and *Gertrude* were the other ships under his command. But this time, in *Burlington*, with five other Yarmouth men in the crew, he and his crew experienced a once-in-a-lifetime horror. Incredibly, no one was more than superficially burned by the lightning. However, it penetrated the deck and set fire to their cargo of cotton between decks, as they were soon to discover.

The story of the eight-day ordeal, trying to combat the fire and keep afloat, was told in an article by Lewis Lovell, a member of the crew who called himself "Decayed Mariner", and by the entries from the ship's log.

Almost at once the captain and first mate carefully examined the area around the mainmast and pumps, but they saw no evidence of penetration below the deck. But at midnight, when the watch changed the crew smelled smoke in the forecastle, and almost at once the mate called all hands on deck; smoke was emerging from the booby hatch aft.

For safety the captain ordered the longboat cleared away and provisioned and the jolly boat (on davits at the stern) made ready for lowering. Then the carpenter bored holes around the mainmast, and a "water tunnel" (hose) was inserted to douse the fire, since the deck was already getting hot.

After a good breakfast of fried pork, all hands met in the captain's cabin, where he spoke to them:

Men, this may be that last time we shall all meet together in this world . . . but we should all remember that we are men, and it is a duty we owe to ourselves and our friends on shore to preserve our lives as long as possible.

Then he read the Sailors' Psalm, number 107, beginning, "They that go down to the sea in ships, and do business in the great waters... He maketh the storm a calm, so the waves thereof are still."

To abandon ship looked to be the best option. Into the longboat went 120 gallons of water, a barrel of salt pork, five barrels of bread, coffee, sugar, etc., as well as a small coal stove. Because the weather was worsening, very gingerly the boat was lowered over the side and veered astern some fifteen fathoms on a five-inch hawser. They lowered the jolly boat, but the tackle fouled and it filled with water, which they bailed out. Then they veered it astern of the other boat.

How to get into the boat? The seas were too tall to bring it alongside. With a lifeline along the spanker (the rearmost sail) boom and a rope with overhand knots in it, the men were able to climb down to safety. Captain Hallett was the last to leave. And thus they left Burlington, with one topsail and the ensign upside down at the mizzenmast head (the universal distress signal).

Captain Hallett decided to stand by until the bark burned to the water's edge and then head for the nearest port, New York or Bermuda. He had his chronometer and sextant aboard. That afternoon the weather cleared, and they warped back to the bark. Climbing back aboard, they found the deck cooler than it had been. So they concluded to try to sail her to the nearest American port.

Getting sail on, and pumping water into the holds (and pumping it back out to keep her afloat) the watch was very busy. One should note here that the pumping was all by manpower.

From this point our author reproduces the ship's logs to tell the rest of the story.

Thursday, March 12: *Commenced with strong gales from the SSW. All hands employed in pumping up water and pouring water below and securing the long boat. . . . At midnight still blowing heavy but not so much lightning. . . . The decks still continue hot and every time the plugs are taken out to pour down water fire and smoke rush out . . . At 5 turn [took] two reefs out of the topsails, set the mainsail, spanker and jib. Deck still hot. . . .*
Friday, March 13th: *Moderate weather and cloudy, let one watch lie down, while the other was pasting up every vent hole below. The decks we think are*

getting cooler; . . . we are in hopes that the plan of stifling the fire will succeed.
Saturday, March 14th: *Commenced with fresh gales and fine weather at 6:30 saw a ship about 8 miles distant. . . . By keeping the blankets around the coats of the mainmast continually wet the coat and mast kept quite cool, but by putting our fingers down the holes in the deck . . . it was impossible to hold them there a moment without getting burned Two brigs passed us standing to the south.*
Sunday, March 15th: *Commenced with moderate breezes. At 7 [P.M.] now blowing a violent gale from the SE. The lightning is terrific. At 4:30 A.M. shipped a sea which filled the cabin and state rooms. . . . At 8 blowing a complete hurricane; . . . Made a drag with a heavy sampson post and made it fast to the bowsprit end. . . . Our storeroom filled with water, our provision near expended. . . . The heat below about the same.*
Monday, March 16th: *Commenced with a perfect hurricane, ship laboring hard, hove to under bare poles, the lea [sic] gunwale under water. . . . There were also three water casks which all went to leeward [washed overboard]. At four A.M. warship to WSW; found the fire had gained on us a good deal A heavy sea running.*
Tuesday, March 17th: *Commenced with strong gales and heavy snow until 5 p.m. all [sic] engaged in pumping up water and turning it below. 5 p.m. smoke not rising quite so fast . . . "[P]umped the ship dry and continued to pour down water at intervals through the night. At nine violent gales from the NW clewed up and furled [almost] all sails. . . .*
Wednesday, March 18th: *Commenced with fresh NE breezes and clear. At 2:30 a perfect hurricane from the NW. . . . Our mainmast works a good deal; think the wedges have burned off and dropped down. . . . All boring new holes in the deck and pouring down water. . . . Midnight more moderate. Cabin filled with gas. . . . Captain Hallett retired at 1 a.m. and calling him at four he was almost dead, falling helpless to the deck. . . . At 10 a.m. saw a sail on our starboard quarter. Hove to and set our ensign union down in the mizzen rigging.*
Thursday, March 19th: *Commenced with fresh NE breezes and clear. At 3 p.m. ship to windward was found to be the St. James of and for New York, one of the London line of packets, Capt Sebor, with emigrants and cabin passengers. On being informed of our distress he immediately lowered his boats . . . and we got out the jolly boat and commenced putting in what few things we had at hand . . . [I]t was impossible to get anything out as the gas and smoke were so strong . . . Ebenezer Gage went down the [forecastle] ladder . . . but had to be hauled up by a rope and he was insane for some time after. At 6:30 we were all on board the St. James. Captain Hallett was the last to leave the ship. . . . and the fire was blazing some ten or twelve feet above the deck. . . . At 10 p.m. she suddenly disappeared from view and the unfortunate Burlington then sunk [sic] to rise no more.*

"Decayed Mariner" had only praise for Captain Bangs Hallett with these final comments about their experience:

I will here simply remark that throughout the time the ship was on fire Captain Hallett acted the part of a true seaman and efficient commander. . . . [K]nowing no earthly power could save a soul on board if it once got control, he was cool and calm as if the ship was sailing with a fair wind and a smooth sea.

A final note on our captain: Retiring after thirty years at sea, he and his wife Anna acquired the handsome Georgian house in Yarmouth Port that now houses the Historical Society of Old Yarmouth. In July 1879 they celebrated their fiftieth wedding anniversary. All of their children, grandchildren, brothers and sisters attended. He lived fourteen years longer, dying at home in 1893, aged eighty-six.

Figure 5-7 The steamer *Massachusetts* towing a whaler out of Nantucket Harbor in a "camel" (a sort of floating drydock) because of shoaling at the harbor entrance. *Courtesy of Peabody Essex Museum, Salem, MA.*

Stove by a Whale
The Essex *Disaster*

Many and strange are the tales of what men can do under extreme conditions at sea. Countless tales of horror, cruelty, and nobility exist. Then there are the tales that are never told: those in which no one survived. The annual tally by Lloyd's of London of vessels lost at sea is often staggering: almost 900 craft lost in one year in the 1890's.

This is the story of what was certainly the most unusual disaster at sea in the nineteenth century, the destruction by a sperm whale of a whale ship and the ninety-three-day ordeal in the crew's whale-boats with almost no supplies.

Captain George Pollard and his twenty-man crew set out from Nantucket on 12 August 1819. Six of the crew were "colored," probably Gay Head natives, since at that time they were in great demand as whalers. In mid-Atlantic a squall threw the ship onto her beam ends (almost capsized) and smashed two of her boats. one they were able to replace in the Cape Verde Islands from a wrecked whaler. Rounding Cape Horn easily, they were able to store 400 barrels of sperm oil before heading out into the Pacific. (See the map of the whole voyage.)

It was a fine day on 20 November 1820, and whales appeared. Every boat took off to leeward in pursuit. Owen Chase, the first mate, struck first, but the sperm whale stove in the boat. By packing the hole with jackets, they were able to get back to the *Essex.*

The other two boats had another whale, and Mate Chase sailed the ship downwind toward them. One of the crew spotted a large sperm whale just off the bow and sang out. This bull whale destroyed the *Essex.* Owen Chase tells what happened next:

The whale spouted two or three times and then disappeared. In a few seconds he came up again . . . and made directly for us at . . . about three knots. . . . [Then] he headed for us with great celerity. I ordered the boy at the helm to put it hard up . . . [but] he came at full speed and struck the ship with his head just forward of the fore chains. The ship brought up suddenly as if she had hit a rock.
We realized at once the dreadful accident that had befallen us. . . . [The] whale had stove a hole in the ship and I *must set the pumps to work. . . . I saw that the ship was settling by the head, so I ordered the recall signal for the boats.*
I had scarcely done this when I saw a whale, apparently in convulsions, about a hundred yards to leeward. [Suddenly someone shouted], "Here he is— he is making for us again!" . . . This time he struck the ship under the cat-head and completely stove in the *bow. He passed under the ship again, went off to leeward, and we never saw him again.*

So began the ninety-three-day ordeal in the open whaleboats. Chase set the crew to clearing away the spare boat and saving anything they could, while the steward rescued two quadrants (a type of sextant), two navigators (mathematical tables), the trunks of Captain Pollard and Chase, and two compasses. That was all.

Essex was filling so fast that they barely managed to launch the spare boat before she tipped onto her beam ends. The other two boats had arrived, to find that in barely ten minutes the ship was doomed. Cutting away the masts partially righted her, and by cutting holes in the deck they could reach 600 pounds of bread and some sixty-five gallons of water for each boat, as well as tools, a musket and powder, nails, and some turtle meat.

Moored to the wreck, the twenty men rigged masts, sails, and higher gunwales for the boats from cedar boards. This careful preparation was what enabled them to survive the storms met during their some 1500-mile ordeal, from which only eight men escaped.

The weather was worsening, and the ship began to break up. Where to head for help? The nearest land 900 miles away was the Marquesas Group, inhabited by known cannibals. The Sandwich Islands were to the northwest, but this was the hurricane season. And there were no charts of this part of the Pacific. So, after long discussion, Captain Pollard decided to head for South America, south and east of their position.

Agreeing to stay together, they set off at noon on 22 November. Food allowances established were one one-pound biscuit and half a pint of water per day.

Figure 5-8 A depiction of the ramming of the *Essex* on 2 November 1820 sinking the ship and bringing about the crew's ordeal. *Courtesy of the artist, Paul Morris.*

Chase's boat had been repaired as well as possible, but it was not too seaworthy. They figured that they had provisions for sixty days. If time ran out, their only hope was to be rescued by a whaler, since there were few other vessels in those latitudes.

Chase's boat began to leak badly, but with the help of the others they were able to make repairs. Then on the twenty-seventh Captain Pollard's boat was attacked and damaged by some large fish; again, by tipping the boat they were able to partially fix the leak. But some of the bread was water-soaked, and eating it caused extreme thirst.

The food problem only worsened. Dolphins played around them, but they could never catch one. A caught sea turtle, cooked in its shell, was consumed, raw blood, entrails, and all. In mid-December the bread ration was halved, and they even scraped off and ate the barnacles on the boats' bottoms.

After a series of gales, Captain Pollard was able to fix their position as some six hundred miles from the wreck— but *south-southwest* of it, almost ninety degrees in the wrong direction. And when the winds died, the enfeebled men tried to row, with little headway. And still they struggled on.

After a month of this torture, on 20 December they saw land; Mate Chase's observations led him to conclude that they had found Ducie's Island, uninhabited and barren of vegetation. Finally they discovered a spring after two days' searching, and some men drank so much water that they nearly died. Hauling up the boats, they repaired them further, and after catching a few fish they cooked them for a few days' more food at sea.

Seven days later the feeble armada put to sea. But three men (William Wright and Seth Weeks of Barnstable, and Thomas Chapple of Plymouth, England) refused to go; they would not risk their lives further in the boats. The Captain left an account of the disaster in a tin box. Their desperate goal was still South America, 2500 miles away.

The hardships only worsened. On 12 January 1821 in a severe storm,

Owen Chase's boat became separated from the others in 32° 16' South, 112° 20' West. On the thirteenth the second mate, Matthew Joy, in command of the third boat, died and was buried at sea, the first of many.

Chase wrote in his diary on 8 February,

Our sufferings were now drawing to a close; a terrible death appeared to await us; hunger became extreme; our speech and reason seem to be impaired.

And on 8 February Isaac Cole went suddenly mad after days of wild hope and utter despair and died "in the most horrid and frightful convulsions I ever witnessed. "As they were burying him, Chase, in utter desperation, suggested that his body become their food. Finally his crew agreed. He records the act:

We separated his limbs from his body, cut off all the flesh, took out the heart, sewed up the remains in canvas, and committed it to the deep, and making a fire partook of it, and preserved the remainder for future use. In this manner we disposed of our fellow sufferer, the painful recollection of which brings to my mind some of the most revolting ideas that it is capable of conceiving.

The next morning the flesh was spoiling, so they cooked it and lived on it for six or seven days.

By the fifteenth the flesh was gone, and they had only two bits of bread left. Their arms and legs had swollen and were very painful. "We were still some three hundred miles from land, " he writes. On the morning of the eighteenth Thomas Nicholson (Nickerson) lay down to die, despite Owen Chase's urgings.

Then, at 7:00 A.M. on 18 February 1821, someone cried out, "Sail ho!" and young Thomas Nickerson stood up to see. Soon the decrepit whale-boat was alongside the brig *Indian*, Captain William Crozier, of London. The three survivors (Owen Chase, Benjamin Lawrence, and young Tom Nicholson) began their recovery with tapioca pudding in tiny amounts. They had sailed some 3700 miles since that fateful November day, ninety days ago.

The other two boats were to experience even more terrible tragedy. When the last of the food gave out, Charles Shorter became the next source of meat, shared between the two boats. Then Thomas Lawson died and was similarly disposed of, as was Samuel Reed's body. Then, on 28 January the two boats were separated by heavy seas, and Obed Hendricks' boat disappeared forever.

By the first of February no food was left. The four surviving men decided to draw lots to be the next victim. Owen Coffin drew the short stick, and young Charles Ramsdell drew the duty of executioner. Captain Pollard offered to take his nephew Owen's place, but Owen refused, claiming his right to give his life for the others. Ramsdell pleaded that he be allowed to replace Owen; Owen again refused and died of a shot to the head. Finally, ten days later Barzillai Ray died, and the two left (Pollard and Ramsdell) lived on his flesh for twelve days.

This was sheer luck, because on 23 February they saw land and were rescued by the Nantucket whaler *Dauphin*. On 17 March 1821 they reached Valparaiso, Chile, two weeks after Owen Chase and his two men (Benjamin Lawrence and Thomas Nickerson) arrived. What a reunion that must have been!

What of the three men left behind? Captain Pollard at once asked for help in retrieving them. The frigate *U.S.S. Macedonian* was at Valparaiso, and Commodore Downes persuaded the captain of *Surrey,* an English ship bound for Australia, to rescue them. On 8 April 1821 *Surrey* picked them up and carried them to Sydney, where the two Americans found a ship bound for Boston.

In port was another Nantucket ship, *Hero,* which had been captured by pirates off Chile. The captain and the ship's boy had been shot, but Obed Starbuck, the mate, escaped and with the other officers retook the *Hero* and sailed her to Valparaiso. The five *Essex* survivors, finding that *Hero* was bound home, sailed on her.

Safely in Nantucket harbor, they found a massive crowd waiting to welcome them. It is reported that when the tragic news went through the crowd, the people silently watched the eight men, out of twenty, walk up the wharf to their homes.

Since that time many mariners have questioned Captain Pollard's judgment in ignoring the Society Islands, relatively close to the wreck. But his logic was perfectly valid: no charts, hurricane season, and cannibals in the Marquesas.

It may be of interest to learn what became of the five survivors of the boat passage. For one thing, they all went to sea. Captain Pollard continued whaling and lost his ship on a coral reef. Ironically, the crew began another open-boat voyage, but the Nantucket whaler *Martha* picked them up after a few days. After that he "swallowed the anchor, " as sailors say, and lived to eighty-one, serving many years as the town's watch.

Captain Charles Ramsdell had a long career, dying in 1866, forty-five years after the disaster. First Mate Owen Chase had a highly successful career in whaling from 1832 to 1840, when he retired; he lived to be seventy-three. Captain Benjamin Lawrence went into the merchant service, retiring in 1841. Captain Thomas Nickerson, after a successful career, retired and died in 1883.

Perhaps because of the strength and courage that these men showed, a fitting memorial might be to list, boat by boat, the names and fates of the twenty men who set out from Nantucket on 20 November 1820:

First Boat

Captain George Pollard, Jr., survived

Barzillai Ray, died, eaten

Owen Coffin, shot, eaten

Samuel Reed, died, eaten

Charles Ramsdell, survived

Obed Hendricks, Third Mate, took over third boat
Seth Weeks, stayed on Ducie's Island, survived

Second Boat
Owen Chase, First Mate, survived
Isaac Cole, died, eaten
Benjamin Lawrence, survived
Richard Peterson, died, buried at sea
Thomas Nickerson, survived

William Wright, stayed on Ducie's Island, survived

Third Boat
Matthew P. Joy, Second Mate, died, buried at sea
Obed Hendricks, from first boat, missing
Lawson Thomas, died, eaten
Joseph West, missing
Charles Shorter, died, eaten
William Bond, missing
Isaiah Shepard, died, eaten

Thomas Chapple, stayed on Ducie's Island, survived

In the captain's boat two survived the entire voyage; in Owen Chase's boat there were three survivors; and the third boat disappeared in a storm on 29 January, with no survivors.

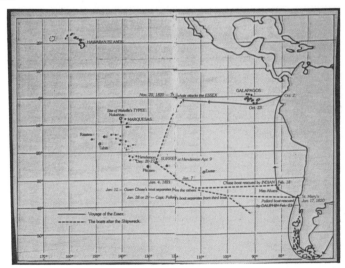

Figure 5-9 Track of *Surrey* and of the boats until their rescue and that of the three who stayed on Henderson Island.

The Great October Gale of 1841

The most dreadful maritime disaster on Cape Cod was the Great October Gale. Truro alone lost fifty-seven men in seven vessels; Dennis lost twenty men and five vessels; Yarmouth lost seven men. The fleet was fishing on the Grand Banks on Sunday, 3 October, when they were hit by a stronger and stronger gale; a hurricane we would call it today. These sloops and schooners were good seaboats — many of them built by the Shivericks in East Dennis— but they were unable to withstand the wind and waves and, one after another, went down.

Damage from the storm in Nantucket Sound and ashore was much less powerful. In Dennis, for example, four schooners were driven ashore, and only six of the twenty-seven vessels moored or anchored in Bass River escaped damage. Ashore, that Monday there were downed trees everywhere, the saltworks along the shore were badly damaged by the wind-driven tides in the bay, and the pier at Nobscusset was damaged. And there was no word from the fleet.

Everyone waited, hoping, praying. And in Dennis word of the disaster finally came with the arrival of Captain Eben Howes's *Villager* at about 5:00 P.M. on Tuesday, 5 October. They were lucky; leaving Nobscusset later than the other boats, while the storm caught them too, they were able to return to Provincetown harbor. Captain Howes told of the loss of *Bride* with eight bodies found in the cabin; *Vestal, Red Wing,* and *Zambucca* had come ashore, badly damaged, but the crews were safe. He had no word on the other eight schooners in the Dannis fleet.

During the next seven days word trickled back that five of the eight were safe, having landed in various places. The other three, *Greek, Isabella,* and *Theater*, were never heard from.

In Truro, by far the worst hurt of the bay towns, the anguish was almost unendurable. Families in this little town lost sons, brothers, and husbands, the oldest forty-one, the youngest eleven. Of the fifty-seven, there were nine Paines, eight Snows, six Riches, and three Atwoods— almost half of the deaths from these four families. One man, Gamaliel Paine, missed the departure of his schooner, on Sunday walked to Provincetown and hitched a ride in another vessel, and then transferred to his own schooner; he was lost.

In 1842 the town of Truro erected a plain marble shaft on a brownstone base, remembering those lost in the disaster of 1841. On the front of the monument is the following epitaph:

Figure 5-10 The obelisk in the Old Burying Ground high above Truro, in memory
of the fifty-seven men lost, with their
names and ages.

Sacred

To the memory of

FIFTY-SEVEN CITIZENS OF TRURO

who were lost in seven

vessels, which

foundered at sea in

the memorable gale

of October 3, 1841.

Then shall the dust return to the earth as it was;

and the spirit shall return to God who gave it.

Man goeth to his long home, and the mourners go about the streets.

The names, with ages, cover the others sides. The lost vessels, with the
number of crew were: *Dalmatia*— ten, including three Snows and three Paines;
Cincinnatus— ten, including a Paine and a Rich; *Pomona*— seven; *Altair*— seven,
including three Rich brothers and a Snow; *Prince Albert*— including two Paines;
General Harrison— probably eleven, including two Snows; *Arrival*— including a
Snow, a Paine, and two, boys eleven and twelve. There were also four boys in their
early teens in the other schooners.

Two accounts of surviving captains, Joshua Knowles of *Garnet* and Matthias
Rich of *Water Witch,* tell in graphic detail exactly how powerful and deadly was the
storm. Here is Captain Knowles's account.

They left Provincetown on Saturday, 2 October, and, with all sail set on the schooner, headed for George's Bank. But by midnight it was blowing a gale, and he took in the mainsail and jib. Early Sunday morning the foresail tore out;. they repaired it. At ten a heavy sea took the boat and davits. Sounding indicating that they were close to shoal water, they tried to claw off but lost every sail but the jib by 8:00 P.M. Sunday.

We could do no more. . . . The next throw of the lead was six fathoms. . . . Put up the helm. Just as she began to fall off, a tremendous sea or a breaker completely buried the vessel, leaving her on her broadside. . . . Brother Zack was washed overboard, but caught the mainsheet and hauled himself on board. The foremast was broken . . . the mainmast [was hauled] out of its step, tore up the deck, swept away the galley, bulwarks and everything clean, and shifted the ballast under the wing (toward the side of the hold, tipping the ship.)

After chopping away all the rigging, shifting the ballast, and repairing the holes in the deck, they found themselves with "a helpless wreck." But, says Captain Knowles, by Tuesday morning the weather was fine, and so they went to work to jury-rig *Garnet.*

We put a stay on the stump of the foremast, set the staysail for a foresail, and the gaff-topsail for a jib, so we could steer. . . . The boys built a fire on the ballast and boiled potatoes, the first mouthful of food since Sunday morning, the third. [With a distress signal flying, they] discovered a sail approaching from the east. . . . I had before determined to abandon my ship [and with my hatchet] let in the blue water and stepped on the boat [from their savior].

Their rescuer was the packet ship *Roscius,* John Collins of Truro in command (a near neighbor of Captain Knowles). One of the mates was another Truro man, Joshua Paine. Needless to say, the men of *Garnet* were generously treated and arrived in New York on 7 October, ending a hideous ordeal with which they struggled bravely for two days.

The ordeal of Matthias Rich and *Water Witch* ended in safety, but the efforts of the crew were equally strenuous. On George's Bank they passed three of the schooners that later disappeared, *Dalmatia, General Harrison, Pomona.* But Captain Rich decided early to run for home, and, driven by the storm, almost ran ashore. Their sails were ripped apart, but with a double-reefed foresail and reefed jib they managed to round the tip of Cape Cod and anchor in Provincetown.

Pomona, who had also headed for safety, was found bottom up in Nauset Harbor, with the crew drowned in her cabin. The same fate happened to *Bride* of Dennis. But her hull was intact, and the Shivericks righted her, rerigged her, and off she sailed again.

Another nearly impossible survivor was *Reform,* Isaac Lewis, master. She was under bare poles, with a drogue (a device to keep the vessel headed into the wind) out. They were so wave-swept that all hands tied themselves down in the cabin, waiting for death. Elisha Paine went on deck and disappeared. Just then a rogue sea engulfed them, dragging the schooner far underwater and bottom up. Water was bursting into the cabin, and with everything adrift the men knew that their time had come. But within a few seconds *Reform* completed a 360° roll and righted herself. Some of the crew climbed on deck to find the masts gone and the line from the drogue wrapped around the bowsprit— evidence of the fact that the schooner had actually rolled 360°.

Search vessels went out trying to find clues; but unless a vessel actually came ashore more or less intact (see above), the search was futile. And all those seasoned seamen (except the lads, of course) lie somewhere in the Atlantic Ocean with their vessels.

Figure 5-11 A close-up of the monument, taken in 1977. *Courtesy of Megan McDonald.*

Loss of the Josephus

An Eyewitness Account

The following account of a maritime tragedy is from the papers of Isaac Small, for many years Marine Reporting Agent at Highland Light in North Truro. His job was to identify vessels as they went past the lighthouse bound for Boston and to telegraph news of their pending arrival to the owners there, to save precious hours in discharging cargo— on the time-honored principle that "Time is Money."

Highland Light was a busy place in those days. When Henry David Thoreau visited there in 1853, he recorded that in ten days 1200 ships had passed the light. And the keepers had to report monthly the numbers of each type of vessel.

The first shipwreck that he can recall was that of *Josephus* early in April 1849. He begins:

The terrible circumstances attending the destruction of this ship were so vividly impressed upon my childish mind, (I was four years of age at the time) that they are as plain in memory as though they had occurred but yesterday.

In a dense fog the stranding of this full-rigged ship happened about a mile north of Highland Light, a half-mile offshore from the future location of the Highland Life-Saving Station. Since 1849 was long before establishment of the nine stations on Cape Cod, there was no one patrolling the beach to see the wreck. Luckily, through a break in the fog the keeper of Highland Light discovered the ship in deep trouble.

Quickly he spread the alarm, and from the nearby farmhouses and North Truro village, two miles away, men came running. They hoped to find some way of helping the helpless men on the ship. But it was already too late; the storm-driven waves were already tearing the ship apart.

Already the masts had fallen, along with the rigging and shrouds. The deck was continually swept by breakers, and many of the crew had already disappeared into the boiling seas. The utterly powerless watchers could hear the desperate cries for help from the few men still clinging to the remnants of deck gear.

Just then, running headlong down the 130-foot cliffs on which Highland Light is built, came two young men who had just returned home from a fishing voyage. They had not even stopped at home, but hearing of the disaster they hurried to the beach. There they discovered a twelve-foot dory hauled up above high tide, the sort of boat used as a tender on a small fisherman.

Seizing the little boat, they ran it down to the edge of the boiling surf. When the watchers on the beach grasped that Daniel Cassidy and Jonathan Collins were going to launch the boat to try to reach the people on *Josephus,* they protested. Said one man, "You're crazy to do this. You can't possibly reach the ship, and your lives will pay the forfeit for your foolish attempt." But the two readied the boat for launching, replying, "We can't stand it any longer to see those poor fellows being swept into the sea, and we are going to try to reach them."

Isaac Small describes what he saw next:

Standing with my mother and holding her hand on the cliffs . . . I saw the little boat, with the two men pulling bravely at the oars. They had hardly gone fifty yards from the shore when a great white cataract of foam and rushing water was hurled towards them. The next instant it hurled men and boat under its sweeping torrent . . . with the overturned boat riding its crest; two human heads rose for a moment through the seething sea, only to be covered by the next on-rushing wave, and they were seen no more.

As darkness fell, the cries for help dwindled and stopped, while the waves continued to break up the ship. In despair, the helpless watchers turned away and walked home. But Enoch Hamilton, the keeper, after tending the lamps at midnight, climbed down to the beach again, with the thought that some of the drowned sailors would have come ashore. A piece of the cabin had washed up; on it was a nearly dead crewman, cut and bruised by the debris through which he had come to shore.

Somehow Keeper Hamilton managed to haul the man up the steep cliff to the light. He put him to bed and called a doctor. And the man recovered eventually— the sole survivor of the twenty-four men aboard. And if we count Daniel Cassidy and Jonathan Collins, the dead numbered twenty-five. A grim statistic, that.

The Giovanni *Disaster*

An Eyewitness Account

It was not the best of weather on 4 March 1875. A howling snow storm driven by the usual winter nor'east gale was hammering Cape Cod. During a lull in the storm the beach patrolman from Highland Life-Saving Station saw a vessel struck hard on the outer bar some three miles north of the station. It was the bark *Giovanni,* en route from Palermo to Boston with a cargo of sumac, nuts, and brimstone. Her sails were gone, her rudder broken.

After the crews of stations 6 and 7 had rushed to the scene and surveyed the problem, they hurried back to haul their beach carts with Lyle guns and gear through deep snowdrifts to the site. Those three miles took hours to traverse because of the snow. The life boats would have been useless; the dreadful sea conditions and the distance to the wreck made that attempt a sure sentence of death for the life-savers.

The only resource was the Lyle gun, which under normal conditions could throw its projectile 1200 feet, but into the teeth of the gale reached far short of that, well over a hundred yards short. Readying another shot, they realized that it was futile; the wreck was already beginning to break up. All the crew could do was watch the tragedy unfold.

First, two men leaped from the after deck house into the boiling sea. They were able to catch hold of wreckage, and they aroused hope in the men on shore when they reached the two-thirds point. But as the flotsam rose above a wave, one man was gone. The other still clung to his wreckage, and as he came closer the life-savers rushed into the surf and pulled him ashore. He was the only one of fourteen aboard to be saved.

When night fell, they lit a huge bonfire on the beach and set up patrols all night long, hoping that some poor devil would make it to shore. But all they saw was pieces of the wreck and its cargo. Not even a single body washed up; storm waves hitting Cape Cod set up a strong north-south current and would have carried the bodies away.

When daylight came, the watchers were astonished to see the after deck house, part of her bow, and part of the foremast. Even more surprisingly, they saw a man jump from the bow and swim through the wild water to the deck house and climb up under a piece of the roof. Our watcher describes the last scene:

That a human being could live through such a night as that . . . seemed incredible. But the chapter of horrors was not yet complete in this wretched disaster. Piece by piece the sea tore away what remained of the wreck until nothing but the deck house roof remained above the sea; . . . Then we saw, clinging to the few remaining pieces of the frame of the deck house . . . four members of the ship's company, but endurance had reached its limits and they were quickly swept from the last possible thing to which they could cling.

Some adverse criticism was directed against the men of the Life Saving corps, for their failure to rescue these sailors, but it was wholly unmerited as the Life Savers did everything in their power or that it was possible to do under the circumstances.

It was one of those terrible marine disasters, of which there are many, where man is a plaything in the grip of the sea when the storm king is abroad in his might.

Captain Baker and Krakatoa

Captain Benjamin Baker of Brewster was a close witness of the worst natural disaster of the 19th century— the eruption of Krakatoa Island off Sumatra. He and his ship barely lived to bring the first report of the disaster to Boston.

Born 29 September 1841, as usual he went to sea as a ship's boy in the ship *Tropic* to Australia. In *Memnon* later, he worked up to mate and then captain for seventeen years, voyaging all over the world. But his most harrowing experience occurred as captain of the bark *W.H.Besse* in 1883.

Lying in Manila for some forty days, he lost several seamen to cholera, then raging in the city. Finally on 27 May 1883 he left for Boston, meeting the clipper ship *Northern Light* and the bark *J.M.Bourne* in the Macassar Straits between Borneo and the Celebes. Sailing along at a good clip, the *Besse* found an uncharted coral reef on 24 June. They were able to float her off that night, but she was so badly holed that round-the-clock pumping could barely keep her afloat. They were ready to abandon ship when two days later a Dutch steamer came along and helped then limp into nearby Batavia on Java for repairs.

Even though the repairs took two months, Captain Baker was charmed with the city, capital of the Dutch East Indies. He calls it quaint, with its typical Dutch architecture, its canals, and "the Yankee horse-cars." Center of this huge archipelago, Batavia was a lively commercial port as well.

Getting underway on 26 August, the captain headed for Sunda Strait, between Java and Sumatra. From noon on they heard what sounded like heavy artillery coming from Krakatoa Island, in the strait. The night was densely dark, with much lightning. The next day they saw a dark cloud bank in the west, that covered the sky.

Alarmed, Captain Baker took precautions: furled all sail and anchored. Luckily, too. For suddenly a powerful squall hit the bark broadside, followed by a heavy shower of dirt and ashes. Pitch-black night fell— ". . . although still daytime, there was not enough daylight to see one's own hand," said Baker. Winds were of hurricane force, and the waves rose high in all directions.

Added to the problems was a stifling smell of sulfur, so strong that they could hardly breathe. The tide was rushing through the strait and the vessel, under bare poles, was pushed along at an incredible fourteen knots (sixteen land miles per hour). Captain Baker describes the overall effect thus:

The shrieking wind, the spuming and churning waves, the murky and impenetrable veil overhead and on every side, and the tons of ashes, pumice stone and earthly fragments that threatened to engulf the poor vessel, combined to daze and appall every soul on board.

In the middle of the afternoon the sky lightened; meanwhile ashes and pumice rained down, covering everything— the deck, the rigging, the masts— to a depth of several inches. The barometer was bouncing like a ball and then settled down. The ship was hove short (ready to break out the anchor quickly and set sail).

All day on the twenty-seventh was dead calm, with the air full of smoke. Huge numbers of uprooted trees and dead fish floated past their anchorage, and the water looked white from the pumice floating on it. As the weather cleared, Captain Baker could see that whole islands had sunk, the whole northwest side of Krakatoa was gone, and two forested islands nearby were completely treeless.

The weather was much the same the next day. Even greater masses of trees, fish, and other debris floated past their anchorage, extending, as they discovered later, over five hundred miles. Late that day Captain Baker decided to get underway, through Sunda Strait. On the thirtieth they were still meeting large trees and debris, and for the first time they found themselves sailing through large numbers of dead bodies. Finally at 10 A.M. the lookout saw the Java lighthouses, and they were through the strait.

With the exception of an unusually heavy squall, *Besse* had fair weather until 7 November, when, northwest of Bermuda, she ran into a hurricane. She lost a topsail but was able to furl all sails as she lurched through several days of heavy gales, pumping around the clock and having to jettison seventy-five tons of sugar to save the ship.

Meanwhile Captain Baker's crew had been sickening fast, perhaps from the cholera or malaria to which they had been exposed in Manila. In fact, when they reached Boston, of the twenty-two-man crew only five were on their feet and able to work. One man, sent to the hospital when they arrived, was nearly dead. Baker had to find temporary crewmen to get the ship unloaded. One Chinese sailor made the appropriate comment: "You bet, you bet we had a hard voyage." Thus Boston received the news of the worst natural disaster of the 19th century.

Captain Baker and the *Besse* experienced only the opening salvo in an intermittent cannonade that has lasted for almost one hundred years. The island volcano began to erupt on 20 May 1883, so powerfully that the blasts were heard one hundred miles away. During the summer it rumbled away now and then, but on 26 August (the very day on which *Besse* left Batavia, repairs done) Krakatoa literally blew up! And on the twenty-seventh the explosions were so powerful that they were heard in Australia *2200 miles away.* Ash from the blasts rose fifty miles into the air.

The physical effects of the explosions were almost unbelievable. It is estimated that five *cubic miles* of rocks, debris, and pumice (lava that has been aerated by the blast so that it is lighter than water) disappeared from the island. After those blasts pumice was so thick on the surface of the ocean that sailing ships were unable to move. There were two and a half days of darkness in the area. The dust cloud spread around the earth several times before dissipating, providing beautiful sunsets for over a year.

But worst of all was the human tragedy. The blast created a *tsunami* (a Japanese word for tidal wave) that reached Hawaii and South America, across the entire Pacific Ocean. Its local effect was a wave *one hundred twenty feet* high, which took 36,000 lives in coastal Java and Sumatra. Of course all life on the island group around Krakatoa was buried under feet of ash and died.

The multiple cones of the Krakatoa volcano were more or less quiet until 1927, when an underwater cone began building a new island, which was named Anak Krakatoa (Child of Krakatoa). By 1973 the island was 626 feet high. One recalls the similar instance in Iceland some years ago, when a volcanic island arose just south of the main island. Even into the 1980's there were occasional minor eruptions. Krakatoa is still very much a dangerous neighbor of those beautiful islands of Java and Sumatra.

Figure 5-11A Prehistoric Krakatoa, geologists believe, was a huge cone-shaped volcanic island. At some time it exploded, digging a tremendous crater in the ocean. Remaining was a ring of island foothills; the rest was gone. Over time two volcanic islands rose in the crater, eventually merging with the largest island volcano. These blew up in 1883, as described by Captain Baker, creating another crater inside the first. Today, Krakatoa is still building and smoking. *Photo by Jan Bayley, 2 January 1995.*

The Loss of the City of Columbus

On 17 January 1884 the steamer *City of Columbus* left Boston for Savannah, Georgia. She was a fine, strong vessel, and her captain, S. E. Wright, had grown up at sea. With years of experience in steamers, he had a fine reputation as a navigator on what sailors consider to be a most difficult stretch of coast. The 2000-ton ship carried 81 passengers and 45 crew, and a third of the passengers were women and children.

Departing at about 3:30 P.M., *Columbus* had a strong northwest breeze behind her, but during the night hurricane-force winds blew up. Rounding the tip of Cape Cod, she steamed down the "backside" and into Nantucket Sound, sighting East and West Chop and Nobska lights on time. Captain Wright set a west-southwest course and went to his cabin to get warm— and fell asleep.

Two hours later he woke to a cry from the mate on watch and saw the buoy on Devil's Bridge (a notorious reef off the southwest tip of Martha's Vineyard) to port, some 300 yards away. Almost at once she struck hard. Reversing engines, Captain Wright managed to back away two lengths. But the bow was badly stove, and she filled and listed to port.

Bedlam erupted as everyone at once tried to reach the few boats there were. Officers and crew did little to organize departure, and the crew monopolized the boats. As passengers came on deck, scores were swept overboard by the breaking seas. Forty men tried to save themselves by climbing onto the deck houses, but those were soon swept away by the waves. Then they climbed into the rigging,

Figure 5-12 The wreck of the *City of Columbus* with the loss of 97 lives, a third of them women and children. *Courtesy of William P. Quinn.*

127

and during the rest of the night one after another fell into the wild waves.

With daylight, Captain Horatio Pease, keeper of Gay Head Light, roused the neighborhood, and a crew of Gay Head natives, led by Joseph Peterson, launched the Humane Society lifeboat. After a half-hour struggle with the seas, they picked seven men from the water and returned to shore. There was so much debris around the hulk that they could not row very close.

A second lifeboat set out, commanded by James Mosier, and at the same time the U.S. Revenue Service (later the Coast Guard) cutter *Dexter* arrived and sent out two boats. One boat, in charge of Lieutenant Rhodes, took off eight men; Lieutenant Kennedy's boat saved five men; the Humane Society boat plucked thirteen men from the seas and took them to the *Dexter*. All of them had to jump from the rigging into the water.

Two men were frozen to the rigging, and Lieutenant Rhodes volunteered to swim to the ship and free them. On his first try he was knocked out by debris and almost drowned. But he tried again and was able to get them down and into a boat; they later died of exposure. Captain Wright was the last to leave the wreck— aside from the sixty-nine people who drowned in their cabins.

The Weekly Mercury published a list of the survivors which is most revealing. Fourteen male passengers were saved (those from the rigging), and seventeen of the forty-five crew (all men) were saved; they were the ones who commandeered the lifeboats aboard. A total of ninety-seven lives were lost, twenty-six of them women or girls, as well as several babies. This was not the *Titanic* spirit of "Women and children first!" Twenty-five bodies were found.

How could such a disaster happen? The Devil's Bridge is a rocky reef, much of which is bare at low water. It reaches out from Gay Head about a half-mile; at that time it was marked by a black nun buoy (the top of which is a tapered cone), at the northwestern end of the reef, anchored in five fathoms (thirty feet). *City of Columbus* had weaved her way through the many dangers of Nantucket Sound, and was almost in open water. But apparently the deck officer was trying to pass the buoy close aboard to save time, and he failed to observe the effects of wind and tide. As a result the ship stranded inside the buoy.

The aftermath of such a tragedy was monumental. Soon after the cutter *Dexter* arrived in New Bedford with the survivors, several shipping companies offered their services to families of the victims. *Monohassett* took family members to the scene the next day, and the buoy tender *Verbena* marked the wreck with an obstruction buoy. Wrecking steamer *Storm King* and tug *Confidence* also arrived.

The wreck's position was unchanged. The tattered jib that had been raised in a vain attempt to break free the night before slatted in the wind. At low water the ship's bow was exposed, and the gilt letters of *City of Columbus* showed along her side. The debris on shore was incredible, and the passengers from *Monohassett*, landed at a pier, forlornly picked at the rubble, hoping to find some memento of their loved ones. Two native women were amassing a woodpile from chairs, timbers, etc.

One survivor, G.I.Whitcomb, from Hudson, Massachusetts, told of his experiences that night. He and a friend were in their berths in the steerage when the ship hit. He quickly dressed and, feeling seasick, went on deck. His story:

"on going forward I saw that the vessel was filling and the water was swashing over the deck. I went up on deck to look for a life preserver. [There were life vests at every bunk in steerage.] . . . *I heard the captain cry, "Don't be alarmed," and then he said, to someone, "We shall have to leave the poor thing."* . . . *At length the steamer righted and I scrambled into the main top, where I remained until about 2 o'clock in the afternoon, when I was taken off.*

A diver from *Storm King*, W.D. Duncan, suited up and dived to see what he could discover of the missing people. But after a few minutes he surfaced and later explained that the currents were so strong that he was in danger of being swept away, and the water was so murky with sand, oil, and ashes that he could not see farther than a foot.

He tried again later and found that nothing remained but the shell of the ship— main deck and all the cabins gone. His search for bodies revealed none; he theorized that the force of the seas was so great that they were all swept away. A search along the shores of Martha's Vineyard found only twenty-five of the ninety-seven lost in the disaster. And not a single life preserver was found either on the bodies or in the debris driven ashore.

A long letter from Captain R.B. Forbes appeared in the *Boston Advertiser* giving his view of who was responsible for the wreck. He felt that Captain Wright was not. He says, in part:

If any blame can be attached to him, it may be said that he should have examined the compass before leaving the wheel house, and the bearing of Gay Head light, and cautioned his officer against going to the southward of his course. I dare say all this was done . . . [But] *in looking over the many statements . . . in the late disaster, I do not see any allusion to blowing the whistle, burning blue lights or rockets, in order to alarm the people about Gay Head . . . If this had been done*, [the Humane Society boat] *would probably have saved more people.*

But Captain Chester, Hydrographic Inspector of the U.S. Coast Survey, makes the point that the Devil's Bridge, being entirely made of rocks, is not susceptible to change as is a sandy bottom. The nun buoy at the end of the shoal was apparently set properly. And therefore, he says,

When the captain set the vessel's course, unless the direction was altered, the vessel was headed directly for Devil's Bridge, and the catastrophe was inevi-

table. It was no fault of the charts. The ship was headed by Captain Wright's first order for the rocks, and he ran on them, as a matter of course.

According to him Captain Wright was totally responsible. But the mate on duty failed to note his position in a place where there were (and are) plenty of lighthouses to use.

Aside from the ninety-seven families who lost someone, several awards were made for heroism or assistance in rescue efforts. The press raised $3500, most of which went to a large number of the natives of Gay head who had helped. The crews of the two Humane Society boats each received $160; some eighty people received sums ranging from $40 to $5 for assistance.

Other awards came from the Boston Humane Society. Lieutenant John Rhode received the gold medal for "heroic exertions at the peril of his own life in rescuing two persons . . . " Captain Eric Gabrielson received the silver medal "for humane efforts on the occasion of the wreck of steamer *City of Columbus.*" The crew of the cutter *Dexter* received $200, to be divided by the captain "according to his judgment of their desserts."

And the Devil's Bridge is still there, waiting for other unwary mariners to find it— as many have done.

Figure 5-13 Map of wrecks and life saving stations, 1903.

The Wreck of the Jason
One Man Survived

    One of the most terrible disasters in the experience of the United States Life-Saving Service on Cape Cod (See map) was the total destruction of the iron-hulled ship *Jason* on 5 December 1893. She carried a cargo of Calcutta jute bound for Boston, with a crew of twenty-four. Already dismasted by a tornado and nearly sunk in the Indian Ocean, the captain had to struggle into the island of Mauritius for repairs.

    Once underway again around the Cape of Good Hope, she made good time until she was some hundred miles off the New England coast. Captain McMillan had had no sights for two days because of very heavy weather. So he altered course to the west, knowing that he would eventually find a landmark. On 3 December he met a New York pilot boat and received information on his position.

    As Jason neared the coast, the weather worsened into a nor'east gale with

Figure 5-14 The wreck of the *Jason*, 5 December 1893, at Pamet River, Truro.

snow and sleet. Then, at about 5:00 P.M., one of the beach patrol from the Nauset Station saw the 1500-ton ship just offshore. This was a disaster ready to happen, and word went via telephone to other nearby stations. They harnessed their horses to the beach carts carrying the lifeboats, readied their Lyle guns and breeches buoy gear, and stood by.

At 7:30 Surfman Honey rushed into the Pamet River Station, shouting, "Hopkins [the other shore patrol] has just burned his [Coston] signal!" Hopkins arrived to report that the ship was on the bars a half-mile north of the station. Keeper Rich and his men rushed to the scene, to find the shore already littered with wreckage, and they could hear the tattered sails rattling in the gale.

Setting up the Lyle gun, they fired a successful shot across the doomed

Figure 5-15 Samuel Evans, sole survivor.

ship. But already no one was alive to respond. By keeping a watch along the beach the life-savers eventually found one man, Samuel Evans, an apprentice seaman, clinging to a bale of jute. He was the only survivor. Later twenty bodies washed up on the beach and were buried in Truro.

The story of what happened on board *Jason* came out when young Evans was somewhat recovered from being nearly frozen to death. The moment the ship struck Captain McMillan ordered the boats lowered. But they were lashed down and covered with ice and snow. A few men struggled to free them, but most climbed into the rigging, lashing themselves in place. They saw the red signal flare on the beach, but a few minutes later this iron-hulled ship broke in two amidships. The main and mizzen masts fell, taking with them all those in the rigging.

Evans was extremely lucky. When he fell into the water he had the presence of mind to grasp at a bale of jute thrown out of the hold when the ship broke. A dizzying ride on the bale finally landed him on the beach, where the life-savers took him to the Pamet Station for resuscitation and recovery.

The Pamet crew kept an all-night vigil with bonfires, hoping that other survivors might land. But there was no one.

Young Evans's father, William Evans, rector of Traegar in England, wrote a letter of thanks to the Life-Saving Service:

My dear Sir,

As the father of the only survivor of . . . the ship Jason, *may I ask you very kindly [to convey] our most sincere and heartfelt gratitude to Captain Rich and one and all of the gallant crew of the Pamet River Life Saving Station for their indefatigable and successful efforts to save the life of our beloved son. . . . [We] deeply acknowledge our debt of gratitude to almighty God, as it was certainly a supernatural escape. . . . Our prayer is that He will reward you all in your important office of saving [lives] . . . .*

Ever yours faithfully,
William Evans

Figure 5-16 Advertising poster of sailings of *Bay State* and *Portland*.

The Portland *Disaster*

The weather history of New England records a number of vicious storms in which large numbers of people and vessels have been lost. In November 1798, for example, storms dumped *six feet* of snow on Cape Cod and drove seven vessels ashore. Twenty-five bodies were found on the beach and buried. In the Great October Gale of 1841 tiny Truro lost seven vessels and fifty-seven men; Dennis lost twenty men and Yarmouth ten.

There were deadly storms in 1851, 1873, and 1886. But none equaled the tropical storm turned hurricane named for the steamer *Portland*, lost at sea with all hands. The U.S. Lifesaving Service annual report tells the story succinctly, calling the storm:

A memorable cyclonic tempest which hit . . .the New England coast . . . in the evening of Saturday, November 26, 1898, and raged with almost unprecedented violence . . . two nights and a day.

Probably this storm will be remembered as [destroying] the Portland with between one hundred fifty and two hundred people. No such appalling calamity has occurred . . . for almost half a century.

When the Portland steamed away scores of sailing vessels were hunting for harbors of refuge. Forty found shelter . . . in Provincetown or Gloucester, while others were crowding on every sail they could safely carry to reach port.

Figure 5-17 *Portland* warping into her berth in Boston. *Courtesy of Barry Homer.*

In all something like one hundred fifty vessels of all types were lost, supposedly safe in harbor or at sea. This was the costliest storm to ever hit this coast. Wreckage was everywhere alongshore from Chatham to Cape Ann, well north of Boston. *Columbia*, a pilot schooner, was well offshore, lost all sails, and drifted onto the beach at Scituate. All five crewmen drowned. For more misery, a blizzard dropped thirty inches of snow. Communications were down everywhere. In fact when wreckage began to appear along Cape Cod's outer beach, the news went to Boston via the French trans-Atlantic cable from Orleans on Cape Cod. Then it came back to New York via the British cable, finally arriving in Boston by telegraph!

The total damage was almost incredible. The estimated death toll was about *four hundred fifty.* The town of Hull, south of Boston, (where the Nantasket roller coaster looked like spaghetti and all the cars were torn off the Ferris wheel) estimated its damage at over $200,000— millions today, and in one small town. Scituate, on the shore north of Boston, suffered even greater damage to houses there.

The Lifesaving Service attempts to sum up the cataclysm:

Against such indescribable pandemonium of wind and sea . . . few craft, steam or sail, could successfully contend on a lee shore [The nor'easter drove right down on the coast of Massachusetts], and . . . the coast, rocks, and islands were strewn with wrecked or disabled vessels, while an uncertain but considerable number founded [sic] far away at sea.

Figure 5-18 *Portland* off Portland Head Light, Maine. *Courtesy of the Peabody Essex Museum, Salem, MA.*

The *Portland* was the largest sidewheel steamer in these waters. Built in 1889, she was 291 feet long, drawing eleven feet. Luxuriously furnished in cherry and mahogany, with velvet carpets, she was the very latest in hull and engine design. She was capable of fifteen knots with the fifteen hundred horsepower engine. She carried sixteen lifeboats and rafts and eighty life vests.

Her captain was Hollis Blanchard, well respected, a ten-year veteran of the company. Known as very cautious, he was a constant visitor at the U.S. Weather Bureau in Boston. So, knowing the worsening conditions on that Saturday evening, why did he sail at about 7:00 P.M.? Hindsight controversy raged over his responsibility for the disaster.

But apparently he believed that the storm was passing— it was actually barely starting to hit— and that it was safe to sail for Portland as planned. The ship was seen by several people, the latest at 11:45 P.M. off Gloucester, when she was described as wallowing badly and with heavy damage to her superstructure. She had made good only some twenty miles in almost five hours.

An experienced captain, Blanchard might well have felt forced to simply head into the ferocious wind and mountainous seas, and thus take a northeast heading. Apparently he did not seriously consider taking shelter in Gloucester, or was unable to in those seas. In any case, to try to turn across the wind and seas could well have rolled the ship over.

Whatever happened in that wild night— any engine failure would have meant destruction— at some time after the 11:45 P.M. sighting and Sunday night, surfmen of the U.S. Lifesaving Service Station at Race Point began to find wreckage on the beach. The first article was a life preserver stenciled "Portland." And several reliable witnesses reported seeing *Portland* off Race Point or hearing a distress whistle (this at 5:45 on the twenty-seventh, almost twelve hours after she had sailed from Boston).

Those last hours aboard the ship must have been a perfect hell for everyone, especially the passengers with little or no experience of the fearful power of the sea, as the ship's superstructure was stripped off, as the luxurious furniture—chairs, beds, and anything loose careened across their staterooms and the saloon and dining room. And Cape Codders believe that the Portland either foundered or drove onto the Peaked Hill Bars off Race Point that Sunday morning. Others believe that she sank long before, very early in the morning, and that she lies quite far from Provincetown, somewhere on Stellwagen Bank.

No one knows just how many people died; the passenger list went down with the ship. Of the total, only sixty bodies floated up on Cape Cod beaches from Highland Light to Chatham— some in life jackets, some fully clothed, some naked.

Repercussions from the disaster were huge. Nobody knew just what passengers had been aboard. A *Boston Globe* reporter named Frank Sibley arrived at the company's offices to get a story on the tragedy. But, amid the crowd of anxious relatives, all asking for their loved ones, Sibley soon saw that first someone had to create a passenger list. So, for almost forty-eight hours, he gathered names and addresses, while other reporters fanned out to get photographs and information to use in news stories.

Figure 5-19 Plaque erected at Highland Light fifty years after the disaster. While the ship sank elsewhere, wreckage and bodies washed ashore along the back shore to Cape Cod.

Over the years since 1898 divers and researchers have searched for *Portland's* grave. The U.S. Lifesaving Service recorded the locations of each piece of wreckage and of bodies known to have come from the ship. Known tidal, wind-driven, and storm-driven currents went into a computer, including the huge surge of storm-pushed water into and out of Cape Cod Bay. Thus was developed a backtrack of debris to where she went down. Fishermen's reports of obstacles found were added. As a result with side-scan sonar they have found a vessel on the bottom that is the size and shape of *Portland*. But final evidence, such as the ship's bell or maker's bronze plate, has not yet surfaced.

So the final solution to the mystery of the *Portland* disaster still fascinates those of us who relish such challenges.

Figure 5-19A The Portland Gale of 1898 destroyed over 100 vessels. But the most notorious wreck was that of the side-wheeler *Portland* lost somewhere on Stellwagen Bank (now a Marine Sanctuary). She disappeared en route to Portland, Maine, with all hands. Bodies and wreckage washed up on Cape Cod beaches. Here is Rufus Snow of Orleans with the massive helm of the steamer, the ship's quarterboard, and other bits and pieces. *Courtesy of William P. Quinn.*

Figure 5-20 Drill of the Monomoy crew, shortly before the disaster in which seven of the crew perished.

Twelve Men Dead
The Wadena *Disaster*

The Monomoy Point Life-Saving Station suffered one of the worst disasters in the service's long and honorable history. Of the entire crew of eight men only one survived the schooner-barge *Wadena* fiasco; the term is used on purpose, because the rescued men *caused* the tragedy.

That man was Captain John E. Ellis, number 2 surfmen, from Harwich, who had joined the service when the station was manned. After the disaster he was named keeper to succeed Captain Marshall W. Eldredge, who died with six of his men. Captain Ellis tells the story.

On Tuesday, March 11, 1902, about one o'clock A.M. the schooner-barge Wadena *stranded during a northeast gale and heavy sea on the Shovelful Shoal off the southern end of Monomoy Island. The crew were rescued by our station crew. The barge remained on the shoal . . ., and wreckers were engaged in lightering her cargo of coal. On the night of March 16 the weather became threatening and all except five of the [wreckers] were taken ashore.* (Note: the station crew believed that all on the barge had left.)

[On March 17] *the barge was flying a signal of distress. [Captain Eldredge directed] me to launch the surf-boat. About two and one-half miles south of the station we took Captain Eldredge aboard and I gave him the steering oar.*

Figure 5-21 Capt. Elmer F. Mayo (standing), the hero of Monomoy, and Surfman Ellis, whom he rescued.

After a hard pull they reached the lee of the barge and tied up. The five people aboard wanted to get ashore soon and were agitated and afraid. The captain told them to get into the boat via the mooring line. All but one slid down without trouble, but the last man, an obese fellow, dropped into the boat and broke a thwart. Told to sit down in the bottom of the boat, they did so.

After casting off, while they were turning the boat shoreward a huge wave hit them, and they shipped a lot of water. When that happened the barge men stood up, in panic, and threw their arms around the necks of the rowers, helpless now to row.

With control lost, sea after sea hit them, and the boat rolled over, spilling everyone into the frigid water. Soon they were among the heaviest breakers. The crew twice righted the boat, but before they could climb in, it capsized again. All clung to the overturned boat, and the five men from the barge were the first to slide off and disappear into the foam.

All of the station crew clung to the bottom of the boat, their strength ebbing fast. The first to go was Surfman Chase, and then Nickerson and Small lost their grip under the pounding seas, which swept completely over them. Next to die was Kendrick, and soon Foye followed. Three were left, expecting at any moment that they would join their comrades.

Rogers hung on amidships, and the captain and Ellis were near the stern. Captain Eldredge called to Ellis to help him get a better grip, and Ellis was barely able to pull him up onto the bottom of the boat. The next sea washed them both off. Ellis somehow was able to regain his hold, but when he looked for the captain, he was holding on to the boom and sail, which had drifted away. That was the last Ellis saw of him.

Rogers asked for help; all Ellis could do was to tell him that they were close to shore, and to hold on. He could not, and, saying "I have got to go," his hands slipped down the slick bottom of the boat and he was gone.

Alone on the bottom of the boat, Ellis was able to grasp the tip of the centerboard. Holding it with one hand, he took off his boots, oilclothes, undercoat and vest. Here is the end of his report of the tragedy:

By that time the overturned boat had drifted down . . . [near] the barge Fitzpatrick, which was also stranded, [and] I waved my hand as a signal for help. I soon saw those on the barge fling a dory over the side . . . but could see nothing . . . until it hove into sight . . . with . . . brave Captain Elmer F. Mayo. He ran the dory alongside of me, and with his help I got into the boat.

To land in the dory through the surf was a perilous undertaking, but Mayo, who is a skilled boatman, carefully picked his way over the rips and headed his little boat for the shore.

Surfman Bloomer of our station . . . when he saw Captain Mayo . . . ran down into the surf, seized the little boat, and helped Captain Mayo to land safely.

Bloomer was told of the terrible tragedy by Captain Mayo, as I was unable to speak at the time. As I have often said, "If the persons we took off the barge had kept quiet as we told them to, all hands would have landed safely."

Seth. L. Ellis
Keeper, Monomoy L. S. Station

Figure 5-23 The United States submarine *S-4* before the collision. *Courtesy of the U.S. Navy.*

The Loss of the U.S.S. S-4

On 17 December 1927 the town of Provincetown was stricken with a tragedy that shook the entire country. The United States submarine *S-4*, rising to the surface, collided with the U.S. Coast Guard destroyer *Paulding* and sank to the bottom about a half-mile south of Wood End Light. Ultimately the entire crew of the sub died on the bottom. There were no escape hatches at that time.

It happened because of a series of human errors. First, the Navy had established a buoyed trial course marked by white buoys in 1909. In fact forty-nine submarines had undergone their standardization trials there. But those buoys were not shown on any chart or mentioned in the *American Coast Pilot.*

Second, neither ship knew that the other was in the vicinity. The Navy tug *Wandank* was there as a tender and should have been flying the distinctive Submarine Warning Flag. It did not. And Navy doctrine and the *International Rules of the Road* require that a submarine must stay clear of surface vessels. She did not.

Third, *Rules of the Road* and common sense require that every vessel maintain a sharp lookout at all times. She did not.

Just how did it happen? *S-4* was testing equipment at various depths on the Navy's measured mile course, and of course she had to swing wide to circle back onto the course. Since the holiday season was near and the rum-runners were stocking up, *Paulding* was on the prowl and was following the prescribed course

Figure 5-24 The United States Coast Guard destroyer *Paulding*, a former Navy "four stacker" of World War I. *U.S. Coast Guard photo.*

into the harbor. She came to a course of 94⁰ at 3:33 P.M., at a speed of eighteen knots.

Four minutes later the lookout sighted on her port bow two periscopes rising from the surface— and only seventy-five yards away. *S-4* was crossing *Paulding's* bow— a clear violation of the rules of the road. There was nothing she could do. The officer-of-the-deck ordered "Right full rudder!" and rang down for full speed astern. At 3:37, with the submarine's superstructure a third of the way out of the water, the collision occurred, the destroyer striking just forward of the four-inch gun on the starboard side. *S-4* immediately sank with all hands.

The captain of *Paulding* lowered a boat at once to try to find survivors and dropped a buoy to mark the sinking, recording the location with cross bearings. Visibility was excellent, but the sea was choppy with many whitecaps, reducing *Paulding*'s chances of seeing the periscopes.

In view of the multiple errors or infractions of law by the Navy on scene and the commander of the *S-4*, the Coast Guard Board of Inquiry concluded that "No responsibility and no blame is to be attached to the commanding officer, the officer of the deck, or any other person on board the *Paulding*."

With the facts of the collision out of the way, we can turn to rescue efforts and its effects on the town. A number of people actually saw the collision, and in minutes, it seemed, the news was everywhere. Almost at once the Coast Guard surfboat headed for the scene. For four hours they trailed a grapnel back and forth, and finally caught. But as the seas made up the grapnel let go.

Figure 5-25 The damage to the bow of the Paulding after the crash. *U.S. Coast Guard photo.*

Navy ships began arriving, including the *S-4's* mother ship, *Bushnell*, and the salvage tug, *Falcon*. The grappling caught again at 11:45 next morning, and by 1:30 the first diver, Thomas Eadie, Chief Gunner's Mate, USNR, in the cumbersome gear of the times, was down on the deck of the submarine. Tapping with a hammer in Morse code, he asked:

"Are you alive?"

"Yes, six of us are alive here," came the reply.

"Everything possible is being done to help you."

"The air is very bad in here. Please hurry."

The weather was deteriorating. And it got worse and worse, so that divers went down at great risk, into water near freezing and with extremely poor visibility. Eadie returned to *Falcon,* having found that only six men were alive in the torpedo room. Then William Carr dived and attached an air hose to the aft air connection; For a half-hour they pumped air into the ballast tanks— only to see a huge air bubble burst the surface; tanks were ruptured.

Chief Torpedoman Fred Michels was the next to descend. After forty-five minutes, he reported that his lines were fouled and he could not clear them. He asked that Eadie come down to free him. Water temperature was 34°. With cutting tools, he descended, to find Mike face-down on deck with his lines totally snarled in wreckage.

In addition, *Falcon* was beginning to yaw and drift on her anchor, jerking on the divers' lifelines. As Eadie sawed away at an angle iron (it took him forty-five minutes in that icy water), he realized that Michels was unconscious. After more struggles, he and Michels came up together, Michels's suit blown up and lying on the surface. Both men were rushed into the decompression tank, and then *Falcon* rushed Michels, almost frozen, to Boston for further treatment. Seeing her leave, the townspeople, not understanding the undersea conditions, became angrier at what looked like a desertion of the sub's crew. Thomas Eadie had been down for one hour and forty-five minutes. Fred Michels had been down for *three hours and twenty minutes.* Sea temperature was 34°, and they were 102 feet below the surface.

Sea-born and sea-bred, the P'towners were in agony for the six trapped men and the apparent slowness of rescue efforts. The departure of *Falcon* was almost the last straw. They were cursing the Navy as only fishermen can curse.

Time was slipping away. Attempts to send air to the torpedo room failed. Meanwhile communication with the trapped men went on:

"How is the weather?" tapped from the sub.

"Choppy," came the reply.

Later on-came the message: "Is there any hope?" A day later came the last tapped message:

"We cannot last beyond six o'clock."

And they did not. The town could not understand and grew even angrier. The Navy, so concerned with its efforts, utterly failed to inform the town why the delays, why the deaths.

Meanwhile a major salvage company in Boston offered its services. But the Navy, with its equipment in New York, chose to refuse the offer and started huge pontoons on their way. A storm came up, the tow broke loose and three long days later the gear arrived.

Figure 5-26 The diving gear of that time was very cumbersome and required air pumped from above through the long hose shown.

Battling bad winter storms, the raising of the *S-4* was a long and dangerous process. The divers had to descend, in near-total darkness burrow under the sub's hull to find and seal all of the openings so that by pressurizing the hull they could raise the submarine. In fact, two sister ships, *S-6* and *S-8*, were ordered to the scene to serve as models for the divers and rescue team.

Fiorello LaGuardia, later the flamboyant mayor of New York, rode the *S-8* to Boston and spoke eloquently on the tragedy. Then, in Congress, he urged passage of "hazardous duty pay" for submariners. Until then enlisted men received *one dollar* per dive; His bill provided them with 25% extra pay for submarine duty; it passed. This move popularized the submarine service.

After the divers removed all but the six bodies in the torpedo room, they sealed the *S-4* on 16 February. Then the pontoons were positioned, and *S-6* provided air pressure at one hundred pounds psi (per square inch). On 17 March 1928 (three months after the accident) *S-4* rose to the surface at 3:00 P.M. The last bodies were removed, and the sub was towed to the Boston Navy Yard to be repaired in drydock.

A final ironic note was the discovery of the probable cause for the loss of most of the crew: the green curtain over the door of the captain's quarters. Lieutenant Commander Jones was in the control room with most of the crew when they were hit. With water pouring in, they tried to close the ventilation valves. But the rising water lifted the curtain, which wrapped around the valve body, jamming it. Unable to free the valve, they all took refuge in the small engine room, soon used up the air, and died.

Figure 5-27 Three months after the accident *S-4* rose to the surface, using air pressure to remove the water.

A sardonic comment on the affair was found in a watersoaked seabag. A long poem describing the "pigboats" began:

> *In the cantakerous mind of the devil*
> *There festered a fiendish scheme.*
> *He called his cohorts together*
> *And they designed the submarine.*

A number of the divers who had risked their lives countless times in those frigid, dark, roiled waters received medals for their heroism. Thomas Eadie, who had recently received the Navy Cross for his work in salvaging the *S-51*, received the Congressional Medal of Honor for his rescue of Michels. Captain Ernest J. King U.S.N., *Falcon*'s commander, wrote that Eadie was:

a real man who deliberately, knowingly, and wilfully took his own life in his hands to respond to the desperate need of a companion diver under wholly adverse diving conditions. . . .Eadie's deed . . . entirely fulfills the law's re-quirement of "extraordinary heroism in the line of his profession."

Distinguished Service Medals went to King and Saunders; Hartley and four other divers received Navy Crosses.

And Provincetown has never forgotten *S-4* and the feeling of utter help-lessness as they watched what they thought were the Navy's fumbling efforts, and could do nothing themselves. At St. Mary by the Harbor church, every year, a memorial service remembers those men dead these seventy years. The colors troop, and Taps sounds out over the town for them. There is also a large bronze memorial plaque on Provincetown's Commercial Street in front of the town hall.

Figure 5-28 Successfully raised, the submarine enters Boston Naval Shipyard for repairs.
Courtesy of the Standard Times, New Bedford, MA.

Figure 5-29 *Andrea Doria*, named for a great Italian admiral of the Renaissance, listing heavily to starboard. Note that the eight port lifeboats are useless.

The Andrea Doria *Disaster*
Bill Quinn: "I was there."

William P. Quinn, a network news photographer forty years ago, had the good luck to be first on the scene. Late on 25 July 1956, two great ocean liners met in dense fog, and one, the Italian Line's *Andrea Doria,* sank in 225 feet of water.

At 10:30 that night, his brother called to tell him that two ships had collided fifty miles south of Nantucket. Immediately he called his pilot, Bill Ketchen, to ready the twin-engine Cessna for a flight to the area. A few minutes later Francis E. ("Dinny") Whitmarsh, Channel 4 news director, called asking about the wreck; Bill told him that he was on it already.

Airborne at about 12:30 A.M., Ketchen and Quinn flew over Nantucket and kept going south. But already the Coast Guard had closed the area around the wreck, so they had to return to Nantucket. At 5:00 A.M. they took off again and flew toward the area, but there was heavy fog, and they could not find the wreck.

From the radio reports they heard that it was forty miles due east of the Nantucket Light Ship. Heading there, they dropped down under the fog layer and spent fifteen minutes shooting pictures. They were the first news plane on the scene.

They saw empty lifeboats and the *Doria* heeled far over to starboard; the Coast Guard Cutter *Hornbeam* was near the stricken ship; and other ships began arriving within hours to rescue nearly all of the 1,709 passengers; fifty-two died, either in the collision or in the water. It was later learned that one passenger had gone to sleep on the *Stockholm* and woke up on the *Doria!*

Since Bill Quinn's job was to get film footage to his network he had to leave

Figure 5-30 The Swedish liner *Stockholm*, with her bow completely crushed. Note the Coast Guard rescue helicopter above the stern. *U.S. Coast Guard photo.*

the scene. As a result of his foresightedness, Channel 4 was the first television station to broadcast news of this major disaster, which fortunately ended with few lives lost. At 9:00 that morning Quinn appeared on Channel 4 to describe what he had seen. The *New York Daily News* plane arrived on scene while Bill was filming; some of his footage shows the other plane.

But how could two great ocean liners collide? They had all the latest navigational gear, including radar, and yet they met. *Doria* was steaming toward New York, the last night out, with much celebration among passengers and crew. The Swedish *Stockholm,* with a reinforced bow for handling ice in northern waters, was headed east, having departed from New York that day.

The cause is still unclear, but there were heavy fog banks that night, through which the ships sailed, and at full speed. In any case, the *Stockholm's* bow tore open the starboard side of *Doria* near the bridge and a third of the way along the forward section. The oil tanks, empty at the end of the voyage, immediately filled with seawater, causing the heavy list to starboard, which disabled the lowering of half of the lifeboats aboard.

Within hours of the crash, ships from everywhere came rushing to the scene to help, and for eleven hours rescue work went on until, at 10:09 A.M., *Doria* heeled onto her beam ends and sank.

The ultimate irony, however, is that her loss was preventable. When *Hornbeam* arrived, early that morning, the Coast Guard planned to take the stricken ship in tow to shallower waters, where she could be salvaged. But since *Doria* was of foreign registry, nothing could be done without a release from the Italian government. It was not until about 9:30 A.M. that the release came through— too late. The main deck was under water; she could not be saved. Minutes after the *Doria*'s

Figure 5-31 The 656-foot ship begins her death roll to the bottom, 225 feet below. *U.S. Coast Guard Photo.*

captain and the last few crewmen arrived on *Hornbeam,* she rolled over and sank.

In the years since that fateful night, many professional divers have descended those 225 feet to explore this colossal wreck. Because of a rumor that the ship's safe contained great treasure, they even salvaged it and on network television opened it— to find little of value.

Figure 5-32 And down she goes, as seen from the Coast Guard amphibian overhead.

CHAPTER
6

Women at Sea

Hannah Rebecca Burgess - Navigator

The story of Hannah Rebecca Burgess reveals itself in her journals, which she left to the Sandwich Historical Society. It is a story of a protected young girl of nineteen who married her distant cousin Captain William Howes Burgess and four years later, far out in the Pacific, when he died, had to navigate the ship to safety. It is a romantic story and a tragedy, all in one.

Rebecca (her preferred name) was fifteen when she first met William, from Brewster, already at twenty a seasoned mariner. She was visiting at the home of her prosperous great uncle, Benjamin Burgess, in Boston. By March of 1850 the two young people were definitely interested in each other. On 4 March, in fact, William wrote a poem in Rebecca's autograph book:

Rebecca

We do not know how much we love.
Until we come to leave,
An aged tree, a common flower,
Are things o'er which we grieve.
There is a pleasure in the pain
That brings us back the past again.

We linger while we turn away,
And memories unmarked till then,
Come crowding around the heart.
Let what will lure our onward way,
Farewell is a bitter thing to say.

He was about to ship out as first mate aboard *Herbert*, under Captain Bangs Hallett of Yarmouth, for the East Indies. That September Captain Bangs went on vacation, turning over the ship to his twenty-two-year-old mate. He took

Figure 6-1 Hannah Rebecca Burgess, 26, taken when she was the same age as her husband. *Courtesy of the Sandwich Historical Society.*

Figure 6-2 Captain William Howes Burgess, taken when he became master of the clipper ship Challenger. *Courtesy of the Sandwich Historical Society.*

her from Boston to Calcutta and back in ten months. It is likely that William had already proposed to Rebecca before sailing, for he returned with dress goods from India for her wedding skirt.

And she barely had time to make the skirt: Rebecca, eighteen, and William, twenty-three, were married two weeks after his return, in the West Sandwich Methodist Church. Her wedding ring was engraved "I will never marry again," for they swore to be true forever. And on the day she was married she began the journal that tells her story.

One of their first excursions was to Medford to see William's new ship, *Whirlwind*, a-building there. Since she was barely framed, the new couple was able to have a long honeymoon before he had to take command of this new clipper. One trip they made was with the annual Cape Cod Association's steamship day trip to Provincetown from Boston. It was a rough, rainy passage across the bay. She writes:

I was rather sick but not having had any breakfast, I could not vomit. There were several ladies on board and we got on finely, first one would run to the closet and heave, then another, Real sport!

On the way home she was again seasick and joked about it:

A gentleman. . . gave me some brandy, which he said would ease me, and it did for I vomited right well. Yes! Lost all my nice dinner for which we paid two dollars.

Despite these discomforts, her final entry for the day was: ". . .it has been the happiest day of my life, may I be thankful for this privilege to God."

In mid-August the Burgesses left by train for Sandwich and then by carriage to William's home in Brewster, to await the launching of *Whirlwind*. A month later they were at the ceremony, to see this 960-ton clipper ship slide into the Mystic River. She was 185 feet long, with a twenty-foot depth. Now came the rigging, done in Charlestown, and by October Captain William (now) was trying to get ready for the maiden voyage.

Meanwhile Rebecca went shopping in Boston with her mother-in-law. Her complaints have been echoed by women since: "Oh! how tiresome is shopping in the city!" That evening, William impulsively bought Rebecca another dress. She says: "William wants me to dress well. He spares no money. He is an obliging husband."

The day before *Whirlwind* sailed in November Rebecca spent on board and sadly said goodbye, as so many Cape wives had done before. Ashore, she returned to Sandwich to live with her parents. And she stops writing in her journal. Almost a year later, on 31 October 1953 she resumes:

A year will soon have past since that trying hour when I took the parting hand of my beloved husband and dropt the silent tear. . . . William will soon return. . . .Oh does it not fill my soul with joy when I meditate on it.

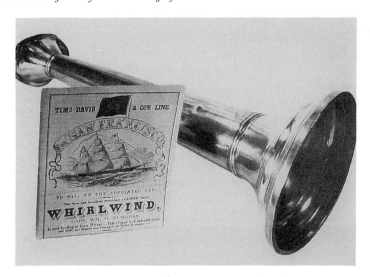

Figure 6-3 Sailing card of *Whirlwind* and Captain Burgess' speaking trumpet. *Courtesy of the Sandwich Historical Society.*

He arrived in New York a month later, and Rebecca met him there. In the interim both had decided that they would not be separated again: she would sail with him on the next voyage, to San Francisco. Meanwhile they boarded at a hotel, where there were other captains and wives, for company. Sightseeing, shopping— a $45 blue velvet cloak that Captain William bought for her which offended her frugal soul—, and going to a play ("I hope it is the last time I shall attend such a foolish place of amusement.") occupied her time while *Whirlwind* was loading. Then she went home to Sandwich to say goodbye to her parents.

The second voyage began on 4 February 1854, and Rebecca suffered badly for the first weeks of rough weather. Everything in the cabin was drenched, and she had difficulty gaining her "sea legs." But two weeks later she is rhapsodizing about the majesty of the ocean and describing the captain's quarters:

The cabin is divided into . . . the forward and after cabin . . . the former is painted with zinc paint of a cream color. . . . The next room [is] altogether different. It consists of mahogany, rosewood and satinwood. On each side of the rooms [are] staterooms, containing two berths each . . . in the after cabin . . . there is a sofa, a large stuffed armchair, an ottoman and a marble-topped center table. Maroon color [is] the furniture in both rooms and of red velvet.

This is not unusual luxury for these ships, for they were also expressions of their owners' wealth in the markets of the world.

Fresh meat consisted of eight pigs (and later three piglets) and four dozen chickens (with roosters); flying fish flew aboard and made a welcome change in the diet; preserved fruit became fruit pies.

Since her religion was so important she was delighted to find that the second mate had an accordion and knew a great many hymns, but she was disturbed that William did not hold services aboard. However, he would do nothing about it.

The workings of the ship fascinated her, and she soon learned all the nautical terms and the names of all the sails. Her journal began to look like the ship's log, in fact, with entries by her husband as to the ship. And she began to study navigation. Nathaniel Bowditch's *Practical Navigator* and Dana's *Two Years Before the Mast* fascinated her.

After two months they were approaching the dreaded waters of Cape Horn. The log entry for Tuesday, 4 April, reports:

Commenced and continued with heavy gales from S and Eastward. Ship close reefed under Main Top Sail and Storm Stay Sail. (Of the more than twenty sails she carried, Captain William dared to carry only two, the topsail to keep the ship from rolling too heavily and the staysail for steerageway.) *A very heavy sea running somewhat irregular. . . . Ends with thick squally weather. Ship under double reefs. For the past three days we have had very bad weather and . . .*

Figure 6-4 Sailing card of *Challenger*, emphasizing speed — most desirable in attracting passengers and freight. *Courtesy of the Sandwich Historical Society.*

it looks very dubious as regards making a fair passage to San Francisco. A quick one is utterly impossible.

On 5 April, with the pumps going every two hours, Rebecca notes in her journal:

I don't like Cape Horn at all if it is like this. We go along for about five minutes very well, then it is pitch! pitch! and . . . all of a sudden your soup is running on your clothes or some hot tea upset.

Well, it is not as bad as it might be yet. . . . I should like to have been on deck. . . although I must have been lashed to the rigging. . . . But I think a few minutes would have completely satisfied me in witnessing a storm at sea.

After two weeks— some transits have taken thirty days!—they broke out into the Pacific, and after a good day's sail found themselves becalmed. Since William's reputation depended on fast voyages, he was most annoyed. But, says Rebecca, "He has left off using profane language, a habit to which most seafaring persons are addicted."

At the end of May the *Whirlwind* received her pre-landing sprucing up, and on 13 May they arrived in San Francisco, to find that other clippers had made even worse time. The journal stops there and does not cover the return voyage. But going home they stopped at the Chincha Islands off Peru and loaded about 1000 tons of guano (sea bird droppings) for fertilizer. On 18 December they arrived in New York, ten and a half months from their sailing date.

On 10 June 1855 Rebecca starts her journal, noting that William has been given command of *Challenger,* a new and extreme clipper, considerably larger than *Whirlwind.* She was 1334 tons, 202 feet long. Rebecca remarks: "I like *Challenger* very much.ˈ She is a much better sailor than the *Whirlwind* and 400 tons larger."

So began a long and tragic voyage. Within a week two seamen were ill with smallpox but recovered. On 2 July a seaman died of an unknown illness and was buried at sea. On 18 August a crewman fell from the topsail yard and was lost. And Rebecca herself was not well and could not shake off her illness.

But she continued to study navigation and began to plot the ship's positions. William would take the actual sight with his sextant, and she would do the complicated figuring. She did not realize how critical this skill would be later.

This was another long, slow trip. *Challenger* fought head winds all down South America; when they rounded Cape Horn they faced head winds up South America's west coast. On 27 September, 116 days at sea, Rebecca wrote:

Oh it is very tedious to be laying [sic] in this place. . . with a headwind and counting each [day] as it passes. We are now the Longitude of San Francisco and heading west. . .and we cannot go northward at all.

At last they sailed into San Francisco, 133 days from Boston.

The next leg of the trip was to go to Hong Kong, returning 350 Chinese coolies to their homes. On 9 November *Challenger* set out, having spent twenty-six days in port, where Rebecca writes that: "I don't think it possible to enjoy myself

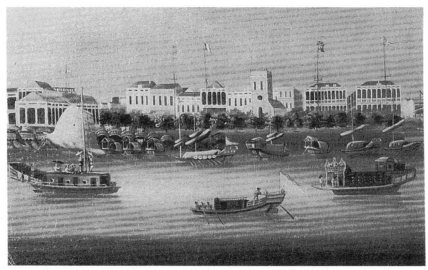

Figure 6-5 The hongs of Canton China, a painting that Rebecca acquired on a voyage there. *Courtesy of the Sandwich Historical Society.*

better in any part of the world than during my last stay in San Francisco." She had regained her health and was enjoying the company of three passengers, Mr. Jackson, who had come aboard in Boston, and the Aldens.

And the ship seemed on a pleasure cruise, with all sails, including the studding sails, set. In twenty-six days she covered 5,051 miles— an average of two hundred nautical miles a day. Then on 19 December they lost another seaman, falling from the topmast rigging. The journal records:

Frederic D. Magoon, seaman . . . was at work setting up the ratlines (rope ladders from the sides of the ship to the masts) *[when he fell, injuring] himself by contact with the spars, as to sink in a moment. No assistance could be rendered. Poor fellow, he is gone, in a moment hurried from time to eternity. . . . May he be at rest with God.*

Arriving in Hong Kong, China in forty days, they discharged the 350 Chinese coolies and then moved upriver to Whampoa, the anchorage for all foreign traders. Captain William went on to Canton, China to arrange a return cargo of tea for London. Just before sailing on 14 January 1856, Rebecca's journal reveals her reaction to China:

I do not like this place (Whampoa) at all and feel no regret in leaving it. . . . I can hardly realize that we have visited the Celestial Empire . . . but I suppose I had too exalted opinions of the place and people. [In Hong Kong] I enjoyed myself very much . . . at the house of Mr. Sturgis. . . .I went to Canton twice but saw nothing to attract save Chinese curios.

I was much pleased with some new words I learnt. . . . "Can catch that pigeon less inside two days" means with Chinese can do or make a certain thing in less than two days.

She made quite a collection of "Chinese curios," which are on display at the Sandwich Historical Society.

Reaching the Cape of Good Hope, *Challenger* ran into such storms that she took fourteen days to round the cape. The journal says that the ship "should never have got round but for the current. The last day it carried us 70 miles in the wind's eye (right into the headwind)." But then they picked up favoring winds and in one day made 296 nautical miles, 1200 miles in a week.

Sometimes William made entries in the journal, too, besides the usual log entries. One of them, a letter addressed to "Dear Wife," saying in essence:

. . . and when there [at home] surrounded by all of your friends except me who will be absent at sea you will be able to form but a slight idea of a lonesome

night at sea and all alone.

Rebecca wrote back a much longer letter :

My Dear Husband, we have been together for 2 years and 6 months, with scarcely a week's separation . . . I have enjoyed luxuries in company with you, William, that bereft of that companionship would bring no happiness. I know that I love the sea. But more I love to be with my Husband . . . I enjoy going to sea because I am with my Husband. With him any place is home.

By 23 April *Challenger* was near the English Channel; with very thick weather Captain William was on his feet for most of four days, until a tug arrived to tow the ship up the Thames River to London, 108 days from China.

There for five weeks, Rebecca in particular became a tourist, visiting the famous places, including the Crystal Palace, built five years before, where she saw Queen Victoria and Prince Albert, a delightful surprise. William was, naturally, doing business. The ship was chartered to go to Callao, Peru, and then to the Chincha Islands for guano, to be delivered to Marseilles, France. For the first time William became sick, diagnosed as "inflammation of the liver." He seemed better by the time they sailed, on 6 June.

Rebecca turned twenty-two on 4 July, and the ship took a holiday, with a special dinner for all. The meal served aft was "boiled and baked chicken, salmon, green peas, and, for dessert, cherry and currant pies."

Cape Horn was more than the usual nightmare: four weeks of struggling with westerly gales and heavy seas. Rebecca writes: "William is discouraged and wishes he was on a farm." Finally, on 20 September, 106 days from London, they reached Callao. By the time they reached the Chinchas on 2 October, William was bedridden, badly dehydrated (as we know now) from diarrhea.

Figure 6-6 The obelisk over William's grave (and her modest gravestone beside it). *Photo by the author.*

Loading of the guano was extremely slow, so that almost two months passed before *Challenger* had 1600 tons aboard and was ready to sail. Meanwhile William had been under the care of a local doctor, with little change. He decided to sail for Valparaiso, hoping for better medical care.

At sea he became even sicker, and Rebecca did her best to care for him with the help of David Graves, the mulatto steward. Since the first mate was not a competent navigator, Rebecca navigated the ship. Then on 11 December 1856, her journal read:

Latitude 33 .02' South Longitude 71 .41' West
19 days from Chincha Islands, 250 miles from Valparaiso.

At 11 P.M. my dear Husband departed this world, apparently at peace with his Maker and in no pain. He was 27 years, 9 months & 14 Days.

They had been married for four years and 128 days. William was buried in Valparaiso, and the American consul, George Williams, arranged for Rebecca's passage home. David Graves stayed with her in Valparaiso, and the first mate, Henry Winsor, was given command. The ship continued her voyage to Marseilles.

Ten days later, en route home, she writes:

. . . He to whom I plighted my youthful heart, for whom I left Parents and my native country, is now no more on earth. William, my dear Husband, let me devote the remainder of my days on earth in cherishing thy memory and may I strive by the grace of God to follow out thy dying injunction, "May we meet in Heaven."

En route to New York on the steamer *Illinois*, Rebecca kept to herself, until the captain asked her to calculate the ship's position, based on his sextant sights. She did so, and the captain exclaimed, "Your work agrees with mine within a mile! You are the only woman I have ever known who understands navigation." She arrived in New York on 27 January 1857 and at once headed for home to tell William's parents of his death.

Once William's body arrived from Valparaiso, Rebecca took great pains in selecting a fitting gravestone. In Boston she chose a tall granite obelisk for his grave in Sagamore and had a farewell poem that she wrote engraved upon it.

The next question was: how to live the rest of her life. She received a "generous reward" for navigating the *Challenger* safely, but when the accounts with the owners were closed she found that they had balanced her "reward" against what was owed Captain Burgess as captain, and she owed them $24.86. Some reward! And finally she found herself with a total of $1630, not much of an estate. But she was able to support herself on the interest from the loans she made to relatives and others.

For the rest of her long life (eighty-three years) she was the center of her family and cared for three generations: parents, brothers, a sister, and their children. Church-loving, she taught a Sunday school class and often invited her class to visit while she told about the wonderful *objets d'art* the she had brought home from her world voyaging.

She continued her journal throughout the years, always noting the anniversary of William's death. And she still wore her wedding ring with the words, "I shall never marry again."

The faithful steward, David Graves, had accompanied her to Boston, and in gratitude for his loyalty she gave him her Bible, upon which she had leaned so heavily. Soon he became steward on *Ringleader* and sailed in her until 1862, when the ship was wrecked on Formosa. Graves and the others survived the wreck.

Later an American visited the wreck site and found the Bible with the inscription: "Presented to David Graves by Mrs. Rebecca H. Burgess, Boston, Feb. 10, 1857." Eventually it came into the hands of Richard Henry Dana, now a Boston lawyer, who advertised for information on Rebecca Burgess. Almost miraculously, she read the notice, wrote to Mr. Dana, and received her Bible. It is part of the Burgess collection at the Sandwich Glass Museum.

When she died, on 13 June 1917, she was buried beside her beloved husband in the Sagamore cemetery.

Figure 6-7 Mary Chipman Lawrence and her Samuel. *Courtesy of the Falmouth Historical Society.*

Mary Chipman Lawrence
Whaling Wife

The whaling industry of the eighteenth and nineteenth centuries subjected the men who sailed the ships to almost unimaginable dangers. Their extremely flimsy wooden ships sailed in totally uncharted seas, risking all for the sake of capturing and killing the grandest animals alive, who would sometimes fight back, as in the case of the *Essex* attacked and sunk by a sperm whale in mid-Pacific.

And rather than stay at home while their men were gone for three or four years, the captains' wives shared their dangers. For example, in the village of Dennis alone almost 150 wives sailed with their husbands. They bore their children, perhaps, somewhere in the Okhotsk Sea, learned to navigate just in case, risked their own female all for the sake of being with their men.

Mary Chipman of Falmouth was one of these women. In 1847 she had married Captain Samuel Lawrence, who that year shipped out in command of the sperm whaler *Lafayette* of New Bedford. Cruising off the west coast of South America until 1850, in the Galapagos Islands he hit a rock and the ship went down. With his reputation badly damaged, he could only find a job as mate.

Later he got a second chance— as captain of the ship *Addison*. Built in Philadelphia, she was 108 feet long, with the figurehead of a woman. Samuel's brother Lawrence had been her captain in 1848. His five brothers were also whalers, and several of their wives had gone to sea. Captain Lewis's wife Eunice, for instance, had made several voyages, and their three children had been born at Tahiti, Norfolk Island (where the descendants of the Bounty mutineers moved), and Honolulu.

What may have decided Mary to go a-whaling was the death of the youngest Lawrence captain, Augustus, who died five months into a voyage in Java, leaving his wife and baby. In any case, Mary faced all the dreadful possibilities and in November 1856 sailed with her captain in *Addison*. Born in Sandwich, she was twenty when they married, and in 1851 she had borne Captain Sam a daughter, Millie, who soon became the ship's mascot.

Thus she joined a growing sorority of captains' wives. The Reverend Samuel Damon, who arrived in Honolulu in 1842 as a missionary, noted in 1852 that:

A few years ago it was exceedingly rare for a Whaling Captain to be accompanied by his wife and children, but now it is very common. . . . [No] less than 42 [whaling families] are now in the Pacific. Just one half of that number are now in Honolulu. The happy influence of this goodly number of ladies is apparent to the most careless observer.

What we know of her is mostly revealed through her journals, kept meticulously during her seven whaling voyages in *Addison*. They reveal her as a sprightly person, loving and courageous, witty and objective about the trials of a whaling voyage. Her picture shows her to be uninterested in dress and adornment. Perhaps her most persistent trait is her devotion to her religion. Minnie, on the other hand, is a somewhat shadowy figure, close to her mother, with whom she does nearly everything. We shall see her proselytizing the crew at one point.

The most valuable quality of Mary's journals, however, is her descriptions of the people and places in the Pacific in the late 1850's, when in fact the "seeking of the cetacean" was on its downward path. We will meet whalers who have been out for several years and still have empty holds. And among the thousands of logs and journals extant, hers is perhaps the most vivid, down-to-earth, sensitive. So we begin the journey on 25 November 1856, when *Addison* left New Bedford harbor.

(An editorial note here: Mary took seven different voyages with Captain Sam. The first few are sufficiently indicative of the quality I have mentioned above. So, to avoid tedious repetition I have omitted the last trips.)

Her first journal begins with a prayer for success— and a report of her and Minnie's seasickness on the first days. But they recovered and developed "sea legs" very rapidly.

November 27. Thanksgiving at home . . . [How 1] should relish a plate of Grandma's nice turkey for dinner. . . . Truly, "they that go down to the sea in ships . . . see the works of the Lord and his wonders in the deep. For he commandeth and riseth the stormy wind, which lifteth up the waves thereof . . ." It sometimes seems impossible that we can live through it, but our gallant ship rides along fearlessly.

"The run down to the bulge of South America was uneventful, except that we are not fortunate with our cooks. Are trying the fourth now (five weeks out)." Their Christmas dinner menu was "roast chickens, stuffed, potatoes, turnips, onions, stewed cranberries, pickled beets and cucumbers, and a plum duff." Her first mention of Minnie is on 26 December. She is very happy, says Mary, having had a real Christmas at sea, and seems to enjoy herself as much as at home.

January 1 [1857]. The past has been an eventful year to us. A father, brother, and niece have been called to the world of spirits: Infancy, Manhood, and Old Age. . . .May He who is the God of the widow and the Father of the fatherless be very near to them.

Mary remarks on the fine singing voices of the crew forward, as they tuned up with "Home Sweet Home" and other favorites. Then she makes an exceedingly astute remark: "I have yet to find out that sailors belong to another class than that of human being . . . I shall not think they are entirely depraved as long as I hear them singing their Psalm tunes."

They spoke their first vessel on 5 January, *Dr. Franklin*, Captain Russell. He came aboard and passed the evening with them and sent her "two dozen nice oranges." Finally, on 13 January they saw their first whales and sent out three boats, but the whales were too fast for them. By this time they were getting short of domestic oil, burning sperm candles supposed to be used for trade.

Figure 6-8 Mary and Minnie Lawrence, three months old. *Courtesy of Francis Freeman Jones.*

One afternoon from the cabin window Minnie showed her doll, Sarah, the rough seas. "Sarah, shouldn't you think I would be afraid of those deep, deep billows? Well, I ain't, for I know there's Somebody up in heaven that will take care of me."

Seven days of very rough weather saw them around Cape Horn, rather than the thirty days that is often the lot of the poor sailorman. Once well into the Pacific they bowled along, sometimes making, she says, 225 miles a day. On 14 February they were running with a large clipper ship and kept up with her.

Paralleling the South American coast, they were at the Galapagos Islands by 5 March and turned west northwest for the Sandwich Islands. Early in March they saw a school of blackfish (a small whale) and were able to take six— which made only about four barrels of oil, their first. Then they began to meet other whalers, *Ohio, Golconda,* and *General Scott.* And the whaling began in earnest. On 13 March they caught two whales, rather small, she says. The next day cutting in (removal of the thick coat of blubber on the whale's body) began, and after the huge slices had been cut up they were boiled in huge kettles to extract the oil. The entire process is a day-and-night struggle, this time yielding sixty barrels.

The crew caught some pilot fish and had them for dinner and then for breakfast. Mary says:

About ten minutes after I had finished my breakfast my face began to burn and my head to ache badly. I looked in the glass and my face was . . . just as red as it could be all over. . . . [Samuel said], "Now I know that we are poisoned by eating those fish. . . . So it went on, until all who had eaten them felt the consequences.

Mary went fishing on 23 March, catching twenty fish so large that she needed help to haul them aboard. Her bait: a piece of white cloth. On All Fools Day she "made our chickens into a pie. The officers said it seemed like home." On Sunday she gave Minnie some Bibles and Testaments, which the girl loaded into her doll carriage and took forward. Soon she was back for another load, which went as rapidly as the first load.

Finally they reached their destination: Lahaina on the island of Maui, the rendezvous for most whalers in the Pacific fleet, anchoring in the roadstead on the afternoon of 17 April. Clearing customs, Captain Sam went ashore to locate a boarding house for themselves. Mary described the house and grounds in great detail, a picturesque "straw cottage" on the beach. The American consul and his secretary were boarding there too.

That Sunday the family went to church for the first time in four months, much to Mary's pleasure. The "Seaman's Chaplain," the Reverend Sereno Bishop, born in Honolulu, preached to a small congregation of native people. Their magnificent singing delighted her, and she was amused by their dress. But within a few

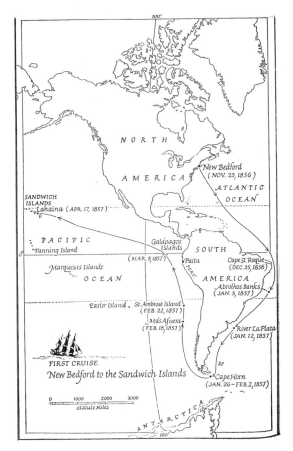

Figure 6-9 First cruise - New Bedford to the Sandwich Islands. *Courtesy of University Press of New Hampshire.*

days she expressed her first opinion of the native people:

From what I saw and heard of them . . . they are a low, degraded, indolent set. . . . Many of them go without clothing; both sexes bathe in the water entirely naked, unabashed. As I am writing, two men are close by my door without an article of clothing. Minnie says, "I have to turn my head the other way." They will lie *and steal whenever an opportunity offers. I am aware that the foreign influence, especially of sailors, has been very bad.*

Her week in Lahaina was sheer delight for Mary. Meeting other whaling wives and missionary wives relieved the tedium of months at sea with mostly only Minnie for company. The weather was fine, with a sea breeze and cool nights, and the town sat at the foot of the mountains at the water's edge, as it does today.

On 27 April they were resupplied and ready to sail. All the foreign residents visited her to say goodbye, bringing little farewell presents for Minnie and her.

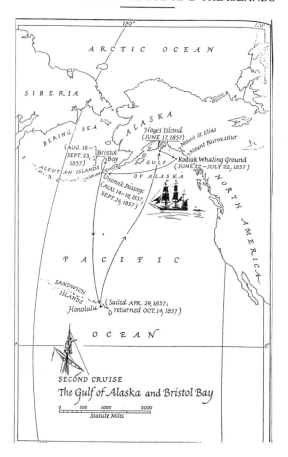

Figure 6-10 Second Cruise - The Gulf of Alaska and Bristol Bay. *Courtesy of University Press of New England.*

Upped anchor and sailed for Honolulu at about five o'clock, arriving the next day. Ashore, they visited the home of the Bateses, which delighted her with its bucolic simplicity. She even found a dandelion in a flower bed; Mrs. Bates told her that she had sent for the seed, to feel like home.

The missionary brig *Morning Star* (on which, incidentally, my great uncle Orramel Gulick served as mate) was in port. This was the vessel named "The Children's Ship" because the school children of Massachusetts had given their pennies toward her building. In fact, Minnie owned stock in her. She was loading for a voyage to the Marquesas and then to Micronesia, with missionary families. Orramel later was ordained and served a long, useful life in the Hawaiian Islands and in Japan.

And thus ends the first whaling voyage of Mary Chapman Lawrence.

The next voyage of *Addison* lasted five and a half months and took them into Alaskan waters and the Bering Sea, still hunting the elusive cetacean. After the poor results from the first voyage, Captain Sam hoped for better fishing there. Their supply of food, described by Mary, is positively mouth-watering. Minnie now had a little dog named Pincher. A few days out, in rough, cold weather she had the stove re-installed in the cabin. She wrote, "Have a nice little stove, a good cozy fire, a kind husband, and a dear little daughter. How ungrateful should I be to complain."

About halfway to the Gulf of Alaska they started seeing whales a-plenty— but they were only finbacks or humpbacks, hardly worth chasing. Other whalers were nearby, the *Benjamin Rush* and *William and Henry,* both "clean," as the whalers say. Mary noted on 25 May that they had been away from home for six months.

Meeting several other vessels, Captain Sam conferred with them, but no one seemed to know where to go next. The ships kept trying but with no success; the whales seemed very shy of the ships. Then they met Captain Lopor in *Sarah Sheafe,* with 800 barrels. On his last voyage he was away for sixty-six months!

Finally on 6 June they were rewarded with a large whale, yielding 155 barrels. After shooting at several whales and having them sink, *Addison* caught another on 21 June as they were entering the Kodiak whaling grounds. It yielded 158 barrels. There were several whalers around them. Very near the land, Mary wrote of the mountains, "height upon height in grand succession rise."

And now their luck changed: a whale on 27 June, another on 29 June, another on 4 July in the midst of their Independence Day dinner of a pair of ducks, stuffed, cranberry sauce, potatoes, pumpkin, and plum duff. On 15 July, they got a cow and calf, 155 barrels, and a total of 600 barrels.

A small delight for Mary and Minnie was a little brown and yellow bird which flew aboard and was caught. Mary turned her work basket into a cage and fed and watered it, but it died on Minnie's birthday, three days later.

Turning west, Captain Sam headed for the Aleutian Islands, arriving off Unimak Passage on 14 August. A brief landing by a boat crew brought back a large bunch of flowers and three kinds of berries.

Frustration set in again, with heavy fog and wary whales. On 19 August fog was so thick that they had to fire guns to help the boats return. Then on 26 August they took a right whale (so-called because it yields the most oil). On the twenty-eighth they awoke to find a "city of ships. Could count fifteen from off deck." Their boats caught a very large one, which sank. But all three boats had lines on him and were able to raise him.

"Plenty of whales in sight today; the sea appears to be full of them," writes Mary on 1 September. But catching them was not so easy. They had to cut loose from a whale that "[used) his flippers quite scientifically." The large whale gave them 300 barrels.

On 24 September Captain Sam decided to head for Honolulu, somewhat satisfied with the take so far. So begins a flurry of preparations for arrival.

October 4. For the last week we have been making rapid progress. . . .We have plenty to do getting ready for port. . . . I am as much hurried in preparing clothes for port as If I were engaged in housekeeping. . . . I put off Minnie's clothes as long as possible because she is growing so fast.

On the fourteenth they arrived off Diamond Head, and as soon as they docked the ship was almost filled with Mary's visitors-and she had not "arranged my toilet," planning to stay aboard all morning. Embarrassed, she rushed to get ready and greet her guests. The next day she found a place to board at $25 per week, with pleasant whaling wife company.

Letters, so uncertain under these conditions, played an important role in whalers' lives. Often months en route, from ship to ship, they meant ties with home: who died, who married. So it was with Mary and her captain. A batch of letters was precious. On 20 October they received a batch, but none when the mail arrived on the twenty-first. Mary laments: "Consequently we must wait until spring for the remainder."

On 22 October brother George arrived in *Harvest*. And Mr. Damon invited

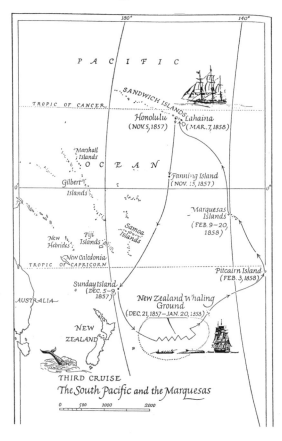

Figure 6-11 Third Cruise - The South Pacific and the Marquesas. *Courtesy of University Press of New England.*

her for a ride, during which they were allowed inside the palace grounds, and Mary remarks that she has seen the king and queen several times. Their stay in Honolulu was a most welcome change for Mary and Minnie. There was a great deal to do: friends to go riding with and visit, attending church (always a source of spiritual delight). She and the captain visited the clipper ship *John Gilpin,* and her comment was: " I wished very much for a small piece of her spacious cabin to enlarge mine a little."

On 5 November, after the pilot boat had left, they found two stowaways on the *Addison.* Having lost five men by desertion, they did not want others' deserters and sent them back via the ship *Black Eagle.* And off they went on their third trip to the New Zealand whaling grounds.

This trip was a long one. It took *Addison* a month to reach Sunday Island, on the International Date line, in an almost straight line from Honolulu. Halfway there Mary notes that a year ago they set out on this odyssey and that they had sailed 36,785 miles so far.

They spent four days there gathering wood and fresh produce and found two Americans living there with native wives and a gaggle of children. Mary sent ashore needles, thread, wax, toys, and books for the children, and the boat returned with a goose, some turkeys, tomatoes, eggs, and bananas from the families.

Leaving Sunday Island on 18 December, they headed for the whaling grounds, due east of New Zealand. On Christmas they had a right royal feast from the food received on the island. "Had a goat killed for the benefit of those living in the forecastle," Mary writes.

The next day they had a gam with Captain Norton of *Falcon.* He had been out over two years and had only 700 barrels. On 28 December they struck a whale, but he fought, and one of the boat crew drowned. This disturbed Mary greatly:

Poor Antone! He came out as one of the cabin boys [and then] went to live in the forecastle. He was so anxious to go out in a boat after whales. He was a smart, active boy of eighteen years. . . .That was a sad day for us, Antone, when thou wast summoned in the mysteries of the unseen world. . . .May God in his infinite goodness have mercy on thy soul.

The next weeks or so were rather humdrum, says Mary, except for very stormy weather. Minnie had been helping the steward, and told her mother that "I think I was something like a missionary. I talked to him about God." Except for one whale that they took, there was no action except storms. On 1 January Mary writes:

Another new year has opened upon us. The old year departed in sadness, for one of our number has left us, never again to return. May not the sad news come to us that any of our loved home faces have passed to the spirit land during the past year.

The weather continued very stormy, so that whaling was suspended. On 15 January *Addison* shipped such a heavy sea that it carried away the bow boat and its davits. On 21 January the captain decided to leave the area; the weather had been too bad for whaling. So they went before the wind northeast toward Pitcairn Island.

Across that empty stretch of ocean they sailed, until on the twenty-sixth they caught up with Captain Curry's *James Maury* and had a fine gam, especially since he had lived in the same boarding house in Honolulu. He had taken only one whale during that season, poor fellow. He told Mary that the price for whalebone had reached $1.50 a pound. Then she makes an interesting feminine and astute comment:

The ladies are to be thanked for that, and I presume all interested in right whaling are truly thankful for this skirt movement. May the fashion long continue. One month today since Antone was swallowed up by the relentless waters.

At last Pitcairn Island hove in sight on 3 February. Sailing around it, they found it uninhabited; the descendants of the *H.M.S. Bounty* mutineers had been moved to Norfolk Island by the British government, since their island could no longer support them. This rocky island has no landing place without a pilot, and so the fruit that they were sure was there was beyond their reach. Captain Sam found that his chronometer was about thirty miles off from Pitcairn's charted position.

Six days later *Addison* made Fatu Hiva in the Marquesas Group, finding another whaler, *Japan*, and the bark, *Glimpse,* with forty passengers headed for California, in the harbor. A wonderful chance to send letters home! A boat filled with "frightfully tattooed men" came out. The one who said that he was chief told them that he would stay aboard while the boats were off getting wood because, he said in pidgin English, "They sava [savvy?] plenty steal."

While they were anchored, the ship was filled with native men; it was taboo for women to use canoes. They brought pigs, chickens, pineapples, and bananas. That afternoon Mr. Kaivi, the "Kanaka" missionary, from Oahu, who had come to Fatu Hiva in *Morning Star,* visited. "Old John," the chief, also came aboard withn his wife, who was wrapped in a red *muumuu* (just a piece of cloth tied around her) and wore earrings of porpoise teeth. She brought gifts of fruit, saying, "Me give you, you give me." Mary gave her some cloth and beads.

Kaivi's first convert, Natua, was aboard for dinner, and he gave a blessing which Mary tried to record as best she could:

O grreat Fader, got no moder, got no broder, got no sister. Make fust de sea, make fust de dry land, make fust de moon and de stars, make fust de trees, den he make man; and now great Fader, give man he belly full. Amen.

That afternoon Mary, the captain, and Minnie went ashore, to find themselves objects of great curiosity. But Mary satisfied her own curiosity and describes the village: bamboo houses, with mats on the pebbled floor to sleep on. Widows scratch their faces as a sign of grief.

They have a number of gods, but the greatest among them is what they call the Sea God, that is, the white man's God, who makes all the powder muskets and ships and cloth. They also have god-men, who talk with the gods and tell the people what to do. When they kill an enemy, they take his body up to a taboo house, and the god-men go there and eat it.

(During World War II, observers noticed that many native societies had an identical belief: all the largesse of war came from the white man's god for the natives' use. This widespread belief was called the Cargo Cult. And here in Mary's journal, a hundred years earlier, is evidence already of the debilitating impact of Western culture.)

There is constant war between the Oomoa Bay people and the others on the other two bays. Deaths are less frequent since they began using firearms (from the whites, of course) than when spears and clubs were their only weapons. Chief John said that they were great cowards: "Me no like fight. Me afraid. Me say me no go. Me sick, me too much sick."

On Sunday, 14 February, most of the crew attended the native church, but the Lawrences did not go, knowing that the congregation would be watching them instead of listening to the preacher. The next day they up-anchored and sailed for Hiva Oa, another missionary station north of Fatu Hiva. There they acquired several barrels of potatoes from the Reverend Mr. Kekela, as well as more bananas, and they met *Nassau,* with only 100 barrels of sperm oil that season. The captain did a lot of trading with Mr. Kekela and was paid by an order on the treasurer of the Hawaiian Missionary Society in Honolulu.

Sailing through the Marquesas Group, they stopped briefly at Ua Pu for more food supplies. While they were there, one of the crew, a Hawaiian, jumped ship. They managed to get twenty-six hogs, forty chickens, 2000 cocoanuts for pig feed, many bananas and plantains, sweet potatoes, and even oranges. Then they headed from Maui with a fair wind, making very good time. The four-month, quite unsatisfactory cruise ended on 7 March 1858, when they anchored in Lahaina harbor. After customs clearance, they learned that they were the fifteenth whaler in port. Thus began for Mary and Minnie a pleasant round of visits from and to other whaling wives. The family moved ashore to the Bigelows' "old straw cottage" on the shore and settled in comfortably.

Three busy weeks went by rapidly. Minnie found several playmates, Mary White, daughter of Dr. White, Lizzie Bigelow, and Mary had a number of congenial friends with whom to catch up on gossip. The great importance of mail is revealed by this passage:

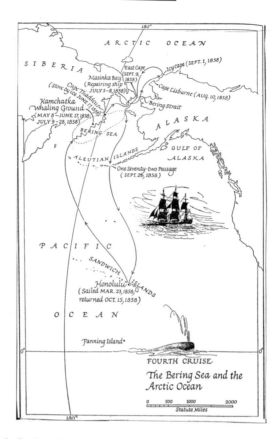

Figure 6-12 Fourth Cruise - The Bering Sea and the Arctic Ocean. *Courtesy of University Press of New England.*

March 12. This morning a schooner arrived with the California mails . . . from Sarah [and] Elizabeth Robinson and a note for Minnie a letter from brother George . . . ; and one from Sandwich from Lizzie. Not a word from Father, Mother, Willie, or Cynthia. I know it is because we were in earlier than we intended. . . . Times have been very hard for the last winter at home.

Another of the very infrequent chances to go to church came on 14 March. Mary writes, "I think I never realized what a privilege it was until since I have become a wanderer upon the sea." she was delighted to see *Speedwell* arrive with Captain and Mrs. Gibbs. Mercy and Mary were schoolmates. Having stopped in the Azores, the Gibbses had had a daughter there named Crianna. The third mate was a Mr. Shiverick, from Falmouth, Mary's home, and a cousin of the Shivericks of East Dennis who were busy building their eight clipper ships. They had a good visit, too.

That night there was an alarm: *Young Hero* was on fire in the harbor, supposedly set by a crewman. With all that oil aboard and oilsoaked decks, the desperate efforts of the crews of several whalers could not contain the flames, and by morning the three masts burned through and fell, and the ship was destroyed.

As the *Addison* was preparing for the next cruise, on the nineteenth the whaler *Omega,* of Edgartown on Martha's Vineyard, arrived with letters from home from Sarah and Willie. When the family moved back aboard, the cooper informed them that they had six newborn piglets; this pleased Minnie, naturally. After extensive farewells *Addison* sailed for the Bering Sea and the Arctic Ocean on 23 March 1858.

This cruise was the longest, most dangerous, and most arduous of the voyages so far, extending up above the Arctic Circle in the relentless pursuit of whales. On a north-northwest course, crossing the International Date Line again, they headed for the Bering Sea whaling grounds north of the Aleutian Islands. They were well supplied with vegetables and fruits, canned goods, and lots of meat on the hoof. After a long haul across an empty ocean, on 3 May, finally, they spoke a ship,

Figure 6-13 Fourth Cruise - The Eastern Siberian Whaling Ground. *Courtesy of University Press of New England.*

Champion, of Edgartown, and had a fine gam. The two captains decided to keep together, "as it is more pleasant to go in among the ice with company than alone and unattended," says Mary. It is also good, prudent sense. Many whalers have been crushed by the ice and the crews lost.

The weather became worse and colder, and on 12 May they were in the ice and surrounded by ships: *Gay Head, Marengo, Omega, America, John and Elizabeth,* as well as their consort, *Champion.* And no whales, until 17 May, when *Addison* took a bowhead after a race with another boat. "Mr. Nickerson got out of his boat to try to shoot him, while another boat crew. . . landed and snowballed the whale probably wounding him severely," says Mary, tongue firmly in cheek.

In the midst of a series of driving snowstorms the ships began to find their whales. Then, on 23 May *Addison* landed another whale. The competition was fierce: sixteen ships all trying for the few whales they saw. Fog, snow, gales, ice: that is the Bering Sea. On 14 June they came up against thick pack ice, through which they could not go.

Three days later *Addison* hit a single ice cake which stove in her larboard (port) bow somewhat. Mary prepared to abandon ship, if necessary. But with almost continuous pumping the vessel could continue. Soon they were able to place a canvas patch over the leak, which almost controlled the problem.

Aside from the occasional ship and a chance to exchange news, as well as nary a whale, they kept heading north when they could, toward Bering Strait between Siberia and Alaska. On 2 July they arrived off Plover Bay, and Mary met her first Eskimos (They call themselves Inuit). Her description:

They are rather a short, thickset race with prominent cheekbones, black hair closely shaved on their heads, except their foreheads, and a yellow complexion. Minnie and myself attracted much attention from them. They were dressed in furs and skins.

It was almost impossible to trade with them: a total language barrier existed, and the Inuit had little to trade except blubber and skins.

Here Captain Sam decided to repair the damage. He borrowed two carpenters from *Benjamin Tucker* and a blacksmith from *James Maury,* shifted cargo so that the port bow damage was above water, and began work. But ice began to drift into the little bay, and *Addison,* tipped to starboard, had to get underway. The next day the ice closed in again in a dead calm; the crew climbed out onto the ice and literally hacked a lane through it to open water. Mary notes that there was about an hour between sunset and sunrise: good working conditions for the repairs. On 11 July, after sixteen days, they were finally whale-hunting again.

That same day they saw seventeen ships and brigs, coming south through the strait: there were no whales to be had in the Arctic Ocean, according to one captain.

Two days later Mary writes in her journal:

July 13. The anniversary of our wedding day and *eleven happy years have they been to us. . . . [Caught] a mussel digger, ripsack, devilfish, or California gray. . . .[Eskimos aboard and] Minnie had a grand time running races with the children. . . .Samuel purchased about eighty pounds of walrus teeth and two splendid bearskins of them.*

On the fifteenth Mary reports that Captain Murdoch of *Nassau* took the captain of the French whaler *Napoleon 3rd,* which had been lost in the ice, and his crew off St. Paul Island and put them aboard the *Nil,* a French whaler. On their return the watering party brought Mary back a bouquet of thirty varieties of flowers. She notes that that gray whale made only twenty-five barrels of oil. That is probably why whalemen gave that gentle giant those derogatory names that she mentions.

The competition continued. There were nine ships at anchor in the bay; the weather was too fierce to catch whales. In late July Captain Lawrence decided to try his luck in the Arctic Sea; six other vessels went along. Then fog and a calm descended, followed by the usual gales and snow. Finally, on 12 August they tied onto a bowhead, and then another, which stove a boat in the struggle. But everybody was smiling for a change. On the sixteenth they landed another.

But all was not happiness. Minnie had a cold that settled in her tonsils. One of the whaling captains had become so despondent about his lack of success that he was often delirious from drink. "Another warning to shun the intoxicating cup. He has a son with him about ten years of age. Oh, that his life may be spared," writes Mary.

On the day that Captain Lawrence decided to leave the Arctic (10 August), suddenly the whales showed up, and all around them vessels were capturing whales—and *Addison* caught none. But on the twelfth Mary writes, "Eureka! Eureka.' A bowhead at last." Again "smiles are radiant with pleasure." On the fifteenth they had another, followed by two more. Then their luck changed again; while others were busy, *Addison* chased in vain.

They had a gam with Captain Hallock of *Emerald,* who told them that *Benjamin Tucker* "In taking [one] whale he had a boat stoven and a man killed. Truly, 'in the midst of life are we in death.'" And a French boat crew from *De Hautpoul,* lost in fog, was picked up by Captain Childs of *William Thompson;* otherwise they would probably have died.

Finally on 8 September, relieved, they started out of the Arctic. They made good time through Bering strait, seeing land on the Siberian side frequently. On 17 September, Mary notes, they "saw the comet" (Halley's). The weather moderated to almost a flat calm for days, as they ghosted along on a southerly course. Mary had been making a black silk basque (a close-fitting bodice) for herself. "After much tribulation and some tears on my part and a few scoldings on Samuel's that I did not have it done in port, I have at last completed it to the satisfaction of all concerned."

Finally, beginning on the twenty-fourth, they picked up a good easterly breeze, with heavy seas, and bowled along, even using their studding sails (extra sails on spars attached to the regular yards of the major sails). Mary reports a total of 700 barrels of oil and 10,000 pounds of bone and congratulates *Addison* for doing so well compared to many of their competitors.

By 10 October port preparations are underway: putting away all the heavy winter clothes and getting their port clothes ready. On 13 October the lookout sighted Oahu, and on the fifteenth, off Diamond Head, the pilot came aboard. A number of ships were arriving: *Marengo, John Marshall, Victoria,* and *Majestic.* The Gibbses aboard *Speedwell* also came in. Captain Lawrence went ashore almost at once to find a boarding house during their stay.

As before, the family settled in for a short, enjoyable stay, meeting old friends with whom they had visited during their previous stays and at points all over the Pacific Ocean and the Bering Sea. But to help my audience understand the trials and dangers of the whaling profession, I believe that I have gone far enough.

However, the Lawrences and *Addison* went on for three more cruises in hopes of increasing the oil that they would take home, and it wasn't until the middle of 1860 that they returned to New Bedford. To close this story it seemed appropriate to include the very end of Mary's journal— the last two weeks before arrival.

June 1. The first day of summer at home, but we have had summer for some time . . . .Packed two large baskets today and filled the commode with light articles to take home with it.

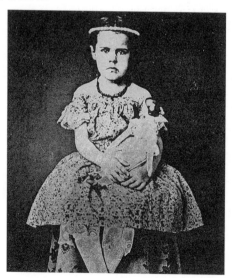

Figure 6-14 Minnie Lawrence with a wreath in her hair, so that she would "look like a Kanaka." *Courtesy of Francis Freeman Jones.*

June 2. Cleaned the after cabin and the water closet today. . . . Also put the medicine chest in shipshape order. . . . Nothing to be seen except gulfweed. . . . Occasionally we get a few pieces for the hogs, hens, and ducks and often find them filled with crabs and very small fish.

    The next few days were filled with further final chores: "I repaired a coat for Mr. Baird and mended our ensign which I think is a disgrace to our country. I have spent a good many hours mending it on this voyage, but it is almost past mending." On 7 June she packed five trunks, a barrel, and two boxes. The next day she cleaned, saying: "Our steward is no hand to clean and takes no interest in making things look nice."

    A tremendous gale and lightning storm, with little thunder, hit them on the ninth. "I never saw such lightning before. The flashes would extend almost entirely around the horizon." And the winds were fickle. That day they made only fifty-five miles by the log. On the eleventh they made only thirty-five miles. "This is a time to cultivate the virtue of patience," she writes. Despite the weak breezes the pilot came aboard at about 9 A.M. on 13 June, and they ghosted into port on the fourteenth. "The pilot could give us very little news," she writes. "Had not a paper on board and did not even know who were the candidates for the presidency."

    Of great importance, of course, was the accounting of the voyage. The standard oil barrel contained 31.5 gallons, and figures for the voyage were 2382 barrels of whale oil, 60 barrels of sperm oil (from at most two whales), and 27,187 pounds of whale bone. This translated into $50,532.79 profit divided among the

Figure 6-15 Captain Samuel Lawrence while he was with the Old Dominion Line, about 1885. *Courtesy of the Falmouth Historical Society.*

Figure 6-16 Mary Lawrence, probably in 1900. *Courtesy of the Falmouth Historical Society.*

officers and crew, 35 3/4% of the total profit. And the total cost of fitting out *Addison* for the trip was $27,654.02. Although these figures are roughly average for such a voyage at that time, the Lawrences were disappointed with them.

At anchor in the Acushnet River, old *Addison,* sails furled for the last time, quickly found herself bereft of crew and cargo. Mary and Minnie went directly to the home of a near relative, George Chipman, in New Bedford. In the almost three years that they had been gone, much had changed. In fashion once, hoop skirts were out, and that cut a large piece out of the whalebone market— although the thriving corset industry was intact. An up-to-date fashionable hat was Mary's first purchase, but Minnie, in her old-fashioned clothes, drew stares. (Yes, even girls' styles changed in three years) The Falmouth green had changed, too. The First Congregational Church, with its Paul Revere bell, had moved to the other side of the green.

The *Barnstable Patriot* did not report the Lawrences' return, but at least Mary discovered that Abraham Lincoln and Stephen Douglas were presidential candidates. In an editorial the *Patriot* predicted dire consequences for the Union if Lincoln were elected.

And they were dire. In 1858 John Brown tried to seize the arsenal at Harper's Ferry. In 1859 the first oil well, in Titusville, Pennsylvania, cast a long shadow over the whaling industry. And in 1861 the states of the South seceded, and the Civil War began at Fort Sumter. That same year the federal government bought a large number of whalers, loaded them with stone (They were called the "Stone Fleet."), and sank them to block the harbor entrances of Charleston and Mobile. Many of them were old friends of the Lawrences'.

Not only that, but the Confederate raiders such as *C. S. S. Florida, Alabama,* and *Shenandoah* prowled the Atlantic and Pacific, destroying whalers in large numbers. *Shenandoah,* unaware of the war's end in 1865, caught the becalmed fleet in the Arctic and burned dozens of vessels after putting the crews on four of the whalers and sending them to San Francisco.

Probably the death blow to the industry occurred in 1871. A fleet of whalers found the Bering Sea ice especially thick. But since they felt that they knew conditions, they followed the summer's retreating ice and began whaling. However, ice came back in and trapped them. Inexorably the ice gripped the ships and squeezed, crushing the wooden hulls. The crews abandoned thirty-four vessels, took to the whaleboats, and made a headlong dash for the few ships outside the ice. Everyone including the wives and their children escaped, but all the ships were lost. Among them was *Awashonks.*

Rerigged as a bark (requiring fewer crewmen) , *Addison* continued whaling throughout the Civil War from 1860 to 1867— a very long voyage indeed. After two more whaling voyages, she "went merchant" and was lost off the Azores in 1875.

Samuel Lawrence continued going to sea, becoming a captain for the Old

Dominion Steamship Line, eventually serving in the company offices ashore. He had moved the family to Brooklyn, where he died "of asthma," at seventy-four. He was buried in the family plot in Falmouth.

Mary, our witty journal-keeper, died in Brooklyn on 3 March 1906 after a long, happy life devoted to her church. Her obituary appeared in the *Falmouth Enterprise* on 10 March 1906:

Mrs. Mary (Chipman) Lawrence, widow of the late Captain Samuel Lawrence, died at her home . . . March 3, age 78 years. Interment was In Oak Grove Cemetery, this town, March 6. She is survived by one daughter, Miss Minnie C. Lawrence, and one brother, William Chipman.

Figure 6-16A Flensing (or cutting in) to remove the thick blanket of blubber from the whale carcass was a most dangerous operation, always done on the starboard side of the ship. These "blankets" were hoisted on deck, to be cut into smaller pieces, which were then melted in huge caldrons for the oil. *From* Maritime Sketches *by Paul Morris, with permission of the author.*

Figure 6-17 The clipper ship *Southern Cross*, burned by a Confederate raider during the Civil War.

Lucy Lord Howes

For many years the East Dennis Wesleyan Methodist Church once a year in July held a special Sunday service called "Old Home Week." In 1942 the theme was "Women Who Went to Sea." One might well be astonished to learn how many women accompanied their men on voyages, bearing children at sea, often sailing with their captains for many years, and given the perils of the age of sail dying with their husbands. A number of women researched the subject and, from just the village of Dennis, arrived at a total of 137 wives at sea, sailing either coastwise or foreign.

One such was Lucy Lord, who in 1860 married Captain Benjamin Perkins Howes. She had no conception of the adventures and perils of going to sea, since she did not come from a sea-faring family. As a matter of course she went with her husband when he became captain of the beautiful clipper *Southern Cross,* which Captain Thomas Prince Howes, also of Dennis, had already taken three times around the world.

When the Civil War began with the firing on Fort Sumter in Charleston, South Carolina, the ship was away from the United States. Captain Howes decided to avoid the Confederate raiders like *Alabama* by staying in foreign trade. That worked for a while, but in July of 1863 the Confederate raider *Florida* caught up with them off the west coast of Mexico.

Captain Howes figured that since his cargo was entirely foreign he would be safe, but to no avail. *Florida* took his cargo as well as Lucy's sea chest contain-

Figure 6-18 The hermaphrodite brig *Lubra*, 318 tons, attacked by pirates on 23 September 1863 off Hong Kong.

ing her trousseau, lovingly handmade. Removing everyone from *Southern Cross,* the Confederates burned their ship. At least they were alive, they thought, as they arrived safely in Brazil. Eventually Lucy and Captain Ben found a ship to return them to Dennis.

The mere fact of a wartime hijacking at sea did not deter Lucy when her husband took command of the bark *Lubra* for a trading voyage to Hong Kong. Having done well, and with a cargo of tea and spices, they sailed on 22 September 1863 for Boston.

One day out, *Lubra*, becalmed, was overtaken by a large number of Chinese pirate craft. There was no way that the ship could defend herself. Some crewmen climbed the rigging trying to escape; others dived overboard. The pirates shot two of those in the rigging and of course captured those in the water. They drove the captain and his wife and child into the cabin, mounting a guard.

After six hour of looting the cargo, one of the pirates entered the cabin and came up to the captain, sitting with his wife and with his child in his arms, and announced that he must die. Leveling the pistol in his hand, he killed him.

After destroying the nautical instruments, they set fire to the bark and left. With great difficulty, led by the first mate, Henry Hall, also of Dennis, the remaining two mates and two seamen put out the f ire and returned to Hong Kong. In Happy Valley Cemetery in Hong Kong are the graves of Captain Benjamin Perkins Howes and his infant daughter Genevieve (Jenny), who had been born six months before in the Hawaiian Islands.

Henry Hall's story deserves telling. Captain Howes, choosing a crew for *Lubra*, chose him for his first mate. Gone to sea early like so many of his peers, he quickly worked up to officer rank. When the pirates attacked, young Henry hid in a barrel and was wounded several times as the pirates thrust their swords between the staves. It was he who navigated the bark back to Hong Kong. Later he testified against the pirates, and they were executed. The whole sea-going fraternity blessed him for it.

Henry returned to Dennis, married, and started a family of three children. But he died in his thirties, possibly weakened by his ordeal. The astounding fact is that when *Lubra* was attacked he was a mere *fifteen years old.*

Lucy Howes, with her daughter Carrie, thanks to a kind offer of another Cape Cod captain, returned to Dennis briefly. But then she moved to Oregon, where Carrie grew up and married a cousin, Charles Wesley Howes.

Figure 6-19 A typical scene of two pirate junks attacking a merchantman. Captain William Sturgis of Barnstable fought off such an attack with cannon; when he returned to Boston, the owners charged him freight for his armament, because he had not told them of his plans. *From Harper's Weekly, 1876.*

Figure 6-20 The fenced graves of Captain William and his daughter Jenny in Hong Kong's Happy Valley Cemetery. *Photo by Jim Carr of Dennis.*

Growing Up at Sea
A Girl's Life

Kate Baker of Harwich spent most of her first twenty-two years at sea, beginning when she was five years old. When she was eighty-one, for her family she put on paper in great detail her recollections of those years. With her girl's eyes she gives us a very different view of what life aboard ship was like in the last quarter of the nineteenth century.

In 1873 Captain James Gorham Baker was in San Francisco with his ship, *Sterling*, waiting for a charter for wheat to Europe. Once before he had taken the family (minus Kate) on a voyage from New Orleans to Le Havre, France, and back to New York. Now it was Kate's turn (with her sister Sue) to travel the oceans of the world.

The transcontinental railroad had only recently been completed, when Mary Doane Baker and her two girls set out from Cape Cod for San Francisco. An arduous trip it was. Even at five, Kate recalls great details: the kindness of the porters in getting milk and food at stations; the stop-over in Omaha; being held up by a washout and having to tramp a long way in the mud to another train; even being held up by a horde of grasshoppers, whose dead bodies made the tracks so slick that the engine could not move.

At Sacramento the Captain met them, and soon they were aboard ship and Liverpool-bound. Kate turned out to have good "sea legs," but her mother and Sue were not so fortunate. School was the first order of business, with their mother as teacher - - and a good one, says Kate.

She had to be quite strict, as there were so many interesting things going on on deck. . . .School began at nine o'clock, just after the morning sight was taken. Mother helped father on that by taking the Greenwich time [from the chronometer] when father called "time." Father took an observation of the sun again at noon. . . .Then the steward rang the bell for dinner. While we ate dinner, the watch below had theirs; then the other watch on deck went below and had theirs. Everything had to go by clockwork and strict discipline was observed in all things.

The girls must have been quite a nuisance to the watches on deck, asking numberless questions as to which "rope" (quickly they learned to say "line") went where, and why. Of course they wanted to climb the rigging— absolutely forbidden. But one day the first mate, Mr. Goodwin, was in the main top, and they persuaded him to pull them up. Lowering a line with a bowline, he pulled Sue up, let her look around, and lowered her. As Kate was half-way up, Captain Baker came on deck, and she was lowered at once. He said, "Go to your rooms until supper," and naturally they went. The mate got a blistering bawling out.

The mates spoiled the girls, making toys such a little cart which, with a little pig for power, gave them rides, bows and arrows, and all sorts of hooks for catching fish and birds. Mr. Goodwin in particular was delighted with them and sang to them. Sometimes when he was on deck, Sue and Kate would go to his room, empty his trunk, and repack it as they thought it should be done. And he never mentioned it.

Livestock of numerous kinds was aboard, and there was milk from goats. On one voyage from Cardiff, England to San Francisco a gentle little Jersey cow gave them fresh milk. In fact, just to say that she had done it, Mrs. Baker made butter off Cape Horn. "Molly" was afraid of storms and would moo piteously; so Captain Baker had a sailor with a lantern sit up with her in her padded stall.

For the first crossing of the Equator they held the ancient ceremony of the arrival of Father Neptune, with his huge wooden razor, to "shave" the "polliwogs" and then dump them into the big tub of water on deck, thus making them "A.B.'s" (able-bodied) seamen. Then the whole crew fooled around until eight bells. By the time Kate grew up, she had been around Cape Horn twenty-one times.

There is never enough water aboard ship, says Kate. The carpenter would dole out just so many quarts per person per day. Once he left the cover off, and a rat fell in. So they boiled all the water thereafter in that tank. When it rained, every possible bucket, spread sails, whatever were used to fill up. Then there was a great washday. The captain's job was to hang out the wash on top of the after house and bring it in when it was dry.

Kate lost her playmate when Sue turned thirteen and left to go to school. She was very lonely, but her much older brother Rufus was second mate, and he helped her by taking pains to be with her during his off-watches; Kate says, "We became very close to one another and real chums."

The itinerary of *Sterling* is typical of merchant ships of that time: in Liverpool, load coal for San Francisco; there load wheat for Cork, in Ireland; from there to London; from there load a cargo of salt for Rangoon, Burma; from there to Baltimore.

The girls were astonished by the strangeness of Rangoon.

We boarded for a while at the so-called best hotel A queer place, all open. . . .It was dirty. We were glad to get back to the ship, under the awnings. A native funeral went by, with much noise and seemingly much pleasure, like the Fourth of July.
We saw the world-famous pagoda covered with gold leaf by natives buying their way into heaven. [At the zoo] a leopard took a dislike to me and tried his best to get at me. . . .[We] learned to like curry. . . .Mother and I just devoured it. The weather was exhausting, and we were glad to start on our way home to Baltimore.

They stayed at home for a while as Captain Baker had a new ship, *Henry Willard,* built for him, in which Kate and her mother made several voyages from San Francisco to Liverpool. Then he had *John Rosenfeld,* a fine, large ship with beautiful appointments. On her Sue, Kate, and her mother sailed to San Francisco, to Liverpool, and back to San Francisco.

Then he went to Washington, D.C. for a load of coal, and en route back the tug towed the ship too close to a rock, and she was lost, along with "all the money he had invested in the ship." After a long dispute over damages, he received only the cost of the tugboat. Kate and her mother lived for a year in a San Francisco apartment while the damage case was being settled. Meanwhile Sue was married to Captain Edward Sewall and went to sea with him in *Solitaire.*

Offered the command of *C.F.Sargent,* in New York, he took the train. At the same time Sue was coming west to join her husband. When the two trains met, Captain Baker persuaded the railroad company to stop the trains, so that he could meet Sue. He found her on her train, to her total surprise, and they had a quick reunion before the trains parted.

Kate's next voyage was in *Kenilworth,* an English-built ship that had burned and was being repaired. Again off they went to Liverpool and then to Calcutta, in India, where for one week the thermometer remained stuck at 120°. Kate had a fine time there.

Peddlers would come on board with their beautiful embroidery. . . .Snake charmers . . .would blow on a pipe Then out would come about a foot of cobra, swaying to the music.

One day a high class native called. He was fine looking . . . in gleaming white robes. We did not appreciate his call as much as we ought to, as we were busy watching a bed-bug on his collar. We were so afraid the bug would fall off! One day the river was worshipped and all beggars had their day. . . .One cannot imagine such fearful loathsome sights. On our return to the ship, our horse dropped dead of the heat.

The river is worshipped; it is also used in many ways: for drinking, washing, washing feet many times a day, and also as a sewer. Natives are always in it bathing.

This was Kate's last voyage. After an uneventful trip home, she and her mother settled down on Cape Cod. Kate missed her travels, but she was aware of her lack of interaction with her peers. Their ships were homes enough, though, with every sort of comfort -- a piano, a sewing machine, books, and games— and no question of housework or cooking!

She wanted to see China, which was the next port after Calcutta. But her mother refused to allow it. She was always sorry that she did not insist, for her father and she were very close. The only times when he punished her — with a rap on the head - was when she was saucy to her mother. This was enough; while the rap did not hurt, she felt guilty.

If her father had completed his last voyage, he would have been around Cape Horn sixty-six times. Only one other captain had beaten that record. Kate sums up his career thus:

He was a popular and successful ship captain, had many friends, was always interested in his officers to help them advance.
Our home on shipboard brought us, I think, closer together than many families. On his last voyage to Honolulu, the ship's cargo of raw sugar took fire. it was smothered and brought under control. The gases of burning sugar entered the cabin and killed father, the first officer, and a young boy. . . The next day he was buried at sea.

CHAPTER 7

Mutinies, Massacres, and Piracy

Privateers or Pirates?

A mere two generations after the founding of the Plimoth Plantation, the colonies became embroiled in a series of wars between the English and the French, and the native peoples, notably the Iroquois, were also drawn in. First there was what was known here as King William's War (1688-1697). The Iroquois were allies of the colonies because they wanted to prevent French expansion from Canada. This was primarily a guerilla war, in which defenseless towns suffered most.

One notable attack was on Oyster River in 1694, the latest of a number of similar attacks. The motive here was a shortage of supplies. And so the French and their native allies nearly wiped out the settlement, killing 104 and capturing twenty-seven others.

After a brief interlude the English and French were at it again in Queen Anne's War (1702-1713). Elizabeth Vickery was on her way to Boston to buy her wedding dress when the packet sloop was taken by a French privateer; the tale of her adventures makes inspiring reading. When the war ended, the French had to give up Hudson's Bay, Acadia, and Newfoundland. And it was thirty-one years before the ancient enemies began what was known here as King George's War. The greatest achievement of the colonies was the taking of the French stronghold of Louisbourg in 1745, the base for French privateers. Peace came in 1748.

The last war before the American Revolution was the French and Indian War, so called, from 1754 to 1763. This time, because of colonial expansion into the Ohio valley, the native peoples were with the French. As a result, finally, even though great atrocities were carried out, the French lost almost all of their American possessions in Canada — and of course the Native Americans were the greatest losers.

The first incident of piracy occurred in 1667, when a sloop captained by William Weeks of the Vineyard went ashore on Pasque Island. Weeks reported to Thomas Mayhew, governor of Martha's Vineyard:

Myselfe and company then went to warm ourselves at an Indian house the
Indians said the Vessell and the goods were theirs, wee answered noe, . . . they
had determined all together we should neither have our vessell or goods, they
would take them.

He then lists everything that the natives removed from his sloop. The list includes
pots and pans, shoes, food, guns, a cloak, and much more. This was too much for
the authorities, who demanded from the sachems full restitution and punishment for
the piracy.

Even the Dutch participated in these depredations. One captain ran into
Tarpaulin Cove, on Naushon, and captured four ketches in retaliation for loss of his
vessel. When he landed with them in New York, the authorities (New Amsterdam
was now New York) confiscated the ketches and returned them to their owners.

As the colonies up and down the coast developed, a growing, active maritime trade grew up. And so also did the attractions of piracy, for both ships and
cargoes were growing larger and more profitable. In fact, by the 1680's there were
many pirates operating in these waters, as well as in the West Indies, where many
pirates had their bases. And with the British navy fighting the French, there was
little maritime law enforcement.

As a partial solution the British approved issuance by colonial governors
and others of "letters of marque," allowing privately owned ships to arm and capture enemy shipping, to be rewarded by a share of the value of ships and cargoes.
Combine them with pirates, and making a living at sea becomes quite hazardous. Of
course, the French too had their privateers skulking along our coasts.

A favorite and strategic spot was Tarpaulin Cove on Naushon. There was
a good inn and a private lighthouse, and a lookout on higher ground had a fifteen-
mile range in either direction. In 1689 Thomas Hawkins and Thomas Pound decided that piracy would be very profitable, and so launched a short and busy career
in these waters.

Another example is the case of the French privateer in 1604. On 7 September word of a French vessel in Vineyard Sound came to Providence, Rhode Island.
Governor Cranston immediately sent out two sloops, commanded by the Wanton
brothers, to find and capture him. On Monday, 8 September, John Wanton found his
quarry and attacked at once, although outgunned. The battle was a draw until
brother William arrived, and the Frenchman hauled down his ensign, having lost the
captain and three men and three or four wounded. The captured sloop arrived in
Newport the ninth, where it was discovered that she had ravaged Block Island in
August and had taken four prizes, two fishermen and two coasters.

In 1711 another French privateer was active in Vineyard Sound. On 4
August she chased a vessel ashore and on the ninth and tenth she took three coasters. Newport responded quickly, and two heavily armed sloops went looking for
her. On 13 August they spotted a sail off Block Island and set out after her, chasing

her for the next two days until, too swift for them, she escaped and they returned to Newport.

A curious sort of piracy occurred in 1721, when Benjamin Norton and Joseph Whipple fitted out a brigantine for trading in the Indies. She was taken by "One Roberts, a pirate," who then captured a Dutch ship with a rich cargo of "Sugars, Cocoa, Negroes, etc." and sailed up to Tarpaulin Cove, intending to sell the cargo. While there he fired at and took two coasters as well and then sent the cargo in sloops to Newport for sale. But someone leaked this secret proceeding, and Customs seized the cargo and later the ship, Captain Benjamin Norton having disappeared.

Even the most notorious of all pirates, Captain William Kidd, came to grief in these water. A Scot, born in Dundee in 1654, in 1689 he participated as a privateer in several attacks in the Indies on pirate bases. But, supposedly, that year his crew, many of them ex-pirates, took over the ship, putting him ashore. In 1691 in New York he married; his license describes him as "William Kidd, Gentleman."

Then in 1695 a privateering voyage in the *Adventure Galley,* 34 guns, 70 men, was planned. Participating as shareholders were a lord, the first lord of the admiralty, the lord keeper of the great seal, the secretary of state, the master general of ordnance, and the king himself, who was to receive a tenth of the profits of the venture— a most distinguished lot.

Sailing from England in April 1696, he recruited another eighty-five men in New York and headed for the East Indies. Kidd later claimed that his men forced him into piracy; whatever the case, soon complaints from the East India Company declared him a pirate. By 1699 Kidd was in New England waters, dropping in to Newport briefly and then going on to Boston with a captured sloop; it was then that he claimed to having been forced by his crew into piracy. But before that he stopped at Gardner's Island, off New London, and transferred to another vessel two heavy chests of unknown contents (treasure?), dropped off more at Orient Point on Long Island, and more at Tarpaulin Cove, en route to Boston.

On 8 July 1699 Lord Bellomont, the governor, reported that he had had Kidd and five or six of his crew arrested and imprisoned, despite his profession of innocence, with many witnesses. Bellomont was not impressed, even though he had written Kidd a letter:

. . . *inviteing him to come in, and that I would procure a pardon for him, provided he were as innocent as Mr. Emot [a friend from New York] said he was. . . . But I quickly found sufficient cause to suspect him very guilty, by the many lyes and Contradictions he told me.*

Lord Bellomont also wanted most eagerly to know about one of Kidd's prizes, the *Quidah Merchant,* left in a creek in Hispaniola, loaded with some £30,000 worth of goods.

The final irony for William Kidd was that Massachusetts had no law against piracy; so the authorities illegally shipped him to England, where he was well and truly tried on multiple charges of piracy and "hanged by the neck until dead."

But the story is not yet over. On 10 July 1699 a crewman of Kidd's, Gabriel Loffe, in a deposition gave a good picture of Kidd's career. After he joined the ship in 1696, they sailed to Madeira, Bonavista, St. Jago (John?), Madagascar, Joanna (Genoa), and Mahilla (Manila), "to cruise for pirates," he says. Off India took a Dutch ship and later an English ship "of 450 tons, Capt. Wright an Englishman from Bengal . . . laden with silks and other dry goods . . . divided among Kidd's crew."

Then they took the *Quidah Merchant,* a large Mocha (Indian) frigate and with her sailed to the Caribbean. "Then he ran his Galley on shore, being leaky, stript and burned her at St. Mary's." At Anguilla in the Antilles they were proclaimed pirates; forbidden entrance at St. Thomas, he abandoned the *Quidah Merchant* in Hispaniola, and in a sloop he bought sailed north, hiding his goods here and there as he went along to Boston.

One chapter of Captain Kidd's story remains to be told: the extent of his pillaging. On 25 July 1699 a list was made by court order; it is impressive, even in an abbreviated version:

In Capt Kids Box	*Gold oz.*	*Sil.oz.*
One Bagg silver bars		*357*
One Bagg Bons pieces of silver		*442 1/2*
One Bagg Bons pieces of silver		*421*
(assorted diamonds and gold]		
Found in Mr Duncam		
Campbell's house		
No 1 One box qt. gold	*58 1/2*	
2 One box qt.	*94*	
(four more boxes)	*211*	
7 One box silver	*203*	
In Capt. Wm. Kid's chest		
(assorted jewels: 82 rubies,		
67 emeralds, silver rings, etc.]		
6 one bagbroken silver		*173 1/2*

[bags of gold bars, dust]   *651*

[bags of siver bars]   *521*

      And that is all that anyone has found of Captain William Kidd's hoard. What happened to the *Quidah Merchant* and her £30,000 will never be known.

      These examples are but a fraction of the privateer/pirate activity taking place in Vineyard Sound, Buzzards Bay, and Nantucket Sound. And after 1775 the British navy and privateers virtually bottled up the whole area, so that the islands especially suffered drastic shortages of food and other necessities. In addition, regular forays upon the livestock of the islands by the British further deepened the critical situation of the islands .

Figure 7-1A A favorite haunt of the pirates of the 18th century was the Caribbean. Several ports in the West Indies were known as pirate rendezvous. Here, a pirate schooner (note the "skull and crossbones" at the masthead) is overtaking a merchant brig, preparatory to looting the cargo and taking the ship to expand their operations, as did Captain Kidd and our own Black Bellamy. *From* Mercantile Sketches *by Paul C. Morris, with permission of the author.*

Captured by Pirates

Warren Lincoln, born in Brewster, was twelve years old when the brig *Iris*, in which he was cabin boy, was taken by pirates. Many years later he wrote in full the story of that horrifying experience.

They sailed from Boston on 1 November 1822, with Captain Freeman Mayo in command. Naturally, for the first three days he was pretty seasick and homesick, since this was his first voyage. On about 20 November, past the Bahamas, he was called at sunrise to tidy up the cabin, set the table, and after breakfast to clear away the dishes and wash them. As he came on deck he heard the first mate say to the helmsman, "They may be pirates," referring to two vessels coming toward them. Cuba was about thirty miles away.

Called on deck, the captain trained his spyglass on them.

Damn 'em, they are pirates! Call all hands on deck . . . ; square the yards, set the foretopmast studding sail; bear a hand!

But there was little wind, and the pirates were rowing their boat faster than the *Iris* could sail. After several cannon balls flew toward the brig, the captain felt it prudent to heave to and wait to be boarded. Young Warren hid his entire fortune of three dollars and some cents in the boatswain's locker.

The pirates, in white duck jackets and trousers (a sort of uniform), crowded the deck of the overtaking craft, which soon was alongside with its twenty-four-pounder (referring to the weight of the cannon ball) on a swivel and several smaller cannons. Six of them swarmed up the gangway ladder. The leader asked about the cargo and spare provisions, saying, "We are a privateer cruising after pirates; have you seen any?" The captain replied, "I might spare you some beef, pork, etc." The pirate lieutenant then told Captain Mayo to stand in for the land, and disappeared into the cabin, reappearing in the captain's best suit. He admitted that they were indeed pirates.

Next, of course, the pirates began ransacking the brig for food and drink. They found a wheel of cheese, hacked it to pieces with their swords, and, having found the keg of rum, started to work on it. Meanwhile the *Iris*, under orders, worked its way along the Cuban coast. When the pirate vessel took off after another victim, the captain and crew planned to overwhelm the careless six pirates on deck, take their weapons, and retake the ship. But the pirates herded the eleven-man crew into the forecastle and locked them in.

When the crew was released, they were sure that they would all be killed. But the freebooters wanted to know where any valuables were. Young Warren Lincoln was threatened with death unless he told. Fearful, he produced his wallet with its three dollars. After a final threat to throw the boy overboard, the pirate let him go. Finally that night they anchored in Matanzas, Cuba, and the pirates stripped everything of value from the brig, fighting over the spoils.

Next morning they sailed to a nearby bay, the pirates' rendezvous. The pirates removed their cargo of axes and nails, and then the pirate leader told his lieutenant (in Spanish) to kill everyone if he found no money in two hours. Captain Mayo told the pirate that there was no money, but if he were let go to Matanzas he could return with whatever the pirate wanted. The leader replied: "Well, you may go to Matanzas. I give you three days, and bring me $6000; if you are not back on the third day, I will kill your crew and burn the *Iris*."

"I shall come back, whether I have the money or not," were the captain's departing words.

Desperately Captain Mayo made the rounds of the port. The governor was not interested; the merchants reluctantly produced some $3000. The American ships in port mustered thirty volunteers to try to recapture the brig, but they were not considered a sufficient force against the pirate stronghold. On the third day he again tried to raise more money— to no avail.

As he was about to leave, the U.S. Navy schooner *Alligator*, with fourteen guns, sailed into the harbor, and Captain Mayo at once went aboard to explain his situation. With the captain as pilot, Lieutenant Allen sailed to the rendezvous, where they found three prizes taken by the pirates and a pirate schooner.

Meanwhile, things were quiet until the morning of the third day, when all hands were locked belowdecks and all the pirates left *Iris*. Pretty soon Crosby, the second mate forced a door and saw the pirate schooner and three boats heading out. The crew all came out on deck, to hear cannon and musket fire around the point.

Then around the corner came a longboat, captured from the *Alligator* by the pirates. They boarded the brig and began attacking the crew, wounding them all. Warren had hidden, but had to come out to find six men waving swords and threatening to kill him. They ordered him to find powder and fire, to burn the brig, but he swore there was none.

The pirates ordered the crew into their longboat, with one pirate at the tiller. Crosby, badly wounded, suddenly leaped at the steersman and threw him overboard, just before the rest of the pirates were about to climb down into the boat. Aiming a musket at the pirates above, he shoved off, and they rowed toward shore. Landing on the point, they hauled up the boat and ran into the bushes.

Crosby, in command, had the crew relaunch the boat; hugging the shoreline, they rowed, wounded as they were, for Matanzas, some thirty miles away. They arrived after dark, were challenged by the sentry on *Alligator*, and were welcomed aboard by their captain, who dressed their wounds.

The experiences of the Navy crew in the battle were harrowing. Lieutenant Allen was killed on his own deck; the two boats chasing the pirates captured one but then drew off with three men wounded. The other pirate vessels escaped.

That afternoon Captain Mayo went aboard his ship, to find it deserted.

Fearing that all were dead, the Navy crew rounded up all the vessels there and returned to Matanzas with Lieutenant Allen's body. And Captain Mayo was astonished to find his entire crew, less one, waiting on shore.

Lieutenant Dale, who had led the boats, now in command, took all the ships' papers and sailed for Charleston, S.C., to settle salvage rights with the government. On the second night out *Alligator,* ran onto a reef off Florida and was lost with all hands. When *Iris* reached Charleston, Captain Mayo bought a musket and a sword for each man in the crew. Loading a new cargo, they sailed for New Orleans under convoy of the U.S. brig *Belvidere*, arriving on 1 February 1828.

Because of the death of Lieutenant Allen, the Navy sent quite a fleet of vessels into the Caribbean and along the Cuban coast and effectively ended piracy.

Warren Lincoln, growing up at sea, became a captain in his turn, commanding the brig *Draco* and the bark *Mary.* On one voyage he took his vessel through the Straits of Magellan, a daring thing to do at that time, for the passage is narrow and dangerous. Because of ill health he left the sea at thirty-five and returned to Brewster, where he opened a grocery business and general store. He died at age eighty-nine.

Figure 7-1 Steamboat Wharf in Nantucket in 1832. At the wharf are the *Telegraph* and *Massachusetts*. The whaler *Lexington* is laid up and the packet sloop *Tawtemo* is about to round Brant Point (far left with lighthouse), headed for Cape Cod. *Courtesy of Paul Morris, the artist.*

The Globe *Mutiny*

Alexander Starbuck describes this event as the "most diabolic affair that ever occurred on board of any whaleship." It was just that.

The *Globe*, Thomas Worth, master, sailed from Nantucket on 20 December 1822, to go a-whaling in the Pacific. Aboard as one of the boatsteerers was Samuel Comstock, born on the island, who became leader of the mutineers. His brother, William, later published a complete story of the horrors, from which this account is taken. Five men deserted in Oahu, and six replacements who were the sweepings of the Honolulu waterfront came aboard.

A little less than a month later *Globe* was cruising in company with another whaler and exchanging visits. Captain Worth had punished a crewman that day. One of the new men was overheard saying that this was "the last time Worth would flog one of the crew." One might wonder if already there was some plot to take the ship.

There was. Comstock had nursed several grievances against the officers. For instance, he had challenged Third Mate Fisher in wrestling, and Fisher had easily bested him. Second Mate Lumbard had done him no harm and had six children at home; the captain had shown him every favor on the voyage. But he went berserk.

Figure 7-2 The early steamboat *Telegraph*, built in 1832, by an unknown artist. *Courtesy of Peabody Essex Museum, Salem.*

As a result that night during Comstock's watch the murders began. He gave Silas Payne a boarding knife, and he had an axe. They would kill the captain and first mate; two others were detailed to take care of the second and third mates. The axe served to butcher the captain, and then Comstock help dispatch First Mate Beetle.

Then, taking two muskets he went into the cabin again. Lumbard asked him if he was going to shoot him; he replied, "I guess not." A struggle over the guns ended when Third Mate Fisher captured one and pointed the bayonet at Comstock's heart. Samuel said that he would be spared if he gave him the gun. Fisher complied,

Figure 7-3 A whaleship outfitting at Straight Wharf for another cruise, about 1850. *Courtesy of Paul Morris, the artist.*

and Comstock immediately ran the bayonet through Lumbard's body. Then it was Fisher's turn to die. Turning his back, the mate said, "If there is no hope, I will at least die like a man." Comstock shot him in the back of the head with a pistol.

Another Comstock brother, George, who had not joined the mutiny, was appointed steward. Later he reported seeing Humphries, a black, loading a pistol. Quickly a kangaroo court found Humphries guilty and hanged him from a yardarm; cut down, his body was dropped into the sea.

On 7 February they sighted the King's Mill Islands and landed on Mili, an island in the Mulgraves. According to William Comstock, his brother's plan was:

. . . to establish himself on one of the Pacific Isles—to . . . induce them to elect him their King— and to live a daring and dreaded outlaw in his adopted clime.

A week later he and John Payne quarreled as Comstock attempted to win over the natives and planned to scuttle the ship. But Payne and the other mutineers decided to kill him, and on 17 February they did so, burying him in the sand.

Now in command, Payne detailed six men under Gilbert Smith to man the ship. Smith's plan was to take her— and so they did. After a long voyage they landed in Valparaiso and were put in irons aboard a ship. A Captain York took the *Globe* back to Nantucket arriving on 21 November 1824, almost two years after she had started the fated voyage.

Furious at the loss of the ship, Payne began fitting the boats he had for ocean travel. Exploring, they came back with two women for their "wives." One escaped, was captured, and was badly beaten for daring to leave. Here began the trouble with the natives.

Next morning they discovered that tools had been stolen from their chest. Enraged, Payne told the natives that the tools must be returned. One man brought back half a chisel. Incensed, Payne put the man in irons and told him he must point out the thieves. Then he armed Coffin, Jones, Hussey, and Lilliston with muskets (but no musket balls), marched to the village, and made the prisoner point out the thief.

Recovering the hatchet, suddenly they were attacked with stones, and Rowland Jones was killed. As they retreated to the tent, the natives followed, ready for war, first tearing one of the boats apart. Then Payne bravely walked into the crowd and conferred with the chiefs.

Returning to the tent, Payne announced the deal he had made with the chiefs. They would be given everything belonging to the whites, and the mutineers would live with the natives and be governed by their chiefs. It would seem that he had been infected by Comstock's dream. Looting began immediately. One old couple, whom William Lay had befriended, took hold of him and led him away from the tent. Perhaps they knew what was to happen next.

Suddenly the natives struck. Another wholesale slaughter wiped out almost every white man. An old woman killed Worth with a spear. Lilliston and Brown (a Sandwich Islander) died within feet of where Lay was being covered by the bodies of the old couple.

When it was over, only Lay and his friend Cyrus Hussey, claimed by another couple, were alive. Allowed to bury their former shipmates, each was allowed to take a blanket, some food, and a Bible. Separated on different islands, they became slaves of the couples who had protected them.

Two and a half years later, on 23 November 1825, Lay heard shouting: a ship had anchored off the island. The natives were planning to board her and kill the crew. Afraid that Lay would betray their plan, they would not let Lay come with them to the beach. A boat from the schooner landed, with armed men, but at night they rowed back to the vessel. It was Lieutenant John Percival's *Dolphin* sent to find the mutineers and bring them to justice.

Searching about for Lay, who had been moved to the far end of the island, by chance, probably, *Dolphin* arrived off Lay's hideout and sent a boat in on the 29th. Lay offered to help persuade the boat crew to come ashore; the natives finally agreed. At water's edge he called to the boat, telling them of the planned attack.

Lieutenant Hiram Paulding, in charge of the boat, landed with his thirteen armed men in the face of several hundred armed and angry natives. Walking up to Lay, he grabbed him and, covering his own body with his prisoner, with a cocked pistol at Lay's ear he marched him to the boat to the utter surprise of the natives—and rowed away with the prisoner. It was a daring, courageous act.

Once freed, Lay told Lieutenant Paulding that his friend Hussey was being held on another island. Forthwith the launch sailed there, only to find that the natives had hidden him. Paulding uttered dire threats of punishment unless they returned him, and the two survivors of the massacre were reunited.

Quickly Percival, using Lay as an interpreter, called a meeting of chiefs on 1 December, on threat of extermination. He told the chiefs that the massacre was taboo among civilized nations and that further such acts would bring horrible punishments.

Then he rewarded the two couples who had protected Lay and Hussey and gave each chief three tomahawks, an axe, beads, and handkerchiefs. In addition he left two hogs and two cats as future food sources, and he planted potatoes, corn, pumpkins, and other seeds, leaving instructions as to how to care for them. Thus he tried to greatly increase the food available on the atoll— mainly fish and coconuts.

Setting sail shortly, *Dolphin* cruised through the islands until 9 December and then headed for the Sandwich Islands (Hawaii) arriving at "Woahoo" (Oahu) on 16 December. Leaving Honolulu on 11 May 1826 and exploring several islands en route, mapping their locations, they arrived in Valparaiso, Chile, on 23 July. Percival and Paulding were convinced that neither Lay nor Hussey had shared in the mutiny, and they so informed Commodore Hull there. The two survivors returned home in Hull's *United States*, arriving in New York on 21 April 1827, four and a half years after the start of the *Globe's* disastrous voyage.

They published their own account of their adventures in 1828, expressing the greatest admiration for their rescuers. In the fashion of the day they entitled it: *A Narrative of the Mutiny on Board the Ship "Globe" of Nantucket [etc-].* . . . And Hiram Paulding also published his journal, entitled *Journal of a Cruise of the United States Schooner Dolphin Among the Islands of the Pacific Ocean and a Visit to the Mulgrave Islands in Pursuit of the Mutineers of the Whaleship Globe.*

The six men who stole the *Globe* and sailed her to South America were also not tried for mutiny.

Figure 7-4 Lieutenant John Percival, U.S.N. in *U.S.S. Dolphin*, assigned to hunt down the mutineers, finally found two innocent survivors in the Marshall Islands in 1826. *Courtesy of the Greenwich Publishing Company.*

Figure 7-5 Figurehead of the *Awashonks*, built in Falmouth in 1830, named for the female sachem of the Sakonnet tribe, who sided with the colonists during the bloody King Philip's War. *Courtesy of the New Bedford Whaling Museum.*

The Awashonks *Massacre*

Thanks to his firsthand account we have an extremely graphic account of one of the bloodiest massacres aboard ship in the literature. Captain Silas Jones, born in Falmouth in 1814, lived to tell the tale. Going to sea at thirteen as steward in the brig *Brunette*, he first met *Awashonks* (the name of a local sachem), Captain Obed Swain, on 6 November 1830, when he joined her as a sailor on a whaling voyage. She was a fine vessel, 341 tons, built of live oak and copper fastened, valued at $48,000 with her gear. Quickly he was named boat-steerer, a most responsible position, and at the end of the voyage the captain recommended him for second mate.

On 28 December 1833 as third mate under Captain Coffin he began his second voyage in *Awashonks*— a voyage to disaster. As for sperm whales, it was a most unsuccessful trip. By May 1835 they left Tahiti on a last attempt at finding oil. In three months they had 400 barrels of oil in the hold. Sailing through the various island groups, they became used to having natives aboard for trading. At the King Mills (King's Mill) Islands they took three whales, and then the wind died. The natives paddled out in great numbers— perhaps a hundred aboard at one time— but all they wanted was food.

On 5 October they were near Baring's Island, supposedly uninhabited, five degrees above the equator. But they found out otherwise. Three canoes of natives came out to the ship and were permitted aboard, the chief leading. Silas Jones describes him thus:

. . . He was decorated with a string of teeth of some fish which he wore around his neck . . . and the lobes of his ears [were] extended to two inches in diam-

eter, in which was placed . . . a roll of plantain leaf. . . . Around his loins he wore a string of grass. . . .The other men were in precisely the same dress with which nature had clothed them.

It being time for dinner, the captain and the mates went below, as did the crew, leaving only Silas and the helmsman on deck. Soon more canoes came out, until some thirty natives were aboard. Dinner over, the captain and mates came on deck, to see the natives admiring the wickedly sharp cutting spades, some fourteen in number. Triangular in shape, the blades attach to fifteen-foot poles and are used to cut up whales alongside the ship.

Then Silas saw several men bringing their war clubs aboard. He managed to wrestle one away, but then he saw the natives making a concerted rush for the spades, and was able to grab one himself. But two natives seized the other end of the shaft and he escaped by hitting one of them hard in the face and jumping into the lower deck of the forehold. There he found four seamen trying to organize a defense. Making a dash for the cabin, they armed themselves with a pair of large pistols, located spare powder and shot, and made a stand. Five or six natives had gathered at the gangway with spades, so they fired into their midst several times, driving them off. A fourth sailor, Lewis, came into the cabin, having had his knee joint cut by a spade. He had been the masthead lookout and eluded the natives by jumping from the rigging, receiving a severe rupture. But he fought on with no indication of pain.

Armed with two pistols, four muskets, and two boarding knives, they were ready for a foray onto the deck when a fifth man, Daniel Wood, made it to the cabin, bleeding from spade wounds. He reported that the captain and first mate had been killed.

From the cabin they could tell that a native was trying to steer the ship, even though there was no wind. Firing several times through the ceiling of the cabin, they decided that they had hit the native there, who it later appeared was the chief. Gaining the deck, the three able men fired several times, and the natives all dived into the water, regaining their canoes and paddling away.

Now that the battle was over, they discovered that the second mate and three seamen had dived overboard and been killed in the water. In addition a boatsteerer named Perkins, who was aloft, took command and braced the main yard and by cutting lines gained some headway on the ship.

Now this twenty-one-year-old third mate was in command. The first problem was caring for the wounded. Six men had died, and of the seven wounded Silas Jones felt that four would survive. One man had had a branch of his jugular vein cut, and after they finally stanched the blood, Silas repaired the cut with his needle. They buried their dead that day in the time-honored way, committing their bodies to the sea.

Silas felt that Lewis's leg should be amputated at once, but he declined,

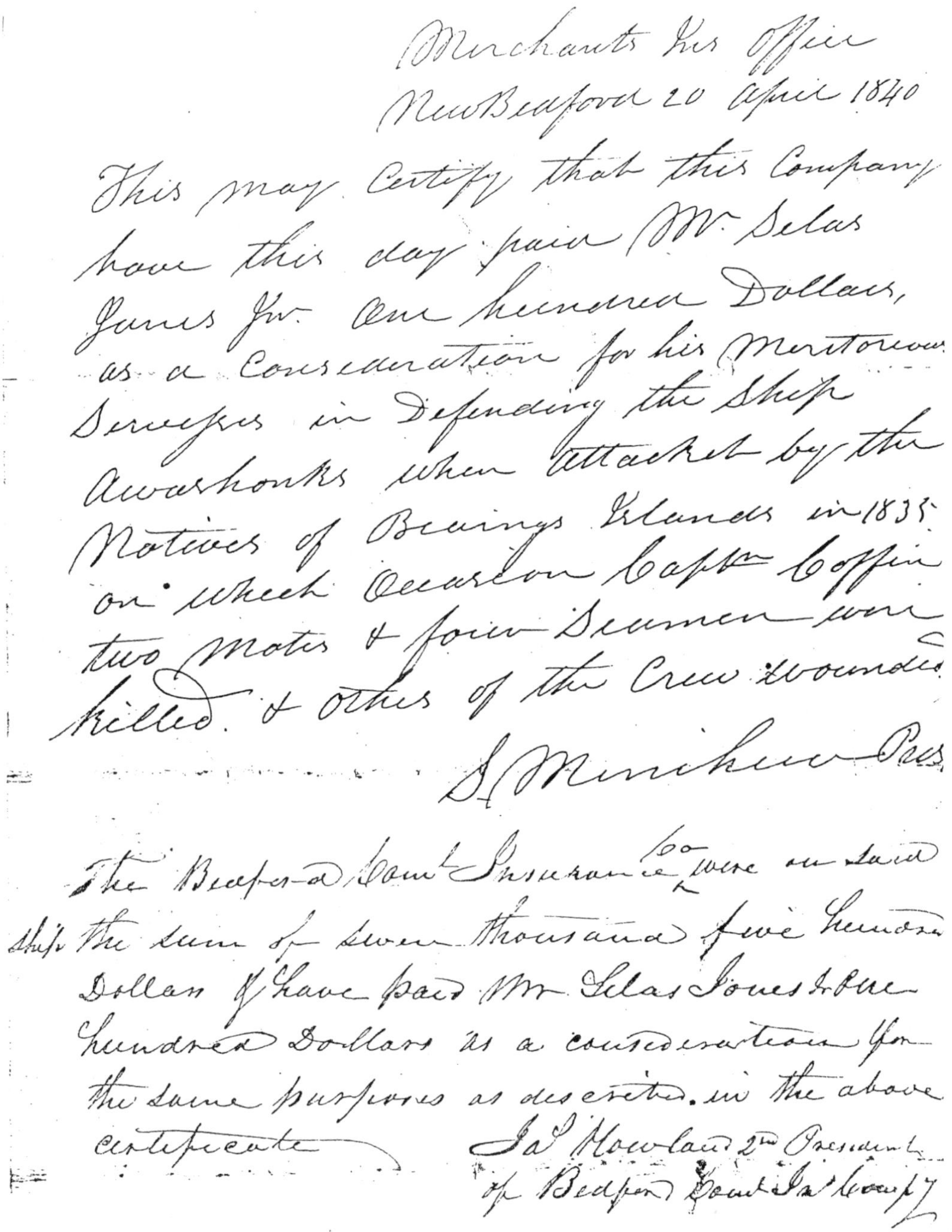

Merchants Ins Office
New Bedford 20 April 1840

This may Certify that this Company have this day paid Mr. Silas Jones Jr. One hundred Dollars, as a Consideration for his Meritorious Services in Defending the Ship Awashonks when attacked by the Natives of Bearings Islands in 1835 on which Occasion Captn Coffin two Mates & four Seamen were killed. & others of the Crew wounded.

S. Minihew Pres.

The Bedford Coml Insurance Co were on said Ship the sum of seven thousand five hundred Dollars & have paid Mr Silas Jones & One hundred Dollars as a consideration for the same purposes as described in the above Certificate

Jas Howland 2nd President of Bedford Coml Ins. Comp.y

Figure 7-6 Certificate of payment on 20 April 1840 to third mate Silas Jones of $100 (a huge amount then) "for his Meritorious Services in Defending the Ship *Awashonks* when Attacked by the Natives of Bearings [sic] Island in 1835 on which Occasion Captn Coffin, two Mates & four Seamen were killed & Others of the crew were wounded." *Courtesy of the Falmouth Historical Society.*

preferring to wait until they reached the Sandwich (Hawaiian) Islands and a surgeon. He died forty days after being wounded. In the case of Wood, Silas decided that the only treatment for a suppurating wound in his back was cauterization. Tying him down, he applied a red-hot iron to the wound; Wood screamed and writhed, and soon he recovered.

After passing several more island groups, and fending off all contact with canoes full of natives, the *Awashonks* arrived in Honolulu on 25 November 1835. Thus ended Silas Jones's first command.

But he was not through with the sea. In 1840 he took command of the *Hobomok* at twenty-six, the youngest whaling captain. And after spending some twenty-five years at sea, in his retirement he served his town of Falmouth and his church in many ways: as a representative to the General Court, and as president of the Falmouth National Bank (among other positions) until his death in 1896.

This account of Silas Jones's ordeal is taken from his verbatim report of the massacre; it was provided by the captain's daughter, Ellen M. Jones of Los Angeles, California.

Awashonks sailed on under a series of captains. A forty-year-old, well past normal retirement, she found herself, with thirty-one other whalers, caught in pack ice in Bering Strait. Slowly the ice crushed the vessels, and the crews seemed doomed. But with great skill they hauled their whaleboats to open water and sailed to freedom, leaving the hulks to the mercies of the ice. Other luckier (or warier) whalers outside the ice took them in, in the tradition of mutual assistance that had existed almost since deepsea whaling began.

Figure 7-7 Captain Silas Jones, veteran of twenty-five years at sea. *Courtesy of the Falmouth Historical Society.*

Figure 7-8 *Awashonks* sailed on, a forty-one-year-old, until her end in pack ice in September 1861, along with thirty other whalers. From one of a series of paintings originally by Benjamin Russell. *Courtesy of the Falmouth Historical Society.*

Figure 7-9 Forced to abandon their crushed ships, all the crews took to their whaleboats and sailed to safety with other more fortunate whalers. *Courtesy of the Bishop Museum, Honolulu.*

The Oeno Massacre
One Man Survived

Whalers well knew the hazards of stopping at unknown islands in the Pacific for water or provisions; an inadvertent visit that was caused by a wreck was quite another matter. The literature of whaling contains stories of a number of disasters in which whalers were murdered by natives.

One of the worst was the case of the Nantucket whaler *Oeno*, of 328 tons, captained by Captain Samuel Riddell. On 4 November 1824 she sailed for the Pacific whaling grounds via the Cape of Good Hope, at the southern tip of Africa. And that was the last that anyone knew of her for almost six years.

In 1830 Aaron Mitchell, the owner, received a letter from William Cary, a crewman, telling of the wreck on Turtle Island and the massacre of the entire ship's company except himself. He was living with the natives on the island. This is his report of what happened.

On 25 March 1825, after a voyage of almost five months, *Oeno* arrived at the Bay of Islands, where two seamen deserted and two English seamen and a native boy replaced them. By 13 April they were among the Friendly Islands. As dark descended Captain Riddell had sail shortened and gave strict orders for a sharp lookout. He was to be called immediately if anything untoward occurred.

At about 2:00 A.M. the helmsman (whose view ahead was heavily obscured) reported seeing white water ahead. Where the lookout was — or what he was doing— is not mentioned. He received no reply. So he called again, perhaps waking the mate, and almost at once *Oeno* piled up on a coral reef. "All hands on deck!" was the cry, but even then waves were crashing across the deck. Clearly, the ship was lost.

The second mate, Drew, was able to launch his boat despite the rough seas, and he and his boat crew found a way inside the reef. After daybreak the other two boats also found shelter there. About nine miles away inside the circular reef, they could see an island. After rowing to it, they saw a man showing them where to land. On the beach were natives "making hostile demonstrations," says our narrator.

The captain did not want to land, suggesting that the boats sail to Wallis Island, a frequent stopping place for whalers. But the first mate, Shaw, maintained that the natives were not hostile and that what seemed to be clubs were sticks of sugar cane. He urged that they land and refit, and when the weather calmed down they could take what they wanted from the ship; then they could go wherever they chose. The captain acceded to those arguments, and they landed.

The captain jumped out and held out his hand; there was no response, but the natives all ran toward the boats, helped beach them, and were permitted to take whatever they wanted from the boats. In return they gave the crew such food as was available. Captain Sam's ticking watch was an object of astonishment and fear to the chief. After trying to show how it worked, he gave it to the chief, who was delighted to have it.

Indicating that the whalers should follow him, he led them to their village housing some fifteen men and boys and ten women. Built on stilts, the houses had heavy thatch roofs and sides of reeds sewn together with coconut fibers. Quickly the crew sat down to a hearty meal. They soon learned that this coral island produced bananas, breadfruit, and coconuts and that the main diet was fish. The only water fell as rain.

Eventually, after an evening of local dancing, the ship's crew lay down on mats in a house to sleep, planning to go out to the ship in the morning. But when they arrived they found that during the night the natives had taken all the firearms and whatever else they wanted. Otherwise, for the next ten days all was peaceful, and the crew was about to add height to the gunwales of the boats when some twenty canoes appeared carrying some eighty men.

Large men, many six feet tall, they were all hideously painted and armed with clubs and spears. The captain met them on the beach, and at first they seemed peaceable enough. But on the second day they turned belligerent and began to take whatever they fancied. Cary says:

Captain Riddell . . . [advised] us not to use force and let them take everything they wanted, and gave his advice for our good as well as his own, as we were without arms and wholly at the mercy of the savages. Well would it have been for the crew had they heeded the advice of our worthy Captain.

Figure 7-10 "The Spermaceti Whale" being attacked by a whaleboat, as envisioned in an 1840 book on natural history. *Courtesy of the Bishop Museum, Honolulu.*

The tension grew, so that most of the crew believed that they would be attacked soon. Everyone but Cary slept in the house; he found a cave and hid there. One of the friendly natives threw a few spears into the house during the night so that the Americans would have some little defense.

The next morning there was a great uproar in the valley below the village. All of the whalers except Cary ran down to see what was the matter; Cary stayed in his cave, and after the noise died down he went to the beach to find signs of a great struggle and found two of his shipmates in a shallow grave; the rest had vanished.

A day later, he was caught away from his cave, and the old chief "adopted" him. Some while later he became the property of a more powerful English-speaking chief from another island, and the *Oeno's* hosts had to give up all that they had looted from the ship. The intruders took him with them to their island and later to Ambow, where he spent seven months. There he had a strange encounter, meeting a canoe with a white man on board. He says:

As they came alongside our canoe the white man reached out his hand and addressed me by name. I was dumb with astonishment. At last he said, "Don't you know David Whippey?" "Yes," I answered, "I formerly knew him. He was a townsman of mine and an old playmate." "Well," said he, "I am that David Whippey."

Figure 7-11 A typical whaler, *Morning Star*, overhauling gear. Note the men on the main foresail yard and the bowsprit. All boats have been removed from the ship's davits. *Care of Barry Homer, South Yarmouth.*

(Whippey had been left there by his captain a year earlier to collect turtle shell, but the ship never came. So Whippey, a favorite of the king, decided to stay on.)

Moving to another island, Raver, in October 1827 Cary finally made contact with the ship *Clay,* which had stopped there for sandalwood and *beche de mer* (a sea cucumber, a great delicacy in the Orient). The two stranded men were hired by Captain Benjamin Vandeford to interpret and help amass a cargo while cruising in the Pacific islands. Then Cary returned to the island and wrote to the *Oeno's* owner of the tragedy, sending the letter via *Clay* while he continued to gather sea cucumbers.

On the *Clay's* next trip, he went along to Manila, where he signed on *Glide* for a while. In March 1831 she was wrecked, but the crew was safe. Finally, after various changes of ship, he shipped aboard the ship *Tybee* of Salem, and on 31 October 1833 he reached Nantucket, nine years after he sailed aboard *Oeno*.

CHAPTER
8

Making a Living

Early Whaling on Martha's Vineyard

The islands off Cape Cod were acquired by the British crown "by right of discovery"; that thousands of people had been living there for many centuries was quite beside the point. So quite offhandedly King James I gave the Earl of Stirling "Pemaquid and its Dependencies . . . together with Long Island and the adjacent islands."

Then in 1641 the earl, probably in need of cash, sold

for forty pounds to Thomas Mayhew . . . and Thomas Mayhew, his son, the Island of Nantucket, with several small Islands adjacent [Martha's Vineyard and the Elizabeth Islands].

Figure 8-1 The Earl of Sterling, who sold to Thomas Mayhew the islands of Nantucket, Martha's Vineyard and the Elizabeth Islands for 40 in 1641. *From Banks' History of Martha's Vineyard.*

That same year Mayhew sold most of his interest in Nantucket to ten men led be Tristram Coffin for thirty pounds "and also two beaver hats one for myself and one for my wife." So, for a net cost of ten pounds he acquired outright Martha's Vineyard and the Elizabeth Islands. He ruled as governor— forget democracy— until his death in his eighties.

The settlers soon found that Martha's Vineyard was poor soil for farming; so they turned to the sea to make a living. They found that the Native Americans on the island had been whaling for centuries, chasing and killing these great animals from their canoes.

Since ancient days men have gone a-whaling. The early Germanic kings and those in Scandinavia hunted this huge game for the oil and the flesh. The English also went after these largest creatures on earth, and Queen Elizabeth I held rights to the tails of all whales caught by her subjects.

Soon after the first settlement in 1642 town records mention the appointment of two men, William Weeks and Thomas Daggett, as whale "cutters." When Thomas Mayhew, Senior, bought land from a sachem in 1658, spelled out carefully was the native right to all "drift whales," those driven on shore. The settlers were entitled to only "four spans round in the middle of every whale that comes upon this shore…"

Since whales were so plentiful, lookout posts along the shore would alert the islanders to sightings, and the small boats would set out. The catch was large. In 1726, for example, eighty-six whales were taken, eleven in one day, a record. An early immigrant noted in his journal that he saw

Figure 8-2 "Cutting In" (peeling the blankets of blubber from the whale before boiling it down for the oil).

mighty whales spewing up water like the smoke from a chimney and making the sea about them white and hoary, as is said in Job, of such incredible signes that I will never wonder that the body of Jonas could be in the belly of a whale.

The first whalers before 1700 are not known, but in 1702 John Butler and Thomas Lothrop appear in the records as having killed three of the "right"' whales (so-called because they yielded the most oil). Evidence indicates that Butler had been whaling for some years before 1702.

Wisely, the settlers employed the natives in the boat crews, because they had far greater knowledge of the habits of these giant cetaceans. And they learned well from the natives. Soon, too, they began to reach farther afield for their prey, going "deep" whaling instead of "shore" whaling. In little sloops and schooners of only twenty or thirty tons they started making forays of two or three weeks.

Thus a whole new industry began. Whale oil needed barrels, and coopers became a part of the maritime scene, as did ship chandlers (marine suppliers), rope-makers, sail-makers, and other occupations serving the fishery. An export market grew up, with Boston as an outlet. Growth spurred growth. The sizes of vessels increased markedly, so that voyages could reach the more distant gathering places of the whales, especially the right and sperm whales. By 1746 the island's whalers were reaching to Greenland and Baffin Bay, by the 1760's the African coast and the Caribbean.

Captain Peter Pease of Edgartown, born in 1732, was one of the most successful of the island whalers. Growing up at sea, like so many of his peers, at thirty he took the sloop *Susannah* to the Virginia Capes and after a successful six-month cruise unloaded his oil in Boston. Thereafter he made a cruise yearly until 1765.

The Revolutionary War nearly wiped out the industry. Whereas, for example, Nantucket and the Vineyard had as many as 125 vessels operating, bringing back in 1769 almost 20,000 barrels of oil, three years later fewer than 100 ships were able to produce less than 8,000 barrels. But not all of the British government was determined to teach the upstart Americans a lesson. The great Edmund Burke rose in Parliament in defense of the Americas, especially the whalers, on 22 March 1775, urging a conciliatory attitude toward their colonies:

Look at the manner in which the people of New England have carried on the whale-fishery. Whilst we follow them among the tumbling mountains of ice, and behold them penetrating into the deepest recesses of Hudsin's Bay and Davis' Strait . . . they are at the antipodes, and engaged under the frozen serpent of the south. . . .Nor is the equatorial heat more discouraging to them than the accumulated winter of both the poles. . . .Neither the perseverance of Holland, nor the activity of France, nor the. . .sagacity of English enterprise, carried this perilous mode of hardy enterprise to which it has been pushed by this recent people, a people who are still, as it were, in the gristle, and not yet hardened into the bone of mankind.

But whaling did not stop. After the war it rebounded to even greater heights and continued through the nineteenth century. Loss of lives and ships was often quite dreadful. For example, in September 1871 thirty-one ships found themselves caught in the ice in the Arctic; every ship was simply crushed, but all the crews escaped in their boats to other whalers south of the ice.

Figure 8-3 A more realistic view of boats attacking a whale.

The Cape Cod Packets

In the early days of our country travel was a real hardship on land. Afoot or horseback, roads were tracks in the sand, streams had to be forded. For example, Yarmouth voted to allow John Miller, their representative to the General Court, two extra days each way to attend the sessions. Later, coach travel to Boston was still a two-day ordeal.

As a result, quickly travel by water for goods and people became the preferred method; shipyards began turning out sloops and schooners for both the carrying trade and for fishing. As early as 1660 these little ships made trips to Boston. Thomas Huckins, proprietor of the Barnstable Tavern, supplied his hostelry with rum in his own vessel. And captains from other towns on Cape Cod Bay began shipping their produce by water and carrying passengers. And someone began calling these little ships "packets."

But "packet" suggests regular scheduled trips, and this began to happen soon after the colonies won their war for independence. Large cash crops of various sorts were being produced. Salt-making, invented by Captain John Sears of Dennis in 1776, by 1800 was a major industry, with some twenty-eight acres of saltworks. Onions had become an export crop, as had flax, and the forests of the Cape produced so much wood that it was often shipped to Boston.

Isaac Bacon of Barnstable is a fine example of a farmer/captain. His onion crops were so good that he took them to market in his own vessel. A careful seaman, on one trip with the boat on a starboard tack, he found the hold filling with water. On the port tack, he discovered that the leak had stopped. So, out in the bay, he lowered himself over the side and found a round hole, source of the leak. Whittling out a plug, he hammered it into the hole and went on his way to Boston.

By the 1830's true packet voyages were being made from many of the towns on the bay. Dennis, for instance, had packet service out of Sesuit Harbor from Captain Nathaniel Hall's pioneering in the 1790's down to 1874, when the *David Porter* made her last run. Judah and Jacob Sears operated in the 1820's, and Dean and Joseph H. Sears began their deep-water careers in packets. There were many others.

The *David Porter*, forty-five years old when she was finally laid up, illustrates the quality of these packets. In 1869, Captain Orren Sears survived a near-hurricane-force gale on 8 September. Trees blew down; roads were washed out. Caught halfway across the bay when the storm blew up, he could only head for Scituate, north of Plymouth. His jib halyard let go, and the main boom and fore gaff broke. Under bare poles, he ran the *David Porter* onto the beach, and at low tide put a ladder over the side and let his passengers walk ashore. On the next high tide the packet floated off, ready for a few minor repairs.

Brewster, next door to Dennis, had nothing but sand flats along its entire

No. 42 Forty two

ENROLMENT, in conformity to An Act of the Congress of the United States of America, entitled "An Act for enroling and licensing ships or vessels to be employed in the COASTING TRADE and FISHERIES, and for regulating the same."

Joseph Huckins of Barnstable

in the State of Massachusetts,
having taken or subscribed the oath required by the said Act and having sworn that he *with Henry W. Hinckley, Lot Gorham
& c., Nelson & c., Seth Parker & c.* all
of *Barnstable aforesaid*
are citizen of the UNITED STATES, sole owner
of the ship or vessel called the *Emerald*
of *Barnstable* whereof *Joseph Huckins*
is at present Master, and as he hath sworn is a citizen of the United
States, and that the said ship or vessel was built at *Saybrook*
in the State of *Connecticut*
in the year *1824* as appears by
*Enrolment No. 7 issued at this office Feb.
27, 1836 now cancelled, property
partially transferred*

And I am having certified
that the said ship or vessel has *one* deck and *one* mast and that
her length is *fifty nine* feet *ten* inches
her breadth *thirteen* feet *eleven* inches
her depth *five* feet *two* inches
and that she measures *Forty seven 64/95* tons ;
that she is a *Sloop* has a *square* stern,
no galleries, and *a scroll* head ; and the
said *Joseph Huckins* having
agreed to the description and admeasurement above specified, and sufficient security having been given according to the said Act, the said
Sloop
has been duly enroled at the Port of
Barnstable

GIVEN under my hand and seal of office, at the Port
Barnstable this *first* day of
April in the year one thousand eight hundred
and *forty*

*Recorded & compared by
. J. Crocker dll*

Figure 8-4 Enrollment document for the famous packet *Emerald* of Barnstable, forty-nine feet, ten inches long, depth five feet, two inches, with a tonnage of forty-seven and 64/95 tons. *Courtesy of the William Brewster Nickerson Cape Cod Room, Cape Cod Community College.*

shoreline. Yet because Chatham and Harwich were close by, the town became a thriving packet port. How did they do it? Between 1820 and 1830 Captain James Crosby and his schooner *Republic* would anchor close in to Point of Rocks, and when the tide went out she would smoothly settle on the sand. Augusta Mayo remembers those days:

We had great enjoyment in riding down to the packet. . . .We would drive up to the vessel's side, climb a ladder, and go on board. While the wagon was being loaded with goods from the hold, we children . . .would go down into the cabin, where Captain Myrick would treat us to pilot bread

Business became so good that the packet owners decided to build a break-water, providing a "sort of" harbor and pier to moor to. Captain Crosby soon had competition from the old sloop *Fame*. Captain Solomon Foster put in bunks and mattresses and refurbished her "in prime order for the accommodation and convenience of passengers." In 1830 her new skipper, Luther Sears, sold her in Boston and took command of the *Patriot*, built for the trade, luxuriously furnished. In the eight-month sailing season (April to November) *Patriot* made forty-two trips. She averaged $400 profit yearly from 1834 to 1839. There were several other packets sailing until 1870, when "packetin'" ended in Brewster.

Orleans, of course, had Rock Harbor, a fine shelter for vessels the size of the packets, and trade was brisk there. The Boston trip was not always fast, however. Albert Smith tells of one such trip that because of calms and contrary winds took forty-eight hours, with a stop at Castle Island. There were only ten bunks for twenty-five passengers, sleeping in shifts, and a fish chowder was made from five fish caught on board. After two nights out on the bay, they arrived off Rock Harbor to find that the tide was out, and they had to row to shore.

Provincetown, the great fishing port of the Cape, boasted one of the loveliest schooner yachts on the bay— *Northern Light*— which under Captain Whitman Freeman in the 1830's made three round trips a week to Boston. No other sailing vessel has equaled that record.

But the most exciting packet competition occurred between Yarmouth and Barnstable. Heavy money changed hands on races back and forth to Boston, and the rival newspapers, the *Barnstable Patriot* and the *Yarmouth Register,* reported the results in great detail.

Yarmouth Port, with a meager harbor at the end of Wharf Lane, had the fastest packets. First there was the *Emerald,* later sold to Barnstable interests, followed by *Eagle Flight*, and finally *Commodore Hull,* the fastest of them all. Barnstable had at various times the *Comet, Globe, Sappho, Henry Clay,* and others. Pride of the fleet was *Mail*, built on the Hudson River especially for the trade.

Such was the fervor built up by these races that an anonymous poet penned this screed, published in the *Patriot*:

The Commodore Hull *she sails so dull*
She makes her crew look sour.
The Eagle Flight *she is out of sight less than half an hour.*
But the bold old Emerald *takes delight to beat the* Commodore *and the* Flight.

(*Emerald,* you will recall, was now a Barnstable packet.)

The *Register* reported in great detail on a race between four packets and a yacht from Boston to Barnstable. Involved were the sloops *Eagle Flight*, and *Commodore Hull* from Yarmouth, *Mail* and the schooner *Sappho* from Barnstable, as well as the yacht *Breeze*. Sailing at about 3:00 P.M., with the wind behind them,

Captain Tom Matthews in *Hull* took the lead at Boston Light and led all the way, even though they had to tack into a southeast wind throughout the night. The *Register:*

Commodore Hull . . . *arrived at the bar before eight o'clock of Sunday morning. The* Flight *arrived at 18 minutes before nine; the* Mail *eight minutes past nine, the* Sappho *at half past nine and the* Breeze *about one o'clock.*

But while the bayside towns handled the Boston run, there was even more activity on Nantucket Sound, where there were good harbors from Woods Hole to Chatham. Shipyards churned out sloops and schooners, and the southside vessels far outnumbered those of the Cape Cod Bay towns. Hyannis had a heavy trade to New York and to the South— so much so that when the railroad reached the village it was laid right down to and onto the pier. Captain Benjamin Kendrick and his *Emulator* had a regular route between New Bedford and Chatham. And at Falmouth half a dozen vessels plied so regularly to New Bedford that they were almost ferryboats.

By the 1870's the heyday of the packets was over. Steam and the railroads were the culprits, especially the latter. Side-wheelers like the *Longfellow, George Shattuck,* the Sandwich Glass Works' *Acorn,* and *Naushon* began operating by 1860. In 1848 the first train arrived in Sandwich, and in twenty-five years the entire Cape was covered. Salt making died out when salt mines were discovered in New York State, and transporting salt was no more.

But what happened to these sturdy, swift craft? Many simply became fishermen on the Grand Banks; others turned to coasting. *Northern Light* came to grief in the Straits of Magellan. Slowly they faded out of the local picture, having served efficiently their communities with their $1.00 fares and $2.50 meals. But beyond that these vessels were so small that no one could demand exclusive treatment. After all, sometimes there were only ten berths and twenty-five passengers!

Figure 8-5 Schooner in the Ice.

SCHOONER IN THE ICE.

The Wreckers

The term "wreckers" conjures up all sorts of negative pictures, including luring ships ashore through the use of false lights. One long-standing Cape Cod legend says that some people used to tie a lantern to a horse's tail and lead it back and forth on the Nauset cliffs. The local term for such activities was "mooncussing." A captain at sea, seeing the light, would think that it was another ship and thus drive his vessel on shore. When Ralph Waldo Emerson visited Nauset in 1850, he reported that "Collins, the keeper, told us he found resistance to the project [building the lighthouse] . . . as it would injure the wrecking business."

But for many years there had been a most stringent law against these criminal actions. Charles Nordhoff reported in *Harper's Magazine* in 1874 that:

In 1825 it was enacted that "if any person or persons shall hold out or show any false light or lights . . . with the intention to bring any ship or vessel . . . into danger or distress, every such person . . . shall, on conviction, be punished by a fine not exceeding four thousand dollars and confinement to hard labor not exceeding ten years."

The reality was quite different. After all, in order to get access to a vessel's cargo, the wreckers must first get aboard and rescue the crew of the stranded vessel; then they must make a deal with the captain or the insurance company to salvage the cargo. The exception might be when the ship and crew were a total loss.

So the term "wrecker" in most cases was merely descriptive. It denoted the occupation of those who dealt with wrecks, salvagers in other words.

SCHOONER GRECIAN WITH PICNIC PARTY ON BOARD.

Figure 8-6 Schooner *Grecian* with picnic party on board.

On Nantucket the south tower of the Unitarian Church for many years provided an excellent lookout. After a storm it would be manned by a man with powerful glasses. Sighting a wreck, the picked crew of (often) as many as thirty men, boatmen or fishermen, would haul the Humane Society boat to the scene and reach the wreck as soon as possible in order to be first for salvage. There was sometimes a race for first place.

A case in point: In February 1863 came word of a wreck off the north shore. Captain David G. Patterson, a noted wrecker, and his crew rowed out to the vessel. But Alexander Dunham, a noted pilot, and a friend in a dory barely beat Patterson to the wreck— and to the salvage rights. The wreckers would reach Peter Folger, the underwriter's agent on the island, to arrange salvage percentages on the cargo.

Only a month later Captain Patterson dealt with another wreck. The Prussian bark *Elwine Fredericke* came ashore on Great Point Rip. Captain David and Captain Aaron Coffin reached the wreck in a dory, after a very dangerous row out, and rescued the captain and fourteen crewmen. A few hours later the bark was a pile of timbers. For this deed the King of Prussia presented Patterson with a silver chronometer watch. The Nantucket newspaper report ended with: "This is a merited testimonial. Captain Patterson . . . richly deserves the thanks of His Majesty, the King of Prussia, in this substantial expression of gratitude." There was no salvage.

Sometimes the Cape Cod wreckers beat out the local crews. For example, on 30 January 1881 the schooner *Uriah B. Fisk,* with a load of guano (bird droppings valuable as fertilizer) hit on Great Point Rip in an ice pack. Patterson's crew was able to remove the captain, his wife, and the crew across the ice. For several days they worked removing the cargo but would not spend nights aboard lest the vessel break up. One evening the lighthouse keeper saw *Red Wing,* of Bass River, nearing the wreck. The Cape Cod crew made off with both anchors, most of the unshackled cable, deck gear, and twenty tons of guano!

Wrecking on Cape Cod tended to be less formally organized; one was not so careful to get in touch with the underwriters' agent. On 15 March 1889 a Cape Cod newspaper republished a long interview with Captain Joshua N. Bloomer from the *Boston Herald.* The captain, called "a genuine wrecker," recalls many of the difficult rescues and salvages in which he was involved.

The Bloomers moved from Chatham to "Whitewash Village", as the Chathamites rather sneeringly called the fishing village on Monomoy. It was there that Captain Joshua learned his trade.

Starting from [the age of fourteen] I have followed a seafaring life, and I think I know every hook and crook of the shoals out there . . .I can truthfully say I have been a "wrecker," having held the steering oar on many trips. To do this means to have the whole care of the boat and saving the lives from the vessels. My first experience was my worst, and it may be of interest to you.

He was twenty-one. One morning he saw a bark ashore off Monomoy. The seas were calm, and they pulled off the crew easily. She was an old vessel, and when, that night, the wind shifted he knew that she would not last long. Next morning a wicked gale was blowing, but they went out and started to "save a portion of her effects" when they saw a brig flying the upside-down flag of distress. Soon she was on the shoals of a wicked gale.

After the men pulled the new metal Humane Society boat down to the beach, of the forty or so wreckers few would volunteer. Finally fourteen did, if young Joshua would hold the steering oar. At first he refused, since he really felt incompetent, but no one else would step up. So he finally agreed.

Imagine my feelings. Not one of the fourteen expected ever to reach land again alive. . . .Oh, didn't it howl! I became almost paralyzed with fear, but stuck to my steering oar. It was pull to the right and ease to the left, pull straight ahead and bail all the time.

Although the bark was only a mile offshore, the men had to stop and anchor several times, to rest from fighting those waves. At last they reached her and tied up, only to be nearly swamped by the biggest wave yet. The first person Captain Joshua saw aboard was a woman; there were two. Riding the waves like a bucking horse, he would pull close and tell the women to jump; they both landed in the boat safely. One by one the crew followed, and they saved every one. Captain Joshua swore that "Never would I captain another boat in such a gale, and I never have in one that equaled it."

His last experience occurred one morning in May (no year is given). The ship *Mary Ann* fetched up on Pollock Rip Shoals. Again the wind was blowing a terrible gale. A large wrecking crew from Monomoy arrived in the schooner *Favorite* and stayed aboard three days. The ship was in good condition and stayed tight.

Given the ship's position, should they save the cargo or the ship? Captain Joshua decided for the ship, and for three days the wreckers threw overboard (since they had no lighter on which to put it) most of her cargo of crockery and iron, to lighten her. Then at a gamble they carried out both anchors to deep water and at flood tide they kedged her off by hauling on the ship's windlass. Slipping the anchor chains and anchors, they sailed *Mary Ann* to Boston.

Later the wrecking crew returned and retrieved the anchors and chain and shipped them to Boston. Meanwhile they were thinking of the fortune in the cargo, now buried under the sand of the shoal. This was a rather common outcome: save the crew, lose the salvage.

Sometimes the wreckers observed downright "piracy," as Captain Joshua called it— the intentional stranding or loss of a ship for profit. In January 1825 the Monomoy crew saw a brig, anchored close in. Since she seemed in no trouble, they ignored her. Soon a stranger approached a wrecker and asked, "Is there a man on the beach that I can hire to run my brig ashore and save the cargo?"

The wrecker replied, "Yes, there are men here to run her ashore where the vessel and the cargo can be saved." But that was not what the stranger wanted. Finally an agreement was reached, and the wreckers ran her ashore and put out two anchors to hold her. She was the brig *Jane* of Halifax, Captain Hugh McManackle. Removing the cargo of flour, corn, and crackers was an easy job. Next the captain had the masts cut away, to fall toward the shore so that the brig would look more like a wreck.

Then he said, "Is there an auctioneer in the party?" And on the spot *Jane* was sold to the highest bidder on the beach. And he got away with it; nobody complained to an insurance company. Later the wreckers learned that he had a new brig waiting in Halifax as soon as he sold the old one.

These men, as exemplified by Captain Joshua, risked their lives to make a living. They had to get out to whatever vessel they were trying to reach, to save the crew, to arrange for salvage of the cargo, if any, or if the vessel survived long enough to permit removal. And they died trying, literally.

Wherever these wreckers operated, their first duty was to save lives. One of the most difficult and unusual rescues was that of the crew and 226 Irish immigrants aboard the ship *British Queen*. Captain Thomas Conway had been at sea for eight weeks from Dublin. Because of bad weather he had had no chance of checking his position, and so when he was able to locate himself he was in the Muskeget Channel, between Nantucket and Martha's Vineyard, and ran aground there on 17 December 1851.

At dawn on the 18th the South Tower watchman spotted the ship, two of its masts gone. A number of boats tried to reach the ship that day, without success; the seas were too powerful. Meanwhile the steerage passengers underwent a night of absolute horror, believing that the ship would break up at any moment. This was a particularly bitter winter; Nantucket Sound was full of ice, and there was no communication with the mainland.

Early on the 19th the steamer *Telegraph* got up steam and towed the schooners *Game Cock* and *Hamilton* over the bar, just clearing it at high tide. Captain David Patterson was aboard the *Hamilton* as agent for the underwriters.

Captain William Patterson in *Game Cock* started for the wreck and, despite the ice, was able to anchor within a half-mile. *Telegraph* could only get within three-quarters of a mile. Captain David in *Hamilton* arrived soon after and as agent took control.

He launched a boat and struggled to the wreck, boarding her by a rope ladder, to find from Captain Conway that the ship was not insured but that rescue was primary. Signals to *Game Cock* brought her to the lee of the wreck, and the immigrants began boarding her. Two people had died during the night and over a hundred were very weak; the thrashing seas made the rescue difficult, but some sixty boarded before *Game Cock* could take no more and headed for the steamer. The tide had changed, and *Hamilton* had a terrible time to lay alongside. Captain Bearse dropped his anchor and paid out his chain, until he lay across the wreck's bow. The passengers and crew had to either jump or be tossed onto the schooner, but not one person was lost. When all were aboard, the schooner returned to harbor.

The passengers were in desperate condition, with only the clothes on their backs, and many were extremely weak from exposure. As word of their plight spread in the town, food, clothing, and money, as well as offers of shelter, poured in. On 25 December the passengers rode *Telegraph* to the mainland and their new homes. Several of the Irish stayed on Nantucket; their descendants are fine citizens of the island today.

Before they left, the passengers inserted this notice in the *Mirror,* which was published on December 27:

We, the shipwrecked passengers of the . . . British Queen of Dublin, deem it our beounden duty to return our most heartfelt and sincere thanks for the cordial and human reception we have received from the . . .Island of Nantucket. To those brave and humane men who came to our rescue . . .we are at a loss to express our gratitude. . . .

And now, preservers of our lives, permit us in conclusion to commit you to the care and keeping of Almighty God. May He watch over you and yours; may He increase your store a hundred fold, and may there be no lack

nor falling off among you.
Signed, on behalf of all the passengers,
Nelson T. Johnson

This was a truly incredible feat of seamanship and organization. And there was no salvage. Someone bought the hull, spars, and rigging "as is" for $250, and by working night and day was able to remove most of the rigging and deck lumber. Overnight the proud ship *British Queen* was no more.

But the demands on the wreckers were not over. Two fishermen stayed on the ship after the people had been removed. They figured that they could make a nice haul of loose gear. But at dark a heavy sea kicked up, and the ship was pounding heavily. Frightened, the two tried to leave in their overloaded boat, but a sea smashed it against the ship's hull. Their partner reported them lost.

The ship was gone by daylight, and the wreckers began an almost hopeless search for the two. Loose ice piled up on the lee shore and out into the Sound. But Captain Bearse in *Hamilton* went out just before dark to search and hours later was ashore himself. Captain David Patterson and another searched the beach on foot and in the moonlight finally saw the boat a quarter-mile out in the ice.

Shouting, they roused the two men at last, and, leaving a man there to keep them awake (for men can fall asleep forever in the cold), they went for a skiff. But when they came back the two had managed with two boards to paddle close enough that the watchman could wade in and help them ashore. They recovered in a few weeks from their crazy ordeal.

The Jacksons
Three Generations of Fishermen

The Jackson family epitomizes the lives of generations of families on Cape Cod and the islands— people who worked hard all their lives, drawing their living from the sea, and contributing to their towns. They are well worth writing about, especially since all three Jackson boys were awarded the Carnegie Medal of Honor (for skill and bravery in saving lives at sea).

An English immigrant, Hiram Jackson and his wife Jane settled in New Bedford so that he could work in the cotton mills. Between 1875 and 1878 three sons were born to them; in fact the middle son, Robert, worked with his father when he was thirteen. Child labor laws were minimal in those days.

When Hiram was thirty-nine he moved the family to Cuttyhunk, where they had spent summers because of his love for hunting and fishing. Now he could fish year-round for a living. The next year he bought a catboat worth $150 and a house and half-acre lot for $278.50. The house is still there, as is the Cuttyhunk Store, now greatly enlarged. Clearly he had worked hard and saved his money.

Although he was an avid sportsman, he was quite inexperienced and often got into trouble taking chances a more knowledgeable boatman would avoid. But he learned, as did his three sons, as they fished and lobstered for a living. Soon they were all skilled on the water. And wife Jane did her part: she opened her house to boarders and developed a reputation for her seafood dinners served every Sunday to the tourists who came from New Bedford on the little steamer *Cygnet*. Hiram joined the Humane Society volunteers.

He was a member of the Society boat crew who went out to try to save the men on the brig *Aquatic*, aground on Sow and Pigs Shoal. The date was 24 February 1893, the weather bitterly cold and stormy. They were nearly alongside the brig when a huge wave capsized the boat and five of the six, including Hiram and Captain Timothy Akin, drowned. The five bodies came ashore and were buried. Hiram was forty-one years old. The five families were left in dire straits; Jane Jackson was perhaps better off, since she owned her house and the three sons were able watermen. Sam was eighteen, Bob seventeen, and Levi fifteen.

Jane remained a widow until 1908, when she married another Englishman, Thomas Bates. The boarding house prospered, and the boys provided the fish and lobsters. In 1898 Sam was still single and had become a surfman in the Lifesaving Service; he owned *Waif*, his father's catboat, and a horse. Bob had married and owned a catboat, too, in which he lobstered full-time. Levi was twenty, had married, and also went lobstering for a living. Sam boarded at home; the others rented homes; Sam served as selectman/assessor from 1909 through 1911.

Sam, the oldest, did not marry until 1912, when he and his bride, Bertha Chase, moved to Edgartown, like his brothers. There he fished from his boat, *Bertha*. But with many of his neighbors like Dave Bosworth, first keeper of the Life-saving Station, the Veeder brothers, George Stetson, and others, he and his catboat would sail down to Chesapeake Bay for the rich spring fishing.

Soon, however, he moved to Nantucket to take advantage of the great flounder fishing in his sloop *Phyllis J.* All his five children grew up on Nantucket. Of the five, Elson became a famous fisherman too, as did grandson Samuel, who at sixteen was the youngest captain in the Swordfish Tournament. One of the best captains on the waterfront, Tobe Fleming, once said that Sam knew the shoals and waters so well that even in thick fog, without electronics, he knew just where he was. His Carnegie Medal of Honor he earned for bravery at sea, and, with his brothers, he became a legendary figure in the islands. He died at the age of 84.

The second son, Bob, in 1896 had married Annie Maud Redding, a Mayflower descendant. They had three children on Cuttyhunk and two more after moving to Edgartown, where the fishing was better. Annie Jackson was not too happy on Cuttyhunk and so was glad of the move after ten years. Bob sold lobsters and swordfish for the going rate of five cents a pound and seldom made more than $1000 a year; despite that low figure, he had managed to save $3000 to start again on the Vineyard. Swordfishing became his full-time profession, in which he was one of the most successful fishermen. For example, in 1919 he landed 20,000 pounds of these great fighting fish. Record catches every year led up to 1926, when in one day he boated 72; the next day he took 42. This record still stands.

Captain Bob made a number of daring rescues, for which he too received the Carnegie Medal. But he also had some close calls. In his sixty-foot schooner *Progress* he was fishing with other boats when, on 10 August 1918, a German

Figure 8-7 Captain Bob Jackson's sword-fishing schooner *Hazel B. Jackson*, in which he established record two-day catches -- which still stand. *Courtesy of Janet Bosworth, Cuttyhunk.*

submarine surfaced, took what supplies they needed, ordered all the crews into their dories, and sank every fishing boat. It was thirty hours before they were picked up.

During the August 1924 storm, which sank a number of vessels, he lashed himself to the wheel and for four hours fought that storm's fifty-foot waves on Nantucket Shoals to bring his new seventy-foot *Hazel M. Jackson* (named for his daughter) home safely. Finally in 1940 he sold *Hazel*— he was sixty-four— and came ashore, but not to a rocking chair. He was out fishing in his outboard regularly until he was eighty-four.

The youngest son, Levi, married an English girl in 1899. He too served in the Lifesaving Service, both on Cuttyhunk and on the Vineyard, after he moved there in 1906. They raised a good-sized family of seven. But he spent a good deal of his time lobstering and later became well known for his expert handling of salvage and wrecking operations in the islands. A particularly valuable perquisite of salvaging was sale of the stranded vessel's masts. Cut away and towed to New Bedford, they sold for $100 apiece. Tied together, they were most useful as work floats in the harbor.

In 1910 Captain Levi was fishing in *Priscilla* when he accomplished an especially daring rescue of the fifteen people aboard *Mertie B. Crowley,* up on Wasque Shoal in January. The Carnegie Medal honored that rescue. Then in 1914 he was given the Humane Society Medal and a check for another skillful rescue of eleven.

Edgartown Captain and Wife Observe Golden Wedding Day

CAPTAIN and MRS. ROBERT L. JACKSON

Figure 8-8 On 15 May 1946 Captain Bob and his wife celebrated their fiftieth wedding anniversary on Nantucket.

The Adventures of LaRoy Lewis

When Captain LaRoy Lewis of Martha's Vineyard died at seventy-seven, he had had a series of unique adventures, and in his later life served his community in many capacities right up until his death. It seems that he could not really retire. Another example is Captain George Pollard, of the *Essex*, one of two survivors, who "beached himself on Nantucket and lived out his life as a night watchman."

LaRoy Lewis's ancestors were Cape Cod people, his great-grandfather being born in Yarmouth in 1698. But in 1715 he moved his family to Tisbury on the Vineyard. His son John was an odd character; at the age of thirty-two he stopped "[dressing] as a woman and was supposed to be such." Then he donned trousers, married Ann Luce, and sired five children.

LaRoy's grandfather and father were housewrights (an old name for builders), and he grew up in a spacious house in Edgartown. Like many of his peers, he went to sea at fifteen and sailed the world for most of his first forty years. Nine years later he was second mate on the whaler *Alpha* of Nantucket, when his first adventure began.

As he told the story in later years, the bark found a pod of sperm whales, and in the ensuing melee LaRoy's boat was smashed by the flukes of the whale. Somehow he was missed in the rescue and spent fourteen hours in the water, clinging to the wrecked boat. The result was a severe case of inflammatory arthritis, so bad that he could not perform his duties. On tight rations, there was no place for an invalid.

On 22 November 1863 *Alpha* hove to off Norfolk Island, northwest of New Zealand. While the bark's log makes no mention of the reason, Captain Caswell went ashore several times. Then the log states that at 5:00 A.M. on the 24th a boat took Lewis ashore and "landed LeRoy [sic] S. Lewis sick with the Rheumaticks, helpless." The next day the whaler departed, and LaRoy was left to the tender

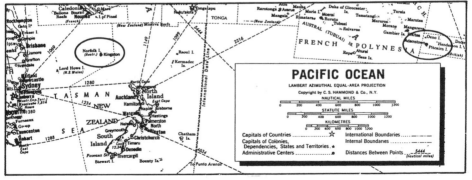

Figure 8-9 Pacific Ocean chart showing Pitcairn Island (first home of the *H.M.S. Bounty* mutineers) and Norfolk Island, 3700 miles away to the west, their new home. It was here that LaRoy Lewis recovered under their care. *Courtesy of the Dukes County Intelligencer.*

227

mercies of strangers, whom he calls "the best people on earth."

Who were they? Nearly all were descendants of the *Bounty* mutineers. And what were they doing on an island 3700 miles west of Pitcairn Island, where Fletcher Christian and his followers had hidden after they had mutinied against Captain Bligh? Nothing was known of the mutiny until Bligh and his boatload of loyal men, having crossed over 2000 miles arrived, exhausted, on New Holland in the Dutch East Indies. The date was 14 June 1789.

Pitcairn was far from an Eden. After nine years only four of the English were alive; all the rest had been murdered. Two of these, McCoy and Quintal, figured how to make "ardent spirits;" McCoy jumped off a cliff in delirium; Quintal "became a raving drunk and a menace to the community," and John Adams and former midshipman Young executed him with an ax. Young died soon afterward, and when the *Topaz* found the island in 1808, only John Adams remained of the fifteen mutineers.

A most unusual man was John Adams. Recruited from the London slums, when he and Young were the sole survivors he learned to read and write from the Bible. And at thirty-six he developed into the patriarch of the clan of Tahitian women and their half-English children. He made sure that they all spoke English and had a sound religious education. He lived for fifty years after the mutiny.

By 1856 the islanders were certain that the 1 3/4 square miles of their island were so debilitated that they had to move. The British government sent a ship and moved all 194 of them to Norfolk Island (see map), an abandoned Australian penal colony. Well supplied with food, 1300 sheep, 430 cattle, 22 horses, pigs and chickens, the colony settled into the empty buildings and began to learn to be farmers.

Seven years later, into this new colony LaRoy Lewis came. He lived with the grandson of John Adams, another John, in officers' quarters along with six of the descendants and Miss Ward, the schoolteacher; she and LaRoy became close friends.

By the time seven months had passed, LaRoy was cured and ready to leave, his rheumatism gone. Probably he cured himself by healthy outdoor work rather than by medical means. And the loving help he received from "the best people on earth" may well have contributed.

However he regained his health, when the bark *Covington* came in for water, he left with her on 14 June 1864. Luckily, he must have found another berth, because in June 1865 the Confederate cruiser *Shenandoah* took the whaler and burned her.

Once back on the Vineyard, it was not long before LaRoy went a-whaling again— as second mate in *Arab*. Then in 1872 we find him master of the whaling bark *Cornelia*. In Talcahuano, a popular provisioning port in Chile, he finally thought to write John Adams a letter of thanks— long overdue— for his stay on Norfolk Island.

There was an almost immediate reply from John Adams. The letter, in the archives of the Martha's Vineyard Historical Society, reads in part:

You scapegrace you, why did you not write before? . . .I would not give the pleasure I received from reading that letter of yours, not for the best fifty dollars that was ever coined in Yankeedom.

He gives all the news: Miss Ward had married; Mr. and Mrs. Levin were killed by "the Maories in New Zealand." And he asks that if Lewis ever came again he bring a "yankee whaleboat." But Captain Lewis never saw the letter for forty years: it had somehow been put into a book, unopened.

The old *Cornelia* was condemned the next year, and after he got home he made several more whaling trips, the last as master of the bark *Mars*. Finaliy in 1890, fifty-one years old, he returned to his home and began a career of community service. By chance in 1912 he opened that book containing the letter; astonished, he read it and replied at once—too late. John Adams had died thirteen years before.

His letter was answered by Cornish Quintal, who had a most complete budget of news. Byron Adams had been killed by a whale; others had died; only Cornish and Polly Adams Christian remained. But worse yet was the fate of the descendants. The Australian government had claimed that they were in

illegal possession . . . [turning them] out of the houses and left in the street at

Figure 8-10 Miss Ward, school teacher on Norfolk Island, who became a close friend of LaRoy Lewis. *Courtesy of the Dukes County Intelligencer.*

*the mercy of others to give them shelter. . . .This is the greatest of the evil days
I have seen and the fine house is rotting down, windows all smash in, cattle
taking shelter in them.*

The Officers' Quarters had become the post office. And despite all that Cornish
could do, they were evicted.

Australian history tells a different story of the ideal life led by the Pitcairners
under government administration. But Alvin Goldwyn, author of this story, inquired
of a former newsman on Norfolk concerning the truth of the history. The newsman
wholly corroborated Cornish Quintal's story, replying:

*The "generally benign image" . . . is [correct for] establishment historians . .
.[who believed that] the Pitcairners were the victims of their own misunder-
standing [as to] the rights to Norfolk they'd been promised. Research . . .
[shows]. . .that they didn't misunderstand at all . . . and that the Australian
authorities have misunderstood, and have enforced their incorrect view.*

Back home in Cottage City in 1879— the town became Oak Bluffs, a much
more dignified name, in 1907— Captain LaRoy held just about every appointive post
in the town. As lamplighter he received $230 a year; for almost twenty years he
was a town constable, posting notices, serving summonses, presiding at polling places.
He was now and then tree warden and cemetery commissioner; but his most important post was that of night watchman for Oak Bluffs, receiving about $450 a year.

Figure 8-11 The Sea View House burned to the ground Saturday night, September 24,
1892. It was located at the head of steamboat wharf and was considered the pride of Oak
Bluffs. *Courtesy of the Dukes County Intelligencer.*

On Saturday night, 24 September 1892, on his rounds he saw lurid red reflections on the heavy clouds, yelled "Fire!" and rang the alarm on box 41. The fire cart responded, but the *Vineyard Gazette* described the scene as "one grand carnival of flame . . . the sky being overcast with heavy clouds, from which at times the rain descended, as if weeping in sorrow over the awful catastrophe."

The fire totally destroyed the Sea View House, a huge wooden hotel, only twenty years old, at the head of Steamboat Wharf. In addition the Casino, another nearby large wooden building built as a roller-skating rink, used later as a summer theater, was gutted. The wharf itself was heavily damaged, as well. This was the worst calamity that had befallen the town since its founding some twenty-five years before.

Perhaps as a reward for his service, futile though it was, he was named janitor and later steward of the fire-house, at $35 a year. Twenty-two years later, in 1915 he resigned. Then, aged seventy-seven, he died in 1916 of "Arterio Schlerosis," having been married to the same wife for fifty-two years.

We do not know what he was doing between 1879, when he came home, and the 1890's— probably more of the same; town reports for those years are missing. And there is little evidence either way as to his circumstances. However, his widow, who lived until 1927, still owned their house (known today as Captain Lewis's house) and had investment income. Son Ira married a Nantucket girl and moved to Cape Cod. His daughter Celina became a high school teacher in Brookline, Massachusetts.

Figure 8-12 The ruins of the Casino. The charred hulk was not removed for more than two years, creating an eyesore for visitors arriving at Oak Bluffs wharf. *Courtesy of the Dukes County Intelligencer.*

This was a survivor, a typical, tough islander who lived through extraordinary experiences and gave back to his town in overflowing measure his small but necessary services. Captain LaRoy Lewis was quite a man.

Figure 8-12A Pitcairn Island, the hideout of the nine remaining mutineers who took over *H.M.S. Bounty* from Lieutenant Bligh on 28 April 1789. Fletcher Christian, leader of the mutiny, found this unknown island, burned the *Bounty*, and with six Tahitian men and twelve women, established a settlement. First knowledge of their existence occurred when Captain Mayhew Folger (There's a Nantucket name for you!) chanced on the island in February 1808. The island is totally rock-bound.

Rum-Running on the Vineyard

The era of the Eighteenth Amendment, banning all sales of alcoholic drinks, saw Martha's Vineyard involved in excitement such as had not been seen since the days of the pirates in the 1700's. With open shores and few inhabitants, the island and Noman's Land nearby were favorite spots for rumrunning, as were many other locations on Cape Cod and the islands. Provincetown was widely known for its participation in the trade.

Quickly an efficient and illegal system grew up to evade the law, which the Coast Guard was working to enforce. Just outside the twelve-mile limit ships from abroad would hover, waiting to transfer their cargoes to small boats for delivery ashore. On dark nights they would slip out to the waiting "mother ships", load up, paying cash, and run for their landing spot, hoping that the Coast Guard would be elsewhere.

Commercial fishermen were some of the best at the trade; they seemed so innocent. Out near the supply ships they would seem to be fishing, until nightfall. Alongside, they would take on their liquid cargo, cover it with tarpaulins and a layer of ice, and then go fishing, stowing the fresh fish on top. Stopped by the Coast Guard, inspection would show nothing but fish and ice. In port, they would sell the fish as usual; then at night they would help load the bootlegger's truck.

But sometimes something went wrong. The *Etta Burns,* a fishing schooner, was on her way to New Bedford in fog when the helmsman dozed off, and she ran aground on the Vineyard. When the Coast Guard heard of the grounding, they sent a cutter to offer to refloat her. But the crew declined, saying that she was leaking too badly. But with no evidence of that claim, the Coast Guard was suspicious, even though all they could see in the hold was fish. Returning in the morning, they found the crew gone. So they removed the thin layer of fish and found the real cargo, which they confiscated. Later it was discovered that the "Scotch whiskey" had come from a floating distillery off Long Island and consisted of alcohol from Belgium and coloring.

Of course the Coast Guard caught onto the fisherman scam. So shortly the rumrunners began building fast seaboats some fifty feet long. Low in the water, with two airplane engines, they could make thirty-five knots or so, even fully loaded. And the Coast Guard could not match those speeds. Or they built strong sea boats that looked like draggers but only pretended to fish.

Frank Butler of the Vineyard, a long-time fisherman, was among the most successful skippers of these new boats. He it was who invented the smoke screen. Dirty engine oil dripped on the hot engines produced a dense cloud of smoke, hiding the fleeing boats that with their speed could outrun their pursuers.

Another clever design was the fisherman with a double bottom. There were two or three feet of space between two hulls, with secret access. But even fully loaded they rode too high in the water. The between-hull space hid the liquid cargo.

———

Figure 8-13 The Coast Guard caught the swift, armor-plated rum-runner *Nola* and sank her with gunfire off Cuttyhunk in 1931. They aimed at drums of raw alcohol stowed on deck. *Photo courtesy of the U.S. Coast Guard.*

To combat all this ingenuity the Coast Guard had to reply on their seventy-five-foot cutters, fine sea boats with a one pounder on the bow, hardly more than an annoyance to the criminals. And they were manned largely by new enlistees, often seasick— and no real problem for the old salts in the trade.

But sometimes the Coast Guard won. They caught the *Tramp* while she was unloading, confiscated her, and used her on patrol. One dark night in December 1931, they saw *Nola*, faster than *Tramp* and armor-plated. Firing her machine gun, *Tramp* pursued the rumrunner. The drums of alcohol on deck, hit by the firing, caught fire, and soon *Nola* was sinking. Frank Butler and his crew were saved. Oddly, He had been captain of *Tramp* originally.

Competition between supply ships was often fierce. Somewhere in Vineyard Sound the steamer *John Dwight* came across the steam yacht *Flit*. A gun battle led to the killing of the entire crew of *Dwight,* as they fought side by side. Afterward the *Flit's* crew opened the steamer's sea valves and sank her. Then they ran their hundred-foot yacht ashore on Noman's Land and abandoned her. She was beautifully furnished, and the manager of the island made several thousand dollars in salvage. Federal divers searched the steamer; several unidentified bodies came ashore and were buried.

Probably the most notorious of the rumrunning captains was Bill McCoy, from New London, Connecticut. When the law got too close he moved to Gay Head. He owned the schooner *Arethusa*, once a Grand Banks fisherman, which he used as a mother ship. His station was roughly twenty miles south of Gay Head, and he did his shopping in the Bahamas— all good drinking booze. He would sell

Figure 8-14 The "mother ship" *Arethusa* would lurk just outside the twelve mile limit of those days. Here, two Coast Guard 75-footers are watching her closely. *Photo courtesy of the U.S. Coast Guard.*

any amount, from a bottle to a boatload. Since he was so far out, he had no worries as to the Coast Guard; he feared hijackers. To discourage them, he kept two men armed with rifles, high up the foremast.

When the weather worsened, cargo transfer was difficult and dangerous. But Captain McCoy solved that problem neatly with a boom supported by the foremast, to which the "rummies" could tie up. Safely away from the schooner, the smaller boats received their loads down a chute from *Arethusa.*

Embarrassed by a first-hand story by a reporter from the *Evening Standard*, Treasury agents found out where he was living. When they asked where McCoy was, his Indian hosts said they had never heard of him; he was upstairs, but without a warrant the agents could do nothing. Later that day he saw the cutter *Acushnet* stop a fisherman and talk to him. He pulled alongside and asked what they wanted. This is what Captain McCoy said to Everett Allen, the reporter:

"What did the cutter want?" I bawled to the master. He was a lean New Englander, salt and dry as a split cod, and he spat over the rail before shouting back: "Wanted to know where Bill McCoy and the Arethusa *was."*

I waited. He spat again. "Told him I never heard of neither of ye," he roared. "Dinged fool!"

They don't breed sqealers among those New England fishermen.

Apparently feeling that things were too hot for him up here, he traded south, still selling excellent Bahamas liquor to all and sundry. One probably apochryphal story is that, while he is long gone, he still lives in American slang. Something that is especially fine is "the real McCoy."

Another story illustrates the dangers of the trade, and the sense of mutual help of the islanders. A large speedboat, the *Allaha*, with two aircraft engines capable of forty knots, was making a run from Captain McCoy's mother ship south of Noman's Land to the mainland, aiming for the Christmas trade in 1926. She got caught in a northwest blizzard and headed for the lee of Noman's Land. But she was not built for such seas and their punishment, so that she began to fill with water.

Soon steering could only be done with the engines, and as she neared the island the crew could only drive her ashore. Escaping the wreck, they made it up the beach, while the boat was crushed by the seas. Later the men on the island were able to salvage her engines.

But that is not the end of the story. A good deal later the *Vineyard Gazette* published a woman's account of what must have been the sequel to the *Allaha* wreck. Sound asleep, she was awakened by a knock on her kitchen door. There were three very wet men, one with a case of pinch bottle Scotch on his shoulder.

She invited them in, to learn that their rumrunner boat (they made no bones as to that) had wrecked. Finding dry clothing, she made coffee and food for them, and they bedded down for the night. In the morning after breakfast a seaplane appeared and landed on the water. Apparently the owners were concerned when the boat did not show up.

Later that day a "small sailing vessel" came, to pick up the cargo— which had been lost. But they picked up the three men and returned to New Bedford. As they left, recounts the farmer, the men

left a very handsome present in greenbacks for the farmer's wife and myself. . . . They were not hardened criminals as most people thought, but very polite and kind-hearted and were always a welcome sight for us on Noman's Land.

CHAPTER
9

Great Seamen

Captain "Mad Jack" Percival

Captain John Percival, United States Navy, in his long and controversial career created a personality and a legend. The first Percival in this country was James. After getting into trouble in Virginia and the Massachusetts Bay Colony, he settled on Cape Cod in 1671 as a farmer and blacksmith. His great-grandson, one of five children born to John (1740-1802) and his wife, Mary Snow (1743-1841), was our John Percival, born on 3 April 1779. The house where he was born, on Scorton Hill in West Barnstable, burned down long ago.

His father, like his peers, went to sea very early, and during the Revolution commanded a privateer, *Anti Smuggler*. Twenty years later, still at sea, he and our

Figure 9-1 Lieutenant John Percival, U.S.N., at thirty-eight having joined the Navy as sailing master when he was thirty. Painted by Ethan Allen Greenwood in 1817. *Courtesy of the U.S. Naval Academy Museum.*

John met accidentally in Bordeaux, France, in 1802 to the great delight of both. He was in desperate straits, and our John put him aboard his ship to go home. He died en route and was buried at sea on 10 August 1802.

Our John also left home early, with almost no formal education, to serve as cabin boy and cook. At sea in the merchant service for sixteen years, he served "before the mast" and worked his way up in the marine hierarchy while wandering the seas. Actual details as to this time of his life are most sketchy indeed.

When he was twenty, in 1800 he spent a brief few months in the Navy as a sailing master at the end of our half war with France. His short stint aboard *U.S.S. Delaware* was more than adequate. He actually began his naval career on 6 March 1809 as sailing master. Thirty years old, a seasoned mariner, much too old in a rank-conscious navy for this lowly position.

One large puzzle in "Mad Jack's" life was when and where he married his wife, Maria Pinkerton, born in 1793. Since official records were no help, the best evidence is the diary of the carpenter aboard *Constitution*. He notes that on 30 September 1845 the crew received extra grog to celebrate Percival's thirty-sixth anniversary. Thus 1809 would be the year that they were married. That was the year (in March) when he first joined the navy.

Three years later the War of 1812 began. If ever there was a lop-sided war this was it. The Royal Navy truly ruled the seas. As Dr. David Long points out in his biography of Captain Percival, "A single statistic to bear this out: in 1812 the Royal Navy possessed twice as many warships in commission as the American Navy had guns." Imagine the British surprise when in 1812 the Americans won three single-ship battles- although they did little but boost American morale.

But by 1814 the British, aside from blockading American ports, had a triple invasion plan. Washington, D.C., was burned, the Canadian thrust was stopped on Lake Champlain, and the overwhelming American victory at New Orleans (in which Jean Lafitte, the pirate, played a part) was the final *coup de grace*, even though the Treaty of Ghent had already been signed, ending the war.

Although he was a very junior officer, Percival showed great seamanship and daring. New York was thoroughly bottled up by a British squadron, with a sloop, *Eagle*, guarding the lower harbor. But Percival had a plan: he borrowed a fishing boat, *Yankee*, recruited thirty volunteers hidden below deck, and with bought livestock on deck sailed out of the harbor. Off Sandy Hook he was spotted by *Eagle*. Her captain, Henry Morris, demanded that they surrender. Suddenly the men below boiled up on deck and began shooting. So surprised was Morris that in minutes Percival had captured *Eagle*, losing not a man, as against three dead, two wounded, and eight captured. Percival sailed both vessels in to the Battery (a fort at the tip of Manhattan) before an ecstatic crowd. For this feat he won his nickname, "Mad Jack."

His superior, Commander Jacob Lewis, U.S.N., praised the feat in a letter pointing out "the service performed in the most gallant and officer-like manner by

Sailing Master Percival." The press trumpeted the deed across the country. But Percival quite justly complained that he received no prize money for three captures.

Itching to get into action, Percival finally got his wish. Commander Lewis Warrington,U.S.N., a former shipmate, chose him for the new sloop *Peacock's* sailing master in early 1814. This was no easy job. Christopher McKee in his book on the navy writes:

A sailing master . . .was charged with [the ship] under the captain, supervised the keeping of her log, oversaw receipt and inspection of provisions and stores and the stowage in the hold, kept the ship in her best sailing trim, and was held responsible for the ship's charts, navigational books, and instruments.

Aboard ship, aside from these duties, he had to withstand much insolence from the lordly lieutenants who outranked him, as well as the midshipmen higher on the social ladder. His sense of inferiority was to last his lifetime and embitter his relations with his fellow officers. His only way out was promotion. And a long haul it was: lieutenant in 1814, commander seventeen years later at age fifty-two, and captain at sixty-two in 1841. There he stopped.

On 12 March *Peacock* sneaked through the British blockade and headed for the Bahamas, to try their luck, and then to Cape Canaveral. There Warrington spotted four ships. They were protected by *H.M.S. Épervier*, under Captain Richard Wales. She had aboard $118,000 in silver and gold. Sending the three merchantmen away, Wales headed for a showdown with Warrington. In opening broadsides *Peacock* lost her foremast and maneuverability. But then *Peacock's* excellent training with her guns paid off. After some forty minutes *Épervier's* masts were largely down on deck or in the water, and over forty shot had penetrated her hull. So, with over four feet of water in her bilges, Captain Wales had to surrender. His men had even refused an order to board *Peacock*.

In his report to the Navy Department Commander Warrington gave great praise to his officers and crew. Among others, he singled out "Mad Jack" thus:

In Sailing Master Percival, whose great wish and pride is to obtain a Lieutenant's commission, and whose unremitting and constant attention to duty, added to his professional knowledge, entitles him to it in my opinion, I found an able as well as willing assistant. He handled his ship as if he had been working her into a roadstead.

Congress was so pleased with this lopsided victory that medals went to the captain and officers and swords to Percival and the midshipmen.

But what to do with the sinking *Épervier*? They put the English crew aboard *Peacock*, plugged the holes in the hull, and jury-rigged sails. Lieutenant Nicholson and a prize crew managed to elude the Royal Navy and sail into Savannah on 1 May. Meanwhile Warrington's faster brig-sloop outran three English frigates and also landed in Savannah on 4 May. The $118,000 treasure was safely deposited in the Planter's Bank. Repaired, *U.S.S. Épervier* joined the Mediterranean Squadron off Algiers (where "Old Ironsides" received her nickname) and, having passed Gibraltar on 14 July 1815, disappeared en route home.

In *Peacock*'s next cruise she took and burned twelve prizes from the Grand Banks to the Irish Sea in five months in 1814. Then in 1815, assigned to Decatur's squadron, Warrington, with Captain James Biddle in *Hornet*, had to set out alone because the flagship, *President*, was taken by the blockading force off New York. *Hornet* had to abort the cruise through jettisoning (throwing overboard) most of his armament to escape a ship-of-the-line. In the Dutch East Indies *Peacock* took three rich prizes. Then Warrington made a large mistake: he fired on the East India Company brig *Nautilus* even though they told him that the war was over. On his return he actually lied about the action in a letter to the Navy Department to cover up his quite callous action.

We must take note that, according to Coggeshall's *A History of Privateers*, while the American navy performed valiantly, it was the privateers (sometimes called legalized pirates) whose impact on the war won it. They destroyed or seized about 1400 vessels, and made insurance costs for English shipping go out of sight. In fact, they were the main reason why England accepted a stalemate situation and signed the Treaty of Ghent.

The war over, "Mad Jack" wanted a new billet. He found one -- again with Warrington -- in *Macedonian*, a Royal Navy frigate that Stephen Decatur had captured. Now *U.S.S. Macedonian*, she was headed for Colombia on a diplomatic mission. A good deal of South America was struggling to become independent of Spain, and many Americans had been imprisoned and property taken.

On 28 May 1816 the ship reached Colombia only to find that the Spanish utterly refused to pay compensation for the losses. So the ship turned around and returned home, to be laid up. Percival received orders to the Boston Navy Yard in Charlestown, under Captain Isaac Hull.

Then on 15 October the Barnstable town meeting adopted a handsome resolution honoring Percival for his exploits in the war. His reply was equally fulsome:

Gentlemen: I have had the honor . . . .to receive the vote of thanks of my fellow townsmen. Permit me through the same medium to tender my acknowledgements. . . . .It has, and ever will be, my highest ambition to merit it and receive the approbation of my countrymen. . . . .And am, respectfully, gentlemen, your obedient servant.

John Percival

Captain Hull in *Constitution* had defeated *Guerriere* in 1812 and became a national hero. He and Percival developed a lifelong friendship during his stay at the yard, and it was Percival whose testimony at Hull's court-martial on charges of corruption at the yard saved him. Both men were eager to make extra money, and this need sometimes got them into trouble.

One bureaucratic blow to Percival he never was able to correct. When he was appointed lieutenant, he was number thirteen, but when the commissions were distributed he found himself number thirty-nine. This meant, of course, that he had lost considerable seniority. And try as he might, he was never able to undo this bureaucratic (or malicious) change.

Again aboard *Macedonion* in 1818, on a mission to protect American interests in Chile and Peru "to afford to . . . the citizens of the United States protection and security, consistently with the law of nations. . .", Percival again distinguished himself. A week out from Boston, the ship ran into fifteen hours of a hurricane that wrecked the frigate. She lost the mizzen mast and jib boom; both masts were sprung; she was in real danger. Then the carpenter began to cut away the mainmast. "Mad Jack" yelled at him, "Avast there, or we shall be in eternity in five minutes!" He oversaw the repairs (splinting the mast) and, according to his official record, "saved the frigate *Macedonian* from being dismasted and lost."

The fighting between the royal Spanish forces and the insurgents was fierce and brutal, as was the infighting between the diplomats and the Navy. In the eight months there little was accomplished except release of a few American prisoners. However, Percival did help to defend against a charge that Commander Downes had violated international law by carrying $500,000 in specie for Spanish merchants.

Ordered home via Panama "to bring a number of invalid seamen home,"

Figure 9-2 *U.S.S. Dolphin* engaging two vessels at once, and winning. *Courtesy of Peabody Essex Museum, Salem.*

Percival became executive officer of the Boston Navy Yard, though suffering from "a liver complaint" and "ague and fever." This was the beginning of physical problems that often during the rest of his career were to severely incapacitate him. There he became embroiled in the nearly continual battles within the Navy for position and power. Men fought duels; courts-martial on trumped-up charges ruined reputations. In 1822, for instance, there were three courts-martial in Boston.

Then Stephen Bainbridge replaced Hull at the yard. And because "Mad Jack" had defended Hull against an attack by Bainbridge, he was in a bad position. In fact, Bainbridge told him to request a transfer— which he did. Hull asked for him in his new command, *United States*, for a voyage to Chile, still trying to protect American interests.

There Lieutenant Percival received his first command, *Dolphin*. When news of the hideous *Globe* mutiny reached the United States, the owners of the whaler demanded that the Navy do something. So Commodore Hull received orders to mount a search for the ship, and he chose Percival and *Dolphin* to find her and bring the mutineers to justice.

After a search covering many of the the island groups of the central Pacific, he arrived at Mili Atoll in the Marshall Islands. There he found evidence of the *Globe*'s presence. Searching, they found Lay, who had been a prisoner of the islanders, and thanks to a bold ruse by Lieutenant Paulding freed him. Lay told him where the other survivor, Hussey was, and the next day Paulding freed him. Everyone in *Dolphin* was convinced that these two were not mutineers. Later Lay and Hussey wrote of their adventures.

Before he left Mili Percival gathered the chiefs of the atolls and made a speech, reported by Lay and Hussey, to the effect that since the islanders had killed the mutineers out of ignorance, they would be forgiven. But if ever they attacked another white man, his country would send a force to utterly destroy the people, and their atoll. If they were kind toward whites, they would return the kindness.

On 9 December 1825 *Dolphin* set sail for Hawaii and home. Ten days en route, "Mad Jack" jumped to avoid the main boom while jibing, fell, and cried, "My God, I have ruptured myself!" He had indeed. A double hernia it was, and the doctor had died on Mili. For the rest of his life he wore a double truss. Thirteen years later, in 1837, he applied for a disability pension, which was granted retroactively to the date of the the accident, 22 December. The amount granted was $12.50 a month.

Satisfied that he had accomplished his mission, "Mad Jack" sailed into Honolulu harbor on 14 January. *Dolphin* was the first American warship to visit, and the Americans came in crowds to see her, although the missionaries studiously ignored her. In April Percival held a royal reception aboard, to which the young King Kamehameha III and his mother Queen Kaahumanuu, the regent, came. They were delighted with the ship.

In 1826 Honolulu was a native village still. The first seven couples of

Christian missionaries, sent out from Boston, had come only five years before, and seven more were to arrive by that date. These first arrivals found a chaotic situation: the old taboos went with the death of Kamehameha I; the idols and temples were in shambles. An ideal time to "civilize" these natives!

The next kings were not strong, and it was relatively easy for the missionaries to begin to impose their ways. They invented the muumuu, a total body wraparound, to cover the women's nakedness, for example, and they required the natives to build "proper" houses, as well as introducing this new single god. And they established new taboos— including a ban on women fraternizing with the ships in harbor. The officers "made out" by taking a "wife" and living ashore; the crews, used to their women aboard, were most unhappy.

Eventually, after Percival had tried very hard to persuade the Queen Regent to relax the taboo on women, On 26 February Percival's crew on liberty, with men from in-port whalers, rioted, demanding women. A nasty confrontation occurred, until Percival arrived. Flailing at his men with his cane, he shouted, "I'll teach you to disgrace us!" In irons, his men returned to the ship and were flogged. Percival apologized to the missionaries but still urged relaxation of the taboo. Shortly several chiefs acquiesced, to the delight of the ships' crews.

The repercussions from this incident were horrendous. The press in the United States, under misionary pressure, condemned Percival. But the businessmen in the islands upheld him; in fact, they begged him to stay longer. So it wasn't until 11 May that *Dolphin* left, finally arriving in Valparaiso, Chile, on 23 June, after ten months. Meanwhile, Commodore Hull was worried about *Dolphin* and ordered *Peacock* to sail to find him. When Percival arrived and told his story, Hull was

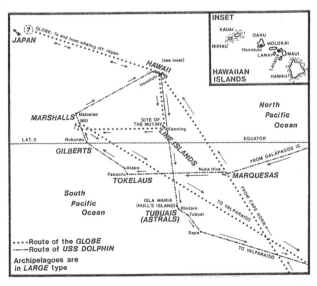

Figure 9-3 Chart of the *Globe's* track (leading to the mutiny) and the track of the *Dolphin,* Percival's first command, in finding the two survivors of the mutiny. *Courtesy of Greenwood Press., Westport, Conn.*

pleased, saying "... it meets with my approbation." And Hull's reports to the Navy Department carefully omitted to mention the confrontations in Hawaii.

Back in Boston, the next two years were legal nightmares for Percival. He had, first of all, made enemies of two captains in Honolulu, involving his rescue of one ship and a large sum of money. These two were to dog "Mad Jack's" footsteps for years. And when he arrived in Boston in *United States* he found himself arrested. A New York newspaper reported the event:

Lieut. Percival . . . whose conduct was so offensive to the Missionaries, arrived. . .and was arrested before landing . . .by writs of individuals for grievances unconnected with the outrage upon the Missionaries. For want of bail, he was committed to prison.

He stayed there nine days. In fact Captain Edwards instituted five different suits against Percival, none of which seemed to be successful. Meanwhile a larger threat loomed: the attack by the American Board of Commisioners for Foreign Missions. This led to a naval court of inquiry in 1828. The three commodores (judges) had some sixteen charges to deal with, which they boiled down to four because of repetitions:

Public and Personal Immorality: The judges decided that the evidence presented was was largely hearsay, dismissing the charge.
Violence in Deed and Language: The court sided with Percival., His defense succeeded.
Interference with Government: The court said that there was "no evidence of [his] having interfered with the government in the manner stated."
Hectoring Witnesses: The court again found for Percival.

As a result a court-martial was "not necessary or proper."

But he was not entirely free. Secretary Southard in 1829 wrote him chiding him for his conduct in Hawaii. And the missionary camp was deeply disappointed and angry; the "cover-up" had succeeded, they felt, and Percival was not cashiered. In fact his promotion to commander was effective on 3 March 1831.

For the next few years we find Percival in command of *Porpoise* and *Erie* in the Caribbean and South America. He was still trying to correct his loss of numbers in rank, still suffering from gout and other problems. But his carrying out of orders was exemplary. He carried out the rescue of the merchant ship *Java*'s crew and its cargo; he salvaged the cargo of *Corsica*; he saved the brig *Rodney*, its crew and cargo, stranded on the Cuban coast. During a slave uprising in Jamaica in 1832, to ensure the safety of American interests he sailed there. But finding no need for intervention, he soon returned to Pensacola. He noted that some 36,000 slaves participated in the uprising. One effect of it was passage by Parliament of abolition of slavery by 1838.

Back at the Boston Navy Yard under Bainbridge, who retired very soon, he had command of *Columbus*, a receiving ship. Its purpose was to act as a "boot camp," training recruits for their shipboard duties. In fact, one of his major concerns was always the education of midshipmen in his commands.

Next in the sloop *Erie*, he spent a year in the South Atlantic, the only U.S. presence in the area. Brazil, too, was in revolt against Emperor Dom Pedro I. Then a strong squadron of French ships arrived. Involved was an old claim of 1815 on France for indemnification for illegal French seizures during the 1790's. Tensions were high between the two countries until in 1834 France paid up.

Then Percival made another political mistake. He inspected the navy warehouse in Rio— and found it a total mess. The officer in charge was cashiered, but his boss, Commodore Renshaw, resented the inspection. Later, on 11 August 1835, gave the *Erie* command to someone else and sent "Mad Jack" home. There had been a number of instances of friction between the two men. It was at this point that Percival applied for his disability pension, which was granted, retroactive to 1825, of $12.50 a month. That meant some $1500 back pay.

A most insightful picture of Percival arose from a dinner aboard the U.S. Revenue Service cutter *Hamilton*, with Nathaniel Hawthorne and Percival as guests. Several hours' conversation elicited this reaction from Hawthorne:

And shortly down comes old Captain Percival a white haired, thin-visaged, weather-worn old gentleman, in a blue, Quakercut coat, with tarnished lace and brass buttons; a pair of drab pantaloons, and brown waistcoat. He has not risen to his present rank in the regular line . . . and has all the roughness of that class of officers. Nevertheless, he knows how to behave and talk like

Figure 9-4 Portrait of the *U.S.S. Cyane* in 1838, one of the ships Percival served on.

a gentleman. . . . Percival seems to be the very pattern of old integrity, . . . to have no ambition beyond his present duties . . . ; at any rate he now passes his life in a kind of gruff contentedness, grumbling and growling, yet in good humor enough.

While Percival was, as usual, fighting to get another sea command, in June 1836 four seamen were severely injured in a train wreck. Crippled and helpless, they appealed to Percival for legal help in getting compensation. The railroad's insurance company offered $12,862, to be divided among the four, at $200 per year. "Mad Jack" became trustee and, to simplify a very long, tortuous story, he never paid them any of their compensation. That amount is listed in his estate at death. He stole their compensation.

His next command was the ship, *Cyane*, as part of the Mediterranean Squadron. Departing in June 1838, he was on his own until Commodore Hull arrived in *Ohio*. In Naples he met *H.M.S. Hastings*, with George IV's widow aboard. He says,

I felt it proper to show every mark of respect . . .[and] *I manned the yards, fired a salute of 21 guns and gave three cheers. The dowager Queen was so pleased that she sent the* Hastings' *captain "to express her personal thanks for the courtesy."*

During this two-year period perhaps his biggest problem was his midshipmen; stuck in grade in a peacetime navy, frustrated, they were always in trouble, quarreling, even dueling, drinking. At the same time his interest in their naval education was paramount. In fact their liberty ashore he tied to their performance in class. The crew, too, was unruly, so that he had to resort to the cat-o'-nine-tails very frequently.

Now pushing sixty, "Mad Jack" was more and more unable to exercise command. Soon after arrival in "the Med," he had to turn the command over to his first lieutenant, Samuel Lockwood, who performed well. Percival's gout, his double hernia, and rheumatism together felled this strong personality, and he received a long leave of absence beginning in August 1839.

After two years in inactive status, during which he received his promotion to Captain in September 1841, he was tired of living at home in Dorchester with his wife and daughter. He began again to importune the department for a command, preferably as a Commodore. Finally given *Franklin*, a ship-of-the-line, on 8 July 1943 he had to recommission her in Boston and outfit her as a receiving ship for recruits. Then on 19 October he received orders as commander of *Constitution*. Quite a quick change here.

She had been temporarily laid up in Norfolk until a decision as to reconditioning could be made. A famous naval architect said that $70,000 would be needed to put her into proper condition for an extended cruise of perhaps three years. But "Mad Jack" made his own survey and produced a figure of only $10,000. One probably apocryphal story tells of his stripping to his "longjohns" and swimming around and under the hull. In any case, his old commander, Commodore Warrington, approved that figure, as did Secretary Henshaw, and Percival became her captain.

By February 1844 (He was almost sixty-five) he reported that the hull was recoppered and caulked, the deck and sides renewed as needed, and other repairs done. The fifty guns were aboard, and "Old Ironsides" was ready for a world cruise. In New York he filled his complement of 450 men.

His orders were to round Africa and stop at Mozambique and Madagascar, Sumatra, Java, Borneo, "Cochin China" (Viet Nam), and the China coast. En route he was to gather all possible commercial, political, strategic, scientific, and cultural information. "The promotion and maintenance of friendly relations would be absolutely essential to the success of his mission."

Before he left, his wife and "adopted daughter" came aboard and stayed for four days, to everyone's delight. Then Henry Wise, an old friend, and his family visited, preparatory to sailing to Rio as American Ambassador to Brazil. Since the family included two girls of marriageable age, Percival warned everyone as to language and behavior.

Figure 9-5 "Old Ironsides", drawn and published by William Lynn. *Courtesy of Peabody Essex Museum.*

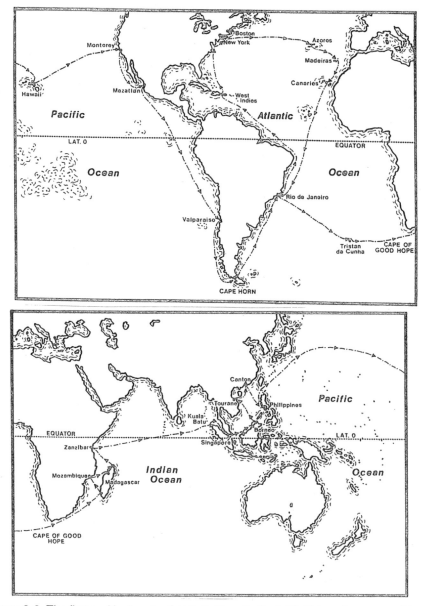

Figure 9-6 The first and last parts of *U.S.S. Constitution's* 52,000+ mile voyage, May 1844 to September 1846. *Courtesy of Westwood Press.*

Percival asked for a small sloop or brig to handle shallow waters in various places. But ultimately his request was denied, and *Constitution* sailed alone on 29 May. Later her near-groundings in the East Indies showed how short-sighted this decision was. The frigate was nearly lost several times for lack of the smaller vessel. Two years and four months later she was to sail safely into New York harbor.

The details of her manning may be of interest. There were thirty-two officers, petty officers, surgeons, etc. Of the 381 sailors, 169 were American. But there were 212 foreigners: 115 English and Irish, 28 Scandinavians, 25 Germans, and a smattering of many others. Five Chinese were to serve as interpreters.

On this solo cruise of 52,370 miles, Percival was alone, with no higher authority. The success or failure of the entire enterprise was in his hands. He was to have little difficulty with his motley crew; his reputation was so great in the forecastle that he "could do no wrong." According to Midshipman Dale's journal, he was "a strict disciplinarian and he was at once beloved and feared by all."

Examples of his concern were seeing to it that the forecastle food was fairly divided, in the tropics painting the ship's hull light gray (instead of the original black) to lessen the heat in the crew's quarters, and even-handedness in punishments. "The cat" being the major punishment, we can compare the roughly seventy uses during the whole voyage to Commander DuPont's forty-one in one month in 1845.

Percival knew well that a busy crew is a contented crew. Thus aside from the regular watches and sail handling, gunnery drills, boarding party drills, and target practice were daily routine. In addition, the multifarious tasks of keeping a huge wooden ship watertight gave little time for grumbling or plots.

The first goal was Rio de Janeiro, to deliver Ambassador Wise to his new post. Percival's sailing route seems roundabout, but in fact the winds and currents make this route the fastest. A few days in the Azores, the Madeiras, and the Canaries made good liberty ports, although the officers were appalled at the miserable poverty, especially in the Azores and Canaries.

After sixty-four days they arrived in Rio, one of the most beautiful harbors in the world, "having," as the captain wrote, "not lost a man either by desertion or death. The Ship had performed every way equal to my expectations." During their five week stay in Rio, Percival's biggest problem was resupply of "Beef, Pork, and Bread" for the long 8000-mile leg to Macao. The government stores were simply inadequate.

Constitution left Rio on 8 September, bound for Madagascar. A month later a heavy storm hammered the old ship, loosening the oakum in the hull. But on 17 October the ship was at anchor off Madagascar. Then on to Mozambique, a Portuguese colony. At each port he met with the governor or consul to discuss increased trade with the United States. It was here that he again displayed his shiphandling skill. With the wind dead ahead, he had to tack many times, coming "within about 2 cable lengths [1400 feet] of the surf, and then we would go about with the surf under our stern," writes a somewhat scared midshipman. Percival was an astute political observer. As well as sizing up the situation in Madagascar, he reported that soon the island would become a French possession; it did.

Now in tropical waters, the usual discomforts aboard a wooden ship in-

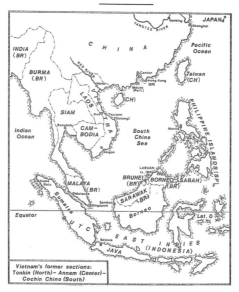

Figure 9-7 The most dangerous part of the voyage through the East Indies with totally inadequate charts. Surprisingly (but for Captain Percival's seamanship) the old ship never ran hard aground. *Courtesy of Westwood Press.*

cluded the hordes of rats and roaches. One captain fumigated his small frigate and wrote that "exclusive of the young . . . [the smoke killed] . . . from twelve hundred to fifteen hundred rats. Percival's naturalist wrote: "The cockroaches eat off the officers' and mens' [sic] toenails while asleep and it was a common thing to hunt for dead mice in the hammocks in the morning."

Sailing north, they next visited Zanzibar, where Percival and his officers dined with the Sultan, met the American and British consuls, and wrote home of the need for a U.S. squadron in the Indian Ocean to protect American shipping interests. The Sultan gave Percival a jeweled sword, which he left to his friend John Bursley in his will of 1861.

After eight days there, *Constitution*, freshly supplied, left on 26 November for the Dutch East Indies. They headed into hotter and hotter weather, nearing 100^0 often. The light hull paint made a great difference to the comfort of the crew, as several people wrote. The ship's clerk noted that after 120 days in the tropics they had not lost a man— an enviable record. But shortly thereafter two men died, and the sick bay was crowded. Percival's many physical problems ganged up on him to such an extent that he had his coffin made and turned the operation of the ship over to his first lieutenant, Amasa Paine.

Finally on 5 January 1845 they reached Sumatra in the Dutch East Indies. Percival's first problem was to reinforce American demands that piracy be stopped. As before, he called the local chiefs together and threatened dire consequences if it were not. His prohibitions worked for a while, but later on the pirates set upon more

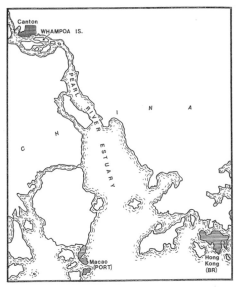

Figure 9-8 This chart shows the problems involved in sailing far up the Pearl River to Canton. *Courtesy of Westwood Press.*

merchantmen.

The next port was Singapore, founded in 1819 by Sir Thomas Raffles and now the premier trading port in the Indies— and the healthiest. The almost month-long stay was a boon to the crew, with liberty ashore, but Percival was still stricken with "an attack of Dystentery [sic], followed by a disease of the liver [and] gout." Amasa Paine had "met his arduous obligation superbly," in navigating and handling "Old Ironsides."

Next came Kalimantan in Borneo. Percival was required to explore chances of greater American trade in this area, where Dutch and English interests predomi- nated. There appeared to be little chance, according to the Dutch governor. And his attempt to negotiate for a coaling station were unsuccessful. Farther north he had no better luck with the English part of Borneo.

Running along the coast, *Constitution* found herself in dangerous waters, with inadequate charts. Several times she scraped on coral or temporarily grounded. In fact, over an eleven day period the old ship struggled with shallow waters. Percival, I am sure, must have thought about his request for a sloop or brig.

Percival's next port of call was "Tourane" (Danang to the thousands of Americans in the Viet Nam War) in Cochin China. This state had been a tributary of China since about 900 A.D. But the Portuguese and French missionaries, begin- ning about 1500, had proselytized so successfully that there were at least 300,000 Christians in the north.

The emperor however, began to attack the priests, executing some and driving many from the country. One such was Bishop Dominique Lefevre, who was sentenced to death. At this point Percival stepped in and committed the greatest blunder of his career. He decided to free the bishop and made a series of dire threats of action against the authorities unless the bishop were free.

But his threats were really empty, and the Chinese simply refused to respond with any action or even discussion. He even took several mandarins hostage, but then released them as he began to realize that, as Dale wrote, "It seems we are doomed to be humbugged by these cunning rascals." From 10 May to the night of 27 May this standoff continued. Finally Percival weighed anchor and, after lobbing a few shots at the fort, sailed for China, humiliated by the refusal of the Chinese to take any action at all. His mistake, of course, was to try to enforce a program without the strength to carry it out.

The bishop survived. The emperor decided not to decapitate him; the French and the British were enough enemies for his regime. Finally the bishop was arrested and turned over to the French authorities aboard *Alcmene*. Eventually of course, the French took over Cochin China as a colony, French Indo-China, although some of the Vietnamese held out until 1890.

How to shed the best possible light on this fiasco? First he won great praise from the French anthorities there, who said that his actions had greatly improved Franco-American relations and ultimately saved the bishop. After many draftings, he sent a long, self-serving report to the Navy Secretary, Dr. George Bancroft, the historian. He wrote on the report: "The Department wholly disapproved of the conduct of Captain Percival as not warranted either by the demands of the Bishop or the law of nations." Later President Taylor sent an envoy to apologize for the actions of Percival. But, typically, they said that they could not receive the letter because no such action had occurred.

Percival's arrival in Canton happened three years after the British launched the "Opium War," to protect their deadly and lucrative trade with China. The Chinese emperor was trying to wipe out the British opium trade, but the British instead wiped out the Chinese fleets and forced a surrender. Five cities were opened to Western trade by treaty, and Hong Kong became a British colony in 1842. By a treaty of 1844 the United States received most-favored nation status and extraterritoriality.

Because of all this diplomatic maneuvering, Percival felt that he had to stay in Canton, far up the Pearl River, for longer than planned. This was a hard time: high heat and humidity, mosquitoes, daily rain storms— and dysentery from drinking river water, though filtered through charcoal. Tensions were high; the merchants asked him to stay on for the ship's calming effect. While waiting, "Mad Jack," as he had once before, raised almost $1800 on board for relief of Pittsburgh's awful fire in April. He asked Chief Justice Lemuel Shaw in Boston to see that the money went to the "proper person in Pittsburgh" and to have a list of the subscribers published there. He also almost became involved in a duel (at age sixty-six) with a naval storekeeper.

Finally, on 1 September, *Constitution* sailed for Manila. En route he came

Figure 9-9 The factories ("hongs") of Canton. *Courtesy of Peabody Essex Museum.*

on a British squadron of six sail and steam vessels. Since the dispute over the Oregon boundary was still unsettled, he prepared for battle, but Admiral Cochrane was delighted to see "Old Ironsides," for he was low on bread and whiskey. Since Percival was well stocked, he provided 14,000 pounds of bread and four hundred gallons of whiskey! A cordial series of meetings occurred, and salutes were exchanged.

Percival stayed in Manila for only nine days and then headed for Hawaii on

Figure 9-10 Captain Percival in late middle age. *Courtesy of the U.S. Naval Academy Museum.*

the great circle route, arriving on 17 October after a miserable, storm-tossed passage. There they were ordered to sail for the west coast and join the squadron there— most disappointing news indeed; they had been gone eighteen months.

While in Honolulu Percival entertained King Kamehameha III and discussed Hawaii's military situation. He recommended developing Pearl Harbor as a major naval port, the first to see its strategic value. Later, in 1887, Hawaii granted a U.S. naval base there. Eleven years later the U.S. annexed Hawaii. But that is another long story. Strangely, no one raised a quibble about "Mad Jack's" previous visit in 1826, when he ran roughshod over the missionaries' plans. Neither newspaper mentioned the affair, although they were published by missionary sons.

Leaving Honolulu on 2 December, the ship bucked storms all the way to Monterey, Mexico, arriving on 31 December. In accord with the ancient military saying, "Hurry up and wait, " for the next three months *Constitution* stayed anchored, idle, in Mazatlan. Then their luck turned, and she was released to go home. Two weeks later the Mexican War started. But they had left on 22 April 1846. And great was the rejoicing thereat!

The voyage home, with stops at Valparaiso and Rio, was so routine that the diarists aboard said very little about it. But rounding Cape Horn on 4 July was difficult. Midshipman Dale wrote: "our Independence Day dinner underwent marvelous transformations and confusions, not to mention . . . turkies [sic] that took wing even from the carver's fork."

On 27 September 1846 "Old Ironsides" came home, after 52,370 1/2 nautical miles and nearly thirty months. One would have hoped for some recognition of the feat; no Boston newspaper even mentioned it. On 5 October the old ship was decommissioned, and Percival went home to Dorchester.

One cannot leave without quoting a midshipman's diary:

. . . she's now come home like her aged Commander [67] to lay her old bones up "for a full due.". . . Every old plank,bolt, spar and rope yarn in her has a share of my love. She's been my Home, my Friend [,] my Pride. . . .I can scarcely bear the idea of leaving her, but I must.

Not quite done with her, Percival took her to Norfolk for repairs. And she sailed on to the Mediterranean in 1848-1851, to Africa in 1853-1855. By 1860 she had become a training ship for the new Naval Academy at Annapolis. And what better school?

Because there was no Navy rule on retirement age, "Mad Jack" after a year of leave started campaigning for the post of commander of the Boston Navy Yard. For two years he pulled every string he had, but in 1849 his old friend John Downes was appointed.

Meanwhile the Treasury Department charged Percival for the pay ($2000) of the *Constitution*'s naturalist, J.C. Reinhart, saying that the appointment was

Figure 9-11 A recent photograph of Captain John Percival's memorial plaque in the West Barnstable Cemetery, facing Route 6-A. *Photograph by the author.*

"without the warrant of law." His only appeal, he realized was an act of Congress, and after several attempts he got his money back in 1848.

Now that he was retired, his activities become hard to trace, even through the 1850's and 1860's. He lived in his lovely house in Dorchester; it burned down some time after 1969. Often he visited West Barnstable, staying with Charles Bursley, his lifelong friend; Bursley at his behest allegedly built the stone walls around the front and side of the West Barnstable cemetery and was never paid by Percival for the work.

In his will he left $2000 for a fund "to be [used] toward paying an adequate compensation to the teachers . . . of [West Barnstable]." And he left $10,000 "for the maintenance of a High School," but with tight restrictions; the high school opened in 1873, long before the money was available. With other acts he was most generous to his town. Other bequests went to organizations there, and generous gifts went to young friends and relatives.

The Percivals never had children, but Maria's niece, Maria Weeks, lived with them for years. "Mad Jack" always referred to her as their "adopted daughter," although not legally. Later she tried to claim his entire estate as his daughter—to no avail.

Mrs. Percival, whose prodigal ways had him in desperation, earned this comment to his lawyer in 1862:

. . . but this is, I suppose [,] a part of <u>the usuages women's zealously looked for as the practical commencement of the millenium [sic] of women's rule and women's happiness</u>.

Note: Emphasis is mine. Percival was not insensitive to the early ferment for women's rights.

That year she died.

"Mad Jack" had outlived all his relatives, as well as his Navy peers such as Hull, Warrington, Downes, and Bainbridge. His last few years were peaceful, and he too died in 1862—on 17 September, almost eighty-three years old. His marriage to Maria had lasted fifty-three years. Given his physical problems—gout, hernias, dysentery, liver problems—it is a wonder he lived so long. He was a tough old bird!

His obituary appeared in Boston and two Cape Cod papers, but at his funeral in Dorchester there were no military men: they were all at the funeral of Major Jesse Reno, killed in action in the West. However, the Barnstable funeral was well attended, and he was buried in the West Barnstable cemetery.

His executor, John Healy, for some unknown reason delayed probate unconscionably until 1889, twenty-seven years after "Mad Jack's" death. The will left a total of $22,500 to five seamen's societies and a home for little wanderers in Boston. In his estate was the $12,756.42 insurance payment for the three disabled seamen, for which he was trustee. He never paid them.

What sort of man was John Percival? A primary trait was his sense of inferiority, with several causes: a grade school education; social inferiority among his peers; a lower middle class family; a naval career "up through the hawsepipe," as sailors say; an education self-achieved. His feelings of paranoia (with considerable cause) hardly endeared him to his superiors, with whom he fought over assignments—as everyone did. And his temper was "on a short fuse" a good deal of the time—caused perhaps by his severe physical problems.

He made three political mistakes: riding roughshod over the Hawaiian missionaries' plans; inspecting the Navy storehouse in Rio and incurring the wrath of his commander; and the Viet Nam fiasco. But that's not bad for an active career of thirty-six years.

He was generous, beloved by his crews because of his concern for their welfare, admired and respected by many of his naval superiors and equals for his bravery and exquisite seamanship. His special concern for his midshipmen's education was remarkable. And his handling of his duties during the "Old Ironsides" cruise was exemplary, barring Viet Nam. He was blasphemous, generous, sly, honest, dishonest. He was in fact, beloved by many, hated by many.

Perhaps the best tribute to him was written by Axel Adlersparre, a young Swede whom Percival met while in *Cyane*. The relationship became one of father-son, so that many years later Adlersparre wrote "Mad Jack":

I have always considered you my guardian angel, to whom, next to God, I am indebted for the happy turn in my destiny. . . . My feelings of love and gratitude will never cease to exist, and my sincere wish is that I may see you once more in this world.

In 1861 Axel sailed into New York in his Swedish frigate and wrote that he planned to be in Boston in 1862; he may have gotten his wish; "Mad Jack" died in September.

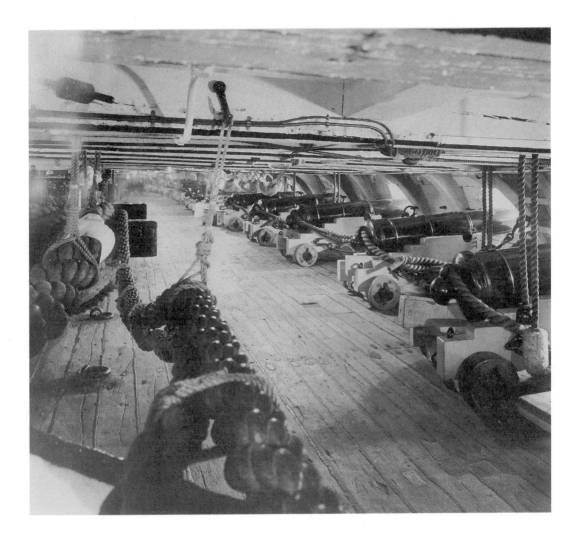

Figure 9-11A The gun deck of *U.S.S. Constitution* ("Old Ironsides") carried 36 cannon throwing twenty-four pound shot, while British ships of the period were armed only with eighteen-pounder cannon. So "Old Ironsides" could pound the British ships into surrender, and with the extra range, have the British shot bounce off her thick oaken hull. *Courtesy of William P. Quinn.*

Figure 9-12 Captain Josiah Richardson in his heyday as master. *Courtesy of the author, Dr. Louis A. Norton.*

A Tough But Tenacious Breed

These words of Samuel Eliot Morison accurately describe the men who plied the oceans of the world during the great days of sail. Whether they fought their way around Cape Horn— often a thirty-day struggle to get from the Atlantic to the Pacific Ocean; or fought the North Atlantic in the packet trade; or specialized in the Far Eastern trade with India and China— ice was a favored cargo to India, for example; or "went coastwise" - the commanders of these vessels were a special breed.

The risks were enormous. Accurate navigation was just being developed; an accurate chronometer was a very expensive essential; charts were often rudimentary at best (During World War II, even, the charts of the South Pacific were often illusional. Off the coast of New Guinea was a legend: *"Reefs Reported by D'Entrecasteaux, 1798."*) In 1830 Lloyd's of London reported 677 ships lost at sea; in 1881, 973. And each captain had to act alone, as best he knew how.

And each Cape Cod and island town's history lists the names of its (often hundreds of) captains. One of the finest was Josiah Richardson, born in 1807 in Centerville. Cabin boy at age eleven, by the time he was twenty-one he was in the coasting trade and the Mediterranean as master of the schooner *Hetty Thom*, sailing out of Duxbury, Massachusetts. Married early, he was a strong family man and a deacon of his church in Shrewsbury.

In 1847 we find him navigating the packet *Walpole*, delivering cargoes of

Figure 9-13 Donald McKay of East Boston, builder of many of the greatest clipper ships, of which *Staghound* was the very first. *Courtesy of the Sturgis Library, Barnstable.*

wheat to Liverpool and bringing freight and passengers back to New York. This North Atlantic route was the roughest, most dangerous of them all, but the packets were stout, fast sailors. The worst problem was finding crews; by the 1850's the only available men were those hanging around the waterfronts, a rough bunch indeed, and the captains had to control them somehow.

A step up was command of the well-known packet *Townsend* in 1849. He was already known as a "gentleman skipper," deeply religious: one of the nobility of masters. Part owner of *Walpole*, he was later hurt badly by her loss at the mouth of the Columbia River, amounting to $10,000— no small amount then. The packets were no real money-makers (too labor-intensive), but, as he wrote his wife in 1849, "It is best to live comfortable, if we die poor." The next year was to belie these sentiments.

This was the year when Donald McKay of East Boston, the master shipbuilder, began his series of great clipper ships. These floating masterpieces were an answer to the rapidly expanding world trade. The first of the series was *Stag Hound*, twice the size of *Townsend*, and a radically different design— so different that many in the field doubted her value. And Josiah Richardson became her captain. A marine underwriter asked him if he were not nervous in such an experimental design, to which he replied, "No, Mr. Jones. I would not go in the ship at all, if I thought for a moment it would be my coffin."

The Boston Atlas on 26 December 1850, praised the ship thus:

This magnificent ship has been the wonder of all who have seen her. Not only is she largest in her class afloat, but her model may be said to be the original of a new idea in naval architecture. She is longer and sharper than any other vessel . . . while her breadth of beam and depth of hold are designed with special reference to stability.

On 1 February 1851 she set out for San Francisco with a crew of forty-eight for the arduous 16,000-mile run around Cape Horn. Because of her already great reputation, her cargo space sold for $1 a cubic foot— an amazing price, amounting to $70,000. Contrast this with the $3,000 Captain Richardson's packet made for a voyage across the Atlantic.

Less than a week out of Boston, *Stag Hound* ran into a powerful gale, losing her main topsail and three topgallant masts. Once repairs were made, Captain Richardson rescued the crew of a Russian ship off Brazil. His log reads:

At 6 A. M. discovered ahead small boat with nine men in it. . . .Took them on board. They were the Captain and crew of Russian brig Sylphide, *loaded at Rio with coffee, bound for Helsingfors. Was upset in a squall four days previous. One man, carpenter, drowned.*

For the rescue he received a letter of thanks from the Russian ambassador via Daniel Webster, then the Secretary of State. Considering all the delays, *Stag Hound* was only a day behind the record when she reached Valparaiso, Chile. And her time of 107 days to San Francisco was a record. The captain wrote the owners: "The ship is yet to be built to beat the *Stag Hound*. I am in love with the ship."

Once unloaded, *Stag Hound* sailed for China for a cargo of tea. Her run back to New York (the "round voyage," as sailors called it) took ninety-four days, a very fast passage considering the winter season. On 24 December 1851 *Stag Hound* secured from sea, having paid for herself and put an additional $80,000 in the pockets of her owners.

But Captain Richardson wanted to spend some time with his family and so resigned his command. He was ashore for all of three months, however. Donald McKay had built the very large packet *Staffordshire*— 1817 tons, 240 feet long— for Enoch Train and Company. Train persuaded Captain Richardson to command her for an envisioned rich world trade and California freight.

Staffordshire sailed on 3 May 1852 with 120 passengers and a full cargo. His passengers were so delighted with their captain that they gave him a silver pitcher "as a slight token of respect for the many kind attentions received at your hands." Sailing like a clipper, she arrived in San Francisco in 102 days, winning the race with Captain Judah P. Baker's *Shooting Star* by three days. Such races were common.

One of the most famous was the race between two East Dennis brothers. Captain Levi Howes in *Starlight* challenged Captain Allison Howes in the East Dennis-built, superb *Belle of the West* to a race from Calcutta to Boston. *Starlight* went down the river twelve hours ahead of *Belle*; they sighted each other three

Figure 9-14 A portrait of *Staghound*, of 1535 tons, built and designed by Donald McKay. *Courtesy of Sturgis Library.*

times during the voyage; and *Starlight* came into Boston twelve hours ahead of *Belle*— a 17,000-mile dead heat!

The San Francisco waterfront was all agog at seeing this imposing, record-breaking packet, and the captain was fawned over by everyone. But his idea of using his fame was to address a Sunday school class. Kittredge remarks:

"Here is an anomaly. . . .A clipper ship captain beats the fleet . . . and spends what time he can spare . . . to bring the Word of God to Sunday School children."

On he went to Singapore and then to Calcutta, and on the last leg of the voyage he made Boston in eighty-three days— the fifth fastest record trip, and in a packet, not a clipper. Careful, even cautious, he did not try for records; he was just extremely skillful. In fact, in foggy weather he stood off Boston for a day instead of risking the ship on the rocks outside Boston.

Next *Staffordshire* took up the Liverpool run, with the idea of selling her, but no buyer appeared. So, on 9 December 1853 Captain Richardson sailed for Boston with 214 passengers and crew and freight. He had written his wife:

I will not go in her [again] at any price. . .Wish I was with you and did not have to make the western passage. . . Life is uncertain and all the property I possess I wish my dear wife and children to have and enjoy.

This sounds like a last will and testament— and in a sense it was.

Figure 9-15 The packet *Staffordshire*. *Courtesy of Sturgis Library.*

Figure 9-16 The loss of *Staffordshire* on Seal Island, off Maine, with the loss of 170 lives. *Courtesy of the author, Dr. Louis A. Norton.*

All was going smoothly until, two weeks out; in a heavy gale *Staffordshire's* rudder sustained serious damage, making the ship difficult to maneuver. Five days later an even worse storm broke off the bowsprit and seriously weakened the foremast by carrying away much of the rigging.

To check on the damage, the captain climbed up to see what could be done. As he was climbing down he lost his footing and fell over thirty feet to the deck, breaking his ankle and spine, according to the surgeon. From his bed he directed his Chief Mate, Joseph Alden, to make repairs.

The story of the wreck comes from the account of Joseph Alden, one of the survivors. Under minimum sail the ship continued westward until, on the night of the 29th, the lookout sighted the lights of Seal Island. But as *Staffordshire*, with her crippled rudder and damaged foremast, struggled to come about she crashed onto a rock, hung there for about five minutes, and then sank bowfirst. In those brief minutes, in the midst of a howling snowstorm, a few boats swung out, but only forty-four survived, including four mates (in charge of the boats).

Josiah Richardson refused any attempt to move him from his bed in the cabin. The *Boston Journal* quoted the chief mate as saying that the captain's last words were, "If I am lost, God's will be done." And so he died as did 169 others.

Forty-four years old, Josiah Richardson had in three brief years shown what the future of American sailing ships was to be. Samuel Eliot Morison summed up this superb achievement thus:

Never, in these United States, has the brain of man conceived, or the hand of man fashioned, so perfect a thing as the clipper ship. . . .For a brief moment of time they flashed their splendor around the world, then disappeared with the sudden completeness of the wild [passenger] pigeon.

The Adventures of Captain Baxter

After fifty-five years at sea, Captain Joseph Baxter of West Dennis decided he had had enough seafaring and came ashore. He was sixty-five. He lived another seventeen years, recollecting his adventures during those long years. And they were many and exciting.

At ten (in 1844) he landed a job as cook on one of his father's ships, like many of his peers. By the time he was nineteen he was mate on the brig *Erie*. On the night of 30 November 1853, the brig was run down and almost sunk by the *Bell Rock*, which was running with no lights. It was a hit-and-run, and three men were found missing, including Henry Baxter, his brother.

Everyone thought they had drowned, but three months later Henry came home with a tale of being rescued by the other ship, of being forced to work their way to England, being refused any pay, and being virtually imprisoned on the ship. Somehow he got away and shipped aboard an American ship to get home.

That winter of 1853 was one of the worst in Cape Cod marine history. Off Cape Cod alone seventy vessels were either wrecked on the beaches or foundered at sea, and that many seamen and fishermen from South and West Dennis lost their lives.

Consequently Joseph decided he'd "sail foreign," with Captain Chase of Harwich in the clipper *Starlight*, bound for San Francisco. His idea of a land of milk and honey was rudely blasted by the reality of the city and its people. He described the place thus:

Gold was there as we had hoped, but there were likewise men. Men from all parts of the earth, of every color, tongue and condition; good men, bad men

Figure 9-17 The clipper ship *Starlight*, of 1150 tons, built in South Boston. Note the extreme flare of the bow. *Courtesy of the Peabody Essex Museum.*

just out of prison, and many who surely should have been in prison. Men with pick, shovel, and an honest ambition, others with dirk, pistol and an unhallowed greed. Every "fortune" had from four to ten men trying to get it by fair means or foul. . . .Where once had stood an old ship [hauled up] on the mud, now is the center of a great city.

Now out of a job, he became cook for a Captain Coleman, trading in the bay area, because he knew how to cook beans! Sailing in the bay and up the rivers, they saw "wild country, for in nearly all the ravines were found beasts of prey and Indians no less ferocious."

After six months with Captain Coleman, he became captain of a sloop and later a schooner and was invited to join the San Francisco Vigilance Committee of some three thousand men, organized to impose the rule of law (illegally) on a totally lawless situation. They organized courts, elected judges, and tried suspected criminals. Conviction meant death by hanging before the day was over.

Finding trade less profitable than expected, Baxter's owners decided to charter the *Nickerson and Baxter* to the Pacific Islands for fruit and turtles. The first stop was Guam, fruitless and turtleless. Then on they went to Saipan, where they met the king. He ordered his subjects to bring all the limes, lemons, and coconuts they could find to the ship.

Being ready to sail, the captain invited the king and his family aboard for a farewell dinner. The king offered the marriageable daughter to Baxter and offered him the kingship if he would stay. Baxter reports:

I told him that this was very unexpected, that I had started out a humble seaman. . . .To become a king had never been any part of my ambition, and that I would want at least one night in which to think it over.

To solve the problem, early the next morning they set sail, planning to go to the Marshall Islands for turtles. But, hit by a typhoon, they were so damaged that they had to limp back to San Francisco.

Now twenty-two, he aimed higher and shipped as a mate aboard the clipper ship *Golden West* for Hong Kong. Buying a ticket for Canton, up the Pearl River, just to see the sights he ran headfirst into the Opium Wars between England and China. Canton had been bombarded by the British fleet, and half the city was in flames. A soldier stopped him and his friends. "He said that a white man's head was worth about five hundred dollars. . . .We thought best not to sell at that figure but wait for a better market." Finally they found a place to sleep in the kitchen of the American consulate, the place being otherwise full.

Off to Macao and Hong Kong by steamer, Baxter and his friends came across a Chinese pirate ship which tried to board them, but with plenty of guns and steam power they easily escaped. In Hong Kong they met and joined a Cape Cod

Figure 9-18 After being offered a Pacific Island crown if he would marry the king's daughter, which he avoided by sailing soon after the offer, he next shipped as mate on the clipper *Golden West,* another Boston-built ship, much larger than his previous berth. *Courtesy of Sturgis Library.*

captain's ship bound for Amoy to carry five hundred slaves to Cuba. These men, many well educated and with property, had signed up for what they thought were good wages. But the slave agents had completely misled them, and the moment the men had signed they were herded into a stockade and treated like the slaves they were.

This was dangerous business, for these men had nothing to lose. In fact the previous slave ship had been destroyed by the slaves, who lost their lives. But on this voyage all went well, and the cargo sold in Cuba for as much as $1000 a head. Baxter was designated policeman and undertaker on the voyage.

This was a "humane" slave ship. The holds were well aired and lighted, and the berths were wider than in the infamous African slavers. One day a barrel a third full of molasses, with a poorly stopped bunghole, was brought out. Because of the opening the molasses was full of beetles and insects— which the Chinese devoured with the utmost delight. Says Baxter, " Chinese are indeed wonderful people as you are always wondering what they will do next." Only ten men died during the voyage.

When Captain Baxter returned to Cape Cod, he and Miss Stanton were married. He was twenty-eight; she was nineteen.

Having sold his vessel, in May 1864 he went to Boston to look for a berth. A Mr. Forbes offered him a job as master pilot of a gunboat. But this was not to Baxter's liking. So he went to Norfolk, Virginia. As he left the ship, an officer stopped him, asking, "Is your name Baxter?" He allowed that it was, and the officer said, "Come with me."

Captain Baxter then found himself essentially drafted for the service. First he served aboard a tug, and then the captain of the gunboat *Brewster* commandeered his services. Attacking Confederate forts, the gunboat received such a beating that she sank; Baxter was picked out of the water by a steamer.

Promoted to full pilot status, he served as pilot or captain of a series of five steamers in action. Ashore, a detective arrested him, mistaking him for John Wilkes Booth, who had murdered President Lincoln. But the commanding general vouched for him and he was released. After further adventures, he received his discharge with ten months of service and headed for Cape Cod.

Never one to settle down for very long, he and his brother, Captain Obed, bought a two-masted schooner and went trading for six years to the Caribbean and South America. Then they had built the schooner *Joseph Baxter*, which they sailed for several years. For the next eleven years he was master of s series of vessels, all in the coastwise trade. On 30 October 1882 his wife, who had been very ill, died, and with little to hold him close he "went foreign" again.

He bought shares in *Ralph M. Hayward*, a barkentine 152 feet long, with a crew of ten, and began a series of trips to Australia, often with cargoes worth $1,000,000. His first trip took ninety days to reach Port Adelaide. His next port was Newcastle, England, where he loaded coal for Hong Kong. Then back to New York he went with general merchandise.

This one trip illustrates the skill and business sense needed by these captains in the days of sail. With only general orders from their owners, and no other communication, they might be gone two years or more, visiting many ports, selling and buying cargoes, and trying to make a profit above the costs of the voyage.

For example, the clipper ship *Surprise* in 1850 on her maiden voyage to San Francisco (and setting a record time) continued around the world. When she returned to New York she had earned $78,000 in freight, paid for her expenses as well as the cost of building her, and netted her owners almost $50,000. Not bad!

On a voyage in 1885 which took fourteen months, the captain's son, Obed, was aboard as mate, and his experiences convinced him not to become a captain like his father. Their itinerary took them from New York to Sydney, to Hong Kong, to Cebu in the Philippines, and back to Boston. They spent twenty-one days becalmed in the Celebes Sea.

Becalmed off the Solomon Islands, they saw the natives come out to trade, but then a pirate galley appeared, rowing fast toward them. Still no wind. Nearer and nearer they came, as Captain Baxter told Obed that this looked like the end. But just then a breeze crept across the water, the sails filled, and they escaped.

At Hong Kong they reported the incident, to learn that a previous ship had met the same cannibals. One crewman fell overboard and was captured. Although the captain tried to recover him, his boat was almost surrounded by the cannibals.

And as they sailed away they could see their shipmate being "speared and barbecued."

In the China Sea, relates Obed, he was on forward lookout when he saw a string of lights ahead. The second mate would not believe him; they were three hundred miles from land. Just then they slid softly up on a coral reef. At daylight they saw a fleet of Chinese boats coming, and off to starboard were three steamer hulks. They had set out a kedge anchor aft in case they could pull themselves off.

Nearly helpless, they watched the pirates climb aboard. The chief told the captain that they would take the ship but return the crew to Hong Kong. From the empty quarterdeck the captain, with a brace of pistols, said, "No, not just yet you won't; wait and see what we would do!"

With the kedge anchor out aft, and all hands on the quarterdeck, next morning the wind came up, the sails filled, and with the capstan taking up the kedge anchor the ship slid off as smoothly as she had slid on. Taken unaware, the pirates, herded on the main deck, started to move, helped off the ship by the crew with their heavy capstan bars.

Once in Hong Kong, Captain Baxter reported the incident and the location of the uncharted reef. The British said that they would send a survey ship out at once to chart the reef. (Incidentally, even during World War II the United States charts of the New Guinea coast were full of legends reading, for example, "Position Doubtful" or "Existence Doubtful.")

Almost home, on 23 December they sighted Long Island's Montauk Point. Suddenly a western gale blew up, and they were driven under bare poles three hundred miles off the coast in a blizzard. Three weeks of head winds and calms later, they made New York. Two of the crew had lost fingers grappling with ice-stiff sails.

After such a long, uninterrupted voyage, they were very short of food. One last barrel of flour from the hold, when opened, foamed up and over the top like a glass of beer. In the bottom were two inches of "livestock" (insects), which they threw over the side. Obed reports that even the bread and boiled salt pork tasted good; their only water was caught in the sails. Having clawed their way back from their slight detour, off Vineyard Haven they flew a distress flag, and a Revenue Service cutter from Woods Hole brought out a profusion of provisions.

Captain Baxter continued, like the Flying Dutchman, to roam the oceans of the world in *Ralph M. Hayward*, and when he finally retired in 1899, aged sixty-five, he had spent all but ten of those years at sea— a remarkable record— and experienced a large segment of our maritime history as well as many singular events.

Finding his health failing, he sold his shares of his ship, rolled his huge collection of charts in canvas bags, locked his sea chest for the last time, and retired to the Baxter homestead in West Dennis. There he spent the rest of his days, enjoying his extended family of children and grandchildren.

Appendix

A Glossary of Nautical and Whaling Terms

Articles of War Rules and regulations covering the behavior of military personnel. Today's Navy's nickname for these rules is "Rocks and Shoals."

Baleen The Baleen whales do not have teeth. Instead the mouth is lined with strips of bone (whalebone) through which the whale strains his food, primarily minute sea creatures.

Bark A three-masted schooner vessel with square sails on the foremast and mainmast and fore-and-aft sails on the mizzen (after) mast. Its advantage is that it can sail with a smaller crew than a ship can; hence it is more economical. *Addison* was rerigged as a Bark on her return to New Bedford.

Barkentine A three-masted vessel with all the three masts rigged with fore-and-aft sails except for the three topmost square sails on the foremast.

Beat Tacking back and forth diagonally across the desired course because of an unfavorable wind.

Binnacle A covered stand mounted forward of the helm (steering wheel) enclosing the ship's compass, with a light inside for use at night.

Blackfish A small whale (often seen on Cape Cod) which townsmen would drive on shore in large herds, to take the oil for their lamps during the 17th and 18th centuries. Whalers took black fish only when other whales were scarce.

Blubber Room A space below the main deck where larger pieces of blubber (whale fat) were cut into smaller pieces (minced) for the *tryworks*.

Boat Steerer A highly responsible, agile man appointed as harpooner and steerer. His station is in the bow with the *iron* attached to carefully coiled rope, ready to strike the whale at the best time.

Bowhead Whale: The "right" whale of the Arctic Seas, so called for the large quantity of oil in its head, as well as baleen.

Brig A two-masted, square-rigged vessel. The *Hermaphrodite Brig's* foremast is square-rigged, its mainmast rigged fore-and-aft.

Broadside Firing all cannon on one side of the ship; or, the whole side of the ship.

Buntline A rope secured forward of a sail to make easier the furling of the sail.

California Gray Whale A relatively small, quick, dangerous whale found in the Pacific from the Arctic to Baja California. Whalers have given it scurrilous names such as *devildish, mussel digger* and *ripsack*.

Capstan A vertical cylinder on which cables or heavy ropes are wound, to raise heavy weights like anchors or sails. Bars slip into square holes in the top, and the crew "walks the capstan round," lifting the weight.

Careen To make hull repairs the ship is rolled onto its side on the shore by heaving on ropes attached to the masts.

Cartel As in the War of 1812, a ship used to make and exchange of prisoners of war.

Chronometer An accurate clock. By comparing local time and Greenwich Mean Time, a ship's *longitude* can be ascertained, thus locating it on the globe.

Clean A whaler still without any oil.

Clipper Ship A vessel designed for great speed, with a very sharp cutwater, large sail area (some clippers mounted six sails on a mast), and eventually a large cargo space. Beginning about 1840, these "Greyhounds of the Sea," as Carl Cutler called them, set extremely fast passages under sail. The American clippers even took over the British tea trade from the Orient; they were able to beat the British ships to England.

Close-Hauled Setting the angle of the sails as close to the direction of the wind as possible.

Cooler The large kettle in which the newly refined oil cools before being poured into barrels for stowage.

Courses The sails on the lower yards. A log will record: "Set courses."

Cut A good haul of whales. Alternatively, to cut the line to the harpoon, abandoning the chase.

Cut In To remove the thick coat of fat from the whale. The whale is secured alongside with chains; men on a staging cut parallel lines on the body; others hoist the large strips of blubber onto the deck; in the *blubber room* men cut up the pieces to a manageable size for the *tryworks* to extract the oil.

Deadlights Heavy covers placed over portholes during bad weather.

Duff A steamed pudding of yeast, flour, water, fruit such as raisins and molasses, considered a real treat by the crews of whaling vessels.

Finback A large *baleen* whale with a small dorsal fin, found from the Arctic to lower California.

Flukes The whale's tailfins. The whale propels himself by waving the flukes up and down, unlike a fish, whose fins wave from side to side.

Flying Colors When a vessel flies its colors it is reporting success. As a whaler's signal it means a full cargo of oil.

Forecastle Pronounced "fo'c'sle." The berthing spaces for the crew. Officers are berthed in *cabins* aft; petty officers, such as boatsteerer, boatswain, cooper have separate quarters in the steerage.

Frigate A relatively small war ship with guns on only one deck. *U.S.S. Constitution,* "Old Ironsides," is a frigate. In today's Navy a frigate is a fast, lightly armored vessel between a destroyer and a cruiser in size.

Galley The vessel's kitchen; also, a vessel with both sails and oars.

Gam The whalers' term for visiting between vessels, a popular and necessary means of both socializing at sea and exchanging information as to profitable whaling areas. Since conditions on many whalers were bad, mutinies were frequent; hence when two captains visited, their first mates went to the other ship, to maintain order, if necessary.

Garboard Streak or *Strake* The row of planks of a vessel's hull next to the keel.

Grampus A small whale, related to the dolphin, rarely sought because of its speed and small quantity of oil.

Greasy A whaling term denoting successful catches; or the description of the vessel while trying out the oil.

Handing a Sail The manual letting out or furling a sail by men on the yardarms.

Helm The term for the steering apparatus.

Humpback A large member of the whalebone family with extremely long flippers and a dorsal fin. It is found in most of the oceans of the world. Whale-watching boats in New England often see the humpback, whose Latin name means "New England Whale."

Iron The harpoon, or the barbed shank of the harpoon, to which the whaleboat's line is attached.

Jury Rig When a sailing vessel is dismasted, as in a storm, repairs are made by "jury-rigging" makeshift masts and sails.

Lay The wages paid a crewman at the end of a voyage, often quite meager, for instance $500 for a four year voyage.

Larboard The left side of a ship, now called port.

Latitude The distance north or south of the equator, measured in degrees. The poles are at $90°$ North or South Latitude. Highland Light in North Truro is at Lat. $42°$ 2.4' North.

League An old measure of distance, about three miles.

Luff To head the ship directly into the wind, so that the wind is on the forward sides of the sails, slowing or stopping a ship.

Longitude The distance in degrees east or west of Greenwich, England, the *zero meridian*. Highland Light is at Long. $70°$ 3.7' W.

Marlinespike A heavy metal tool shaped like a large awl, used to work with heavy cordage, for instance making eyes at ends.

Packet A vessel traveling on a scheduled route carrying passengers and cargo. Until the arrival of the railroad on Cape Cod the best way to travel to Boston was by packet schooner from the ports of Cape Cod Bay. Fare was $1.00. There were also famous trans-Atlantic packet lines such as the Black Ball Line.

Schooner A vessel with two or more masts (up to seven) rigged fore-and-aft, requiring a very small crew and hence economical. Most Cape Cod fishing vessels were two-masted schooners.

Sextant An instrument covering a sixth of a circle, with reflecting mirrors and a curved scale of degrees, for measuring angles horizontally or vertically to establish a vessel's position at sea.

Scuppers The holes for draining water from the weather deck.

Shark For whalers, the salesmen who meet vessels in port to persuade crews to patronize certain boarding houses or marine suppliers.

Ship A three-masted vessel with all masts square-rigged.

Ship of the Line The battleships of the 18th and 19th centuries. They were full-rigged ships, with three decks mounted with guns. Crews often numbered as many as 450, including companies of marines, as in the case of *H.M.S. Somerset,* which was lost on Race Point, Cape Cod, in 1787.

Sloop A small, single-masted vessel, rigged fore-and-aft.

Slops The clothing and equipment store aboard ship, where crewman could buy (often at very high interest) clothing or gear, charging it against their *lays.*

Slush A whaling term for the left-over cooking grease from the *galley*, used to grease the masts.

Speak When meeting another vessel, to exchange information by either voice or flag signals.

Sperm Whale One of the family of toothed whales, large and very dangerous. "It can whip a boat in two with one flap of its strong tail, or bite it in two with its sharp teeth. In its head… there is a reservoir of oil and spermaceti… we cut a hole in its head and dip it out by the pailful, and sometimes we get ten or twelve barrels." (from *A Good Catch*).

Starboard The right side of a vessel.

Studding Sail Light-weight sails rigged out from yardarms to get maximum power from fair winds.

Sulphur Bottom The whalers' name for the great *blue whale*, the largest cetacean of them all. He is rarely taken because of his size, speed, ferocity. When killed, *blues* tend to sink.

Try Out Boiling the blubber to extract the oil. Even the leftover flesh, after removing the oil, was used for fuel in the *tryworks*.

Tryworks The large firebox and the huge kettles, mounted on the main deck, in which the oil was extracted from the blubber.

Turn Flukes A whaling term describing the moment when a whale rolls over after dying.

Universal Distress Signal When a vessel was in trouble it would fly the United States ensign upside down at the after mast.

Voyage A whaling term for the entire time a vessel is away from its home port. Mary Chipman Lawrence's journal is broken into eight different cruises within one voyage.

Waif The taker of a whale who has to leave, to pick up boats, for example, will declare the whale a waif by placing a flag on the body, claiming ownership.

Waist The main deck of a sailing ship between the foremast and the mainmast.

Whaleboat A double-ended, strongly built boat designed to be rowed or sailed. Whalers could carry as many as six boats in cradles and slung on davits ready for instant lowering when a whale is sighted. All necessary equipment was stowed: oars, sails, harpoons, tubs of line attached to the *iron*, knives, lances. Usually there were six oarsmen and the *boatsteerer*.

Figure A-1 Coast Guard Stations warn mariners of dangerous weather conditions by flying a variety of flags. Here the Chatham Station is warning of hurricane conditions. *Courtesy of William P. Quinn.*

Bibliography

Athearn, Edwin. "Rumrunning Not a Job for the Faint of Heart." Edgartown, MA: *Duke's County* Intelligencer, August 1996.

Bartlett, W. Randolph. "Lorenzo Dow Baker: Yankee Entrepreneur." Mystic, CT: Mystic Seaport, *The Log,* Spring, 1987.

Basile, John. "Reunion Ends 35 Years of Guilt." Yarmouth Port, MA: *The Register,* 31 July 1997.

Bird, Delores, ed. *Early Encounters: From the Papers of W. Sears Nickerson.* East Lansing, MI: Michigan State University Press, 1994.

Bosworth, Janet. "The Cuttyhunk Coast Guard." Cuttyhunk, MA: n.p., n.d.

————. "The Jackson Family." Cuttyhunk, MA: Cuttyhunk Historical Society, n.p., n.d.

————. "Tom Jones, Hero of Cuttyhunk." Cuttyhunk, MA: n.p., n.d.

Bradford, William. *Of Plimoth Plantation.* Boston: Wright & Potter Printing Co., 1901.

Clark, Admont G. *Lighthouses of Cape Cod, Martha's Vineyard, and Nantucket: Their History and Lore.* Hyannis, MA: Parnassus Imprints, 1992.

Dalton, J.W. *The Life Savers of Cape Cod.* Orleans, MA: Parnassus Imprints, 1991.

Emerson, Amelia Forbes. *Early History of Naushon island,* 2nd ed. Boston: Howland and Company, 1981.

Ferriter, C.A., RADM, USN (Ret.). "90 Days over the S-4." Dublin, N.H.: *Yankee Magazine,* June 1964.

Gibson, Marjorie Hubbell. *H.M.S. Somerset: 1746-1778.* Cotuit, MA: Abbey Gate House, 1992.

Greenhow, Robert C. *The History of Oregon and California.* Boston: Charles C. Little and James Brown, 1844.

Harwich Historical Commission. *Harwich Men of the Sea.* Harwich,MA: n.p., 1935.

Hassell, Martha. *The Challenge of Hanna Rebecca.* Sandwich, MA: The Sandwich Historical Society, 1986.

Howes, Osborn. *The Story of My Life.* Boston: L. Barta & Co., 1894.

Lawrence, Mary Chipman, Stanton Garner, ed. *The Captain's Best Mate.* Dartmouth, NH: The University Press of New England,1966.

Long, David F. *"Mad Jack:" The Biography of Captain John Percival, USN, 1779-1862.* Westport, CT: Greenwood Peress, 1983.

Mahoney, Haynes R. *Yarmouth's Proud Packets.* Yarmouth Port, MA: The Historical Society of Old Yarounth, Inc., 1986.

Norton, Louis A. "A Captain from Cape Cod." Peekskill, NY: The National Marine Historical Society, "Sea History 75," Autumn 1995.

O'Neil, Neva, *Master Mariners of Dennis.* Dennis, MA: Dennis Historical Society, 1965.

Paulding, Hiram, LT, USN. *Journal of a Cruise of the United States Schooner Dolphin.* Honolulu, HI: University of Hawaii Press, 1970.

Quinn, William P. *The Grounding of the* Eldia *on Nauset Beach.* Orleans, MA: Lower Cape Publishing, 1984.

_____. *The Salt Works of Historic Cape Cod.* Hyannis, MA: Parnassus Imprints, 1993.

Railton, Arthur. "A puzzling Piracy off Tarpaulin Cove." Edgartown, MA: *Duke's County Intelligencer,* November 1991.

_____. "Six Island Whalemen Murdered in History's Most Brutal Mutiny." Edgartown, MA: *Duke's County Intelligencer,* August 1989

Reid, Nancy Thacher. "Dennis Historical Society News Letters." Dennis, MA: Dennis Historical Society, January, February, and March 1982.

Rich, Shebnah. *Truro, Cape Cod: or Land Marks and Sea Marks,* 2nd ed. Boston: D. Lothrop and Company, 1884.

Small, Isaac E. *Shipwrecks on Cape Cod.* Chatham, MA: Chatham Press, 1970.

Stackpole, Edouard A. Life *Saving—Nantucket.* Nantucket, MA: Nantucket Life Saving Museum, 1972.

_____. *The Loss of the Essex.* Nantucket, MA: Inquirer and Mirror Press, 1935.

Starbuck, Alexander. *The History of Nantucket.* Boston: C.E. Goodspeed, 1924.

Swift, Theodore. *Stories of Yankee Shipmasters.* Yarmouth Port, MA: The Historical Society of Old Yarmouth, Inc., n.d.

United Stated Coast Guard. *Board of Inquiry into the Sinking of U.S.S. S-4.* Washington, DC: United States Coast Guard, 7 May 1928.

VanRiper, A. Bowdoin."His Majesty's Sloop Falcon, Scourge of Vineyard Sound. Edgartown, MA: *Duke's County Intelligencer,* August 1986.

Webber, Bernard C. *Chatham: The Lifeboatmen.* Orleans, MA: Lower Cape Cod Publishing Co., 1985.

Winthrop, The Honorable Robert C. "Explorations of the Northwest Coast of the United States." *Historical Magazine,* vol. VIII, September 1970.

Index